WAR OF THE
U-BOATS

WAR OF THE U-BOATS

British Merchantmen
Under Fire

by

Bernard Edwards

Pen & Sword
MARITIME

First published in Great Britain in 2006 by
Pen & Sword Maritime
an imprint of
Pen & Sword Books Ltd
47 Church Street
Barnsley
South Yorkshire
S70 2AS

ISBN 1 84415 501 3

Typeset in Sabon by
Phoenix Typesetting, Auldgirth, Dumfriesshire

Printed and bound in England by
CPI UK

Pen & Sword Books Ltd incorporates the imprints of Pen & Sword
Aviation, Pen & Sword Maritime, Pen & Sword Military, Wharncliffe
Local History, Pen & Sword Select, Pen & Sword Military Classics and
Leo Cooper.

For a complete list of Pen & Sword titles please contact
PEN & SWORD BOOKS LIMITED
47 Church Street, Barnsley, South Yorkshire, S70 2AS, England
E-mail: enquiries@pen-and-sword.co.uk
Website: www.pen-and-sword.co.uk

We are a seafaring race and we understand the call of the sea. We account you in these hard days worthy successors in a tradition of steadfast courage and high adventure, and we feel confident that that proud tradition of our island will be upheld today wherever the ensign of a British merchantman is flown.

WINSTON CHURCHILL TO ALL
BRITISH MERCHANT SEAMEN
JULY 1941

Author's Note

This is a revised and extended edition of a book first published in 1989 under the title "The Fighting Tramps".

Contents

Glossary

Nautical Terms

Abaft:	Behind, in relation to something on the ship.
Abeam:	At right angles to the fore and aft line of the ship.
Aft, After:	Towards the stern.
Airpipe:	Ventilation pipe leading from ballast or fuel tanks to the deck.
ASDIC:	Submarine detection gear based on subsonic transmission.
Astern:	Behind the ship.
Azimuth:	Compass bearing of the sun or stars, etc.
Beam ends:	When a vessel rolls very heavily to one side or the other she is said to be 'on her beam ends'.
Bilge:	Channel at bottom of hold or engine-room into which surplus water drains.
Binnacle:	Pedestal which holds ship's compass.
Black Gang:	Firemen and Trimmers.
Block:	Pulley through which rope or wire runs.
Boat Deck:	Deck on which lifeboats are stowed and boarded.
Boat Stations:	Stand by on boat deck to abandon ship.
Broach-to:	To swing beam-on to wind and sea.

Bulk cargo:	Loose homogeneous cargo, e.g. sugar, grain, ores, etc.
Bulkhead:	Steel or wooden partition between compartments.
Cargo liner:	Ship employed on a regular and advertised trade.
Clipper stern:	Cutaway stern reminiscent of the old clipper ships.
Coaming:	Steel parapet around a hatchway.
Collision bulkhead:	Steel watertight bulkhead nearest to the bows.
Corvette:	Handy type of submarine hunter of around 900 tons. Extensively used by Royal Navy for convoy escort duties in Second World War.
Davits:	Light cranes on which ship's lifeboats are suspended.
Deck service line:	Pipe which carries sea water from engine-room to deck for fire-fighting or washing down.
DEMS:	(Defensively Equipped Merchant Ships.) Initials used to identify Royal Navy and Royal Artillery ratings seconded to merchant ships to man and maintain guns.
Derrick crutch:	Crutch-like support into which cargo derrick is lowered and secured when not in use.
Dog watch:	The 4–8 pm watch is sometimes divided into two 'dog' watches. The first dog watch is 4–6 pm, the second 6–8 pm.
Dunnage:	Rough-sawn planks of wood used in stowing cargo.
Eight bells:	Struck to signal the change of watches, i.e. at midnight, 4 am, 8 am, noon, 4 pm and 8 pm.
ETA:	Estimated time of arrival.
Fall:	Wire or rope purchase used for raising or lowering weight.
Flush deck:	Deck running from bow to stern without interruption of forecastle or poop.
Focke-Wulf Condor:	German long-range reconnaisance bomber.

Forecastle:	Crews' quarters at fore end of ship.
Forecastle head:	Raised deck at fore end of ship.
Fore deck:	That part of the main deck forward of the bridge.
Freeboard:	Distance between main deck and waterline.
GRT:	Gross registered tonnage.
Gunwale:	The uppermost planking of an open boat.
Hatch beam:	Portable steel beam supporting hatchboards.
Hatchboard:	Heavy, steel-banded wooden board used to cover hatchway.
Hatchway:	Opening in deck giving access to hold.
Heave to:	To stop the ship at sea.
HF/DF:	High Frequency Direction Finder.
Jolly boat:	Small general purpose boat.
JU 88:	German twin-engined bomber and torpedo-carrying aircraft.
Lascar:	Indian Seaman.
Lighter:	Barge.
Light ship:	Ship without cargo.
Main deck:	The principal deck of a vessel having several decks.
Marline spike:	Pointed steel tool used to open the strands of a rope or wire when splicing.
Middle Watch:	Midnight to 4 am and noon to 4 pm.
MTB:	Motor torpedo boat.
Painter:	Lifeboat rope used to secure alongside or when towing.
Poop:	Raised deck at after end of ship.
Scotch boiler:	Smoke-tube boiler widely used in merchant ships.
Scupper:	Drains at ship's side and in holds to carry off water.
Serang:	Indian boatswain.

Sloop:	Naval escort vessel, usually of about 1,000 tons.
Smoke float:	Buoyant pyrotechnic giving off dense orange smoke. Standard equipment for ship's lifeboats and liferafts.
Taffrail:	Top of ship's rail, usually made of teak.
Thwart:	Transverse stiffener in lifeboat that serves as seat.
Tiger Bay:	The Butetown district of Cardiff.
Tramp:	A merchant ship which is not engaged in a regular trade but carries cargo to any destination required.
Trim down:	As in the case of a submarine, to fill ballast tanks in order to partly submerge the hull.
Well deck:	Space on the main deck, either between the raised forecastle and the bridge, or between the latter and the poop.
Whistle lanyard:	Thin wire stretching from the bridge to the operating valve of ship's whistle on funnel.
Windlass:	Steam or electric winch used for raising anchors.
Woodbine funnel:	Tall, thin funnel peculiar to many tramp ships. The great height provided natural draught for the boiler furnaces.
W/T:	Wireless telegraphy.

Merchant Navy Ranks (in order of seniority)

Captain/Master:	In command.
Chief Officer/ First Mate:	Senior deck officer. Responsible for the maintenance of the hull and decks and all cargo work. Usually keeps 4 to 8 watch on bridge.
Second Officer/ Second Mate:	Navigating officer. Keeps 12 to 4 watch on bridge.
Third Officer/ Third Mate:	Signals officer. Keeps 8 to 12 watch on bridge.

Apprentice:	Deck officer in training and indentured to shipowner.
Cadet:	Deck officer in training.
Radio Officer:	Operates and maintains wireless telegraphy equipment.
Chief Engineer:	Senior engineer officer. Responsible to Captain for smooth running of engines and auxiliary machinery.
Second Engineer:	Senior watchkeeper in engine-room. Usually keeps 4 to 8 watch. Responsible for engine-room maintenance and cleanliness.
Third Engineer:	Keeps 12 to 4 watch in engine-room. Also responsible for electrical repairs.
Fourth Engineer:	Keeps 8 to 12 watch in engine-room.
Fifth Engineer:	Usually on day work in engine-room, or on deck as required.
Chief Steward:	In charge of catering.
Boatswain:	Senior rating on deck.
Carpenter:	Responsible for all woodwork and plumbing above decks. Sounds ballast and fresh water tanks.
Quartermaster:	Steers ship and keeps gangway watch in port.
Able Seaman:	Certificated seaman.
Ordinary Seaman:	Uncertificated seaman.
Deckboy:	Seaman in training.
Donkeyman:	Senior engine-room rating.
Fireman:	Attends to boiler furnaces.
Trimmer:	Supplies firemen with coal from bunkers.
Greaser:	Responsible for oiling and greasing machinery.
Chief Cook:	In charge of galley.
Second Cook:	Assists chief cook and bakes bread.
Assistant Steward:	Cleans officers' cabins and serves in dining saloon.

Chapter One

To War

In the halcyon years leading up to World War II, Britain's merchant ships dominated the world's seaborne trade. British shipowners waxed fat, re-investing their profits in new tonnage, and their horizons became even wider. It was claimed that, on any one day, some 2,500 ships flying the Red Ensign were at sea or at work in the various ports of the world. Such prestigious liner companies as P & O, Ellermans and Blue Funnel took the cream, but it was the old tramps of Runcimans, Ropners, Radcliffes and their many contemporaries that carried the greatest burden of the trade – and subsequently profited most.

Ironically, the men who sailed in these ships – the men who created the wealth – were those who benefited least. The general public saw them as a necessary evil; lower-class civilian sailors hawking their rust-bucket ships around the trade routes of the world to the greater glory of King and Empire. Shipowners exploited them, judges and titled ladies equated them with the scum of the earth. They drank, they fought and they fornicated, keeping solvent countless dockside pubs and whorehouses from Cardiff to Canton. Yet at their job they were the best the world has ever seen, resilient, resourceful, innovative and blessed with an unfailing sense of humour. Such were the men who crewed Britain's tramp ships of the 1930s.

The average British tramp of the day was of about 5,000 tons gross, blunt in the bow, rounded in the stern and capable of carrying a vast amount of general cargo. She boasted a forest of spindly derricks, her decks were cluttered with steam-belching winches, and her tall masts and funnel were reminiscent of a bygone age. Her propulsion unit, crammed into the smallest possible compartment to avoid wasting precious cargo space, was usually a basic but reliable triple-expansion, steam-reciprocating engine. Fed by three Scotch boilers, into the hungry furnaces of which her 'black gang' of scrawny firemen shovelled best Welsh steam coal, this ponderous machine produced a top speed of eight to nine knots – when the weather was kindly.

Accommodation for her crew was often no more than an afterthought, as though the shipowner was reluctant to burden his ship with structures that earned no freight – as indeed he was. The ratings lived in a dark, airless cavern under the forecastle head, sleeping in two tiered bunks that rose and fell with every swell passing under the bow. Her deck officers – the ruling hierarchy – bunked amidships, directly below the bridge, in cabins just big enough to swing the proverbial cat, of which there were always two or three on board to keep at bay the army of voracious rats that inhabited the cargo holds. Engineers spent their off-watch time in similar cabins perched on top of a steamy engine-room, beautifully warm in the British winter, but uninhabitable in the tropics. Only captains and chief engineers enjoyed the luxury of their own bath and toilet; the rest took their place in the queue in the alleyway.

Navigational equipment was of the most rudimentary, conforming only to the minimum requirements laid down by the omnipotent Board of Trade, namely a magnetic compass, a deep-sea sounding lead and an alert lookout man. That is not to say that the standard of navigation was any the less for such limitations. Sextant and chronometer were put to good use, and it is much to the credit of their masters and deck officers that the tramps wandered to the far reaches of the earth and back with remarkably few casualties by stranding.

Unlike their more privileged sisters, the cargo liners, tramps had no regular or recognised itinerary. They were, for the most part, engaged in the cross trades, often leaving British shores laden down to their marks with Welsh coal and thereafter working the charter market between the diverse ports of the world, earning their keep as they went. It was not unusual for a ship to be away from her home port for up to two years, shuttling coal from Barry to Rio de Janeiro, wheat from the River Plate to Shanghai, sugar from Surabaya to Bombay, and so on, ever circling the globe in search of employment.

Wages and conditions of service for the men sailing in the tramps were usually the minimum allowed under British law. A first mate holding a foreign-going master's certificate could expect to earn about £23 a month, an ordinary seaman £6. For these princely sums they were expected to work up to ten hours a day, seven days a week, and at any other time the safety of the ship or cargo required. There was no paid leave at the end of a voyage, no matter how long it lasted. If a man wished to spend time with his family, he had no alternative but to quit the ship and go off pay. While at sea, medical attention was confined to that which could be provided by the master of the vessel, whose expertise depended on his familiarity with the Ship Captain's Medical Guide, the Board of Trade's 'bible' on the treatment of the sick and injured. Yet treatment on board was often preferable to that offered by the half-trained quacks who masqueraded as company doctors in the far-flung outposts of the Empire. But afloat or ashore, baffling illnesses were frequently diagnosed as malingering, and woe betide the man who contracted 'lady sickness', as the seaman's shore-going occupational hazard was delicately described. VD was considered to be a self-inflicted disease, and the shipowner was not obliged to pay for the treatment of such.

The diet of the tramp ship men – again dictated by the Board of Trade – would not have been acceptable in many Victorian work-houses. Salt beef, salt pork, potatoes half rotten after a few weeks in the locker, haricot beans, split peas, rice and oatmeal were the staple fare at sea, and in port were supplemented with –'when procurable at a reasonable cost' – a limited amount of so-called fresh meat and fresh vegetables. Much of the food supplied by ship's chandlers, who regarded pigs and seamen as being roughly on a par, was of such poor quality that no self-respecting landsman would allow it near his plate. Nevertheless, even in the tramps, the time-honoured British sense of fair play prevailed and provisions, issued daily or weekly, were meticulously doled out by the pound and pint under the eagle eye of the ship's chief steward. It was their more fortunate brothers in the cargo liners, where a much higher standard of feeding was enjoyed, who coined the phrase 'pound & pint ships' to describe the Board of Trade scale.

Without the benefit of air-conditioning, the tramp-ship men sweated out their lifeblood in the tropics. Deaths from heat exhaustion, especially in the engine-room department, were commonplace. In the depths of winter they hovered on the fringe of hypothermia, their suffering only sometimes eased by a cranky, inefficient steam-heating system. In port, after working hours, both heating and electric lighting were often turned off in the interest of fuel economy, leaving them huddled around smoking oil lamps in overcoats and mufflers.

Little wonder that, in Britain alone, there were more than 150 charities dedicated to the care of merchant seamen.

What induced these men to sign on voyage after voyage, sure in the knowledge that they would endure such discomforts and indignities? Were they masochists, or just plain simple? Far from it. The 1930s had seen years of worldwide economic depression, and the threat of unemployment was still a strong incentive, though by no means the main driving-force. The sea was in their blood, as it always had been in all successive generations of this island race. For the tramp-ship men, the sea held no image of romance – this they knew existed only in the fertile imagination of the fiction writer; but there was adventure to be had in plenty, and by this prospect they were all too easily seduced. They lived in a harsh, demanding environment, often akin to a prison afloat, but it was a well-ordered society, which looked after its own, and who knew what adrenaline-stirring challenge or sumptuous delight lay over the horizon? The awesome roar of the hurricane, the insidious, blinding fog that muffled the approach of danger – or perhaps the arms of a beautiful Japanese whore, whose gentle ministrations healed all wounds and stilled all longings. For the seaman, the horizon was always beckoning.

When war came in 1939, the tramp-ship men, like all British merchant seamen, took it in their stride. As civilians following an occupation demanding so much for such niggardly rewards, they might have been excused if they had been loath to face the additional dangers brought by war. Yet never once did they hesitate. No British merchant ship was ever held in port by its crew, even at the height of the Battle of the Atlantic, when to cross that ocean in a slow-moving merchant ship was to walk hand in hand with death for every minute of the day and night. Nor, when there was a need to supply arms to the Soviet Union via the Arctic route, did they flinch. German surface ships and aircraft, based in northern Norway, savaged them without mercy, while the ever-present U-boats continued to snap at their heels like the Hounds of Hell. Of those who died – and they were legion – the fortunate fell to the guns and torpedoes of the enemy, the luckless froze to death in minutes in the icy waters of the Arctic Sea. Those who were spared to reach their goals often endured round-the-clock bombing by German aircraft while in port. But the greatest indignity many of these men suffered was to be treated by their erstwhile Russian allies as outcasts, tainted by the dread disease of capitalism.

Not that they fared any better at the hands of their own kind. Under British law, when a merchant ship was lost, even in wartime, the shipowner's obligation to pay wages to its crew went with it. There were some who took a more philanthropic view, but others closed the books the minute the ship disappeared beneath the waves. To die in the water unemployed was a distinction often awarded to British merchant seamen. Those who survived a sinking found their ordeal was by no means over when they reached the shores of Britain: they were sent home in the clothes they stood up in, with a free railway warrant and half a crown in expenses to speed them on their way. It was almost as though their country was ashamed of them. And yet, they still went back to sea, some staying ashore only long enough to get together some new kit.

Undoubtedly the greatest strains of the war fell on the shoulders of the masters and deck officers of the tramp ships. Their charges were slow and maneouvred like the lumbering barges they were. Station-keeping in convoy was for these men an unending ordeal. On a dark, moonless night it required nerves of steel and the eyes of a cat; in poor visibility or stormy weather it was an impossibility. They straggled, they romped and they veered, becoming the easiest of targets for the stalking U-boats. The men in the engine-room suffered the tortures of the dammed, never knowing when a torpedo might tear through the thin plates of the hull, sending their ship plunging to the bottom before they had a chance to reach the first rung of the ladder to the deck. Burdened, as they so often were, with heavy bulk cargoes, the tramps sank like punctured tin cans filled with lead shot. For those who took to the lifeboats or rafts, the process of dying was more prolonged. Lacking protection from the sun and storms, striving to exist on rations measured in ounces per day, many eventually succumbed to exposure, starvation, thirst or sheer mental exhaustion.

By the time the war finally ended, 29,180 British merchant seamen had lost their lives in the conflict, almost fifty per cent of them in the tramp ships. Within the pages of this book an attempt has been made to bring to life the stories of some of these men and their ships.

Chapter Two

A Game for Gentlemen

The dark clouds of war were brushing the hilltops of Europe when, shortly after nightfall on 19 August 1939, seventeen sinister black shapes slipped out of Wilhelmshaven, motored in line astern across Jade Bay, and fanned out into the North Sea. The cream of Admiral Dönitz's undersea battle fleet was on its way to take up station off the western approaches to the British Isles. In its midst was U-33, commanded by *Kapitänleutnant* Hans-Wilhelm von Dresky, who, by his own admission, was a reluctant warrior.

It was not that von Dresky's courage or loyalty to his own country was in question, nor did he lack confidence in his crew or his boat. His men were hand-picked from the elite of the *Kriegsmarine,* and U-33 was as formidable a weapon as any man could wish to command. Displacing 740 tons and 220 feet long, the new Type VII U-boat had a maximum range of 6,500 miles, with a top speed of 17 knots on the surface and 7½ knots when submerged. She was armed with an 88 mm deck gun, one 37 mm and two 20 mm anti-aircraft guns, and five 53 cm torpedo tubes. Von Dresky's problem was that he could just not see any reason for open conflict between two nations as closely linked as Britain and Germany.

To the U-boats, as they exchanged their last guarded signals before dispersing into the dark night, the threat of war was very real. Some 4,500 miles to the south-west, on the West Indian island of Cuba, a very different atmosphere prevailed. Here the sun was still high in a cloudless sky, the surf boomed good-naturedly on the white sands and the talk was of tobacco, sugar and the price of rum. In Puerto Padre, a small harbour on the north-east coast of the island, the British ship *Olivegrove* was loading a full cargo of raw sugar which she had been chartered to carry to Europe.

The 4,060-ton *Olivegrove,* built by Lithgows on the Clyde in 1929, and managed by David Alexander & Sons of Glasgow for the Grove Line, was very much the archetypal deep-sea tramp of her day. Her wide-bellied hull fell only a little short of the rectangular, her accommodation was equally unattractive, and her triple-expansion steam-reciprocating engine cranky and under-powered. But, despite her graceless lines, the *Olivegrove* was well cared for, her black hull and white superstructure showing only the minimal signs of rust and her teakwood bridge-house in a good state of repair and freshly varnished. She was grandly classed by her owners as a 'general trader', which in effect meant she was on the market to carry anything anywhere, providing the price was right and the water deep enough. Of her crew of thirty-three, the majority were Scots, as would be expected of a Glasgow ship, with a sprinkling of English, Irish, Tiger Bay Arabs, and the inevitable 15-year-old galley boy from Barry in South Wales, from which port she had sailed in ballast in late July of that year.

On the lower bridge of the *Olivegrove,* her master, 46-year-old Captain James Barnetson of Leith, paced the scrubbed wooden deck deep in thought, stopping from time to time to run a critical eye over the slings of bagged sugar as they came swinging over the ship's rail. His mind was grappling with two problems, both complex and both disturbing.

Uppermost in Barnetson's thoughts was the weather, for early autumn in the West Indies is a time of danger, when hurricanes spawned in the open Atlantic to the east of Barbados sweep north-westerly, bringing with them devastating winds, mountainous seas and torrential rain. Cuba stands square in their path, and to be caught in harbour during such a storm could spell disaster for the *Olivegrove.* Had the time been thirty years on, Barnetson would have been able to call on a highly sophisticated weather forecasting organisation backed by satellites, but in 1939 he had only the barometer and his own experience to warn of approaching danger.

He was unlikely to rest easy until his ship was loaded and heading for the open sea.

And then there were storm clouds of another kind gathering on the world's horizon. Since Neville Chamberlain had returned from Munich in September 1938 waving his worthless piece of paper and promising 'peace in our time', the momentum of German expansionism had been speeding up. Czechoslovakia had gone the same way as Austria, and it seemed that Poland was about to follow suit, flattened under the marching jackboots of Hitler's legions. For the second time in a generation the talk was of war between Britain and Germany, and this troubled James Barnetson greatly. In the Great War of 1914–18, such had been the horrors of trench warfare on the Western Front that the sacrifices made by Britain's merchant seamen had gone almost unnoticed, in spite of the loss of 2,479 ships and 14,789 men. Barnetson had been a young man in that war and had good cause to remember the hideous toll it had exacted among his shipmates. It was his fervent hope that such a thing would never happen again, but he knew in his heart that it was now as inevitable as the coming of the next dawn.

The *Olivegrove* sailed from Puerto Padre on the afternoon of 22 August and, loaded down to her tropical marks, wallowed like a heavily pregnant duck as soon as she left the shelter of the land. It was obvious to Barnetson that his ship would not break any records on the run to the north, but he was well used to this state of affairs. His immediate and most pressing objective was to clear the mass of cays and islands that make up the archipelago of the Bahamas, for here, caught by a hurricane, the *Olivegrove* would have no room to maneouvre.

As it turned out, Barnetson's fears proved groundless. The weather remained fine and calm and, thirty-six hours after leaving Puerto Padre, the *Olivegrove* was clear of the Bahamas and settled down on her long, diagonal run across the Atlantic. In accordance with common practice in the charter market, where cargoes often change hands overnight, the port of discharge for the *Olivegrove*'s cargo had not yet been declared. She was heading for 'Land's End for orders', meaning Barnetson would be notified by radio of his destination only a few days before reaching British waters. By past experience, those on board knew this would almost certainly be

London, Liverpool or Glasgow, with the ship's Scottish home port being a hot favourite. Whatever decision was taken by the wheelers and dealers of the Baltic Exchange, ahead of the *Olivegrove* lay a voyage of 3,700 miles, sixteen or seventeen days' steaming, in which a great deal might happen.

Oblivious to the stratagems of man, the *Olivegrove* pushed north-eastwards under an untroubled sky, dipping her blunt bows into a boisterous sea with gay abandon. It was as though she sensed she was on her way home. The miles seemed to fly by, and before long the homeward-bound spirit was rampant throughout the ship. Paintbrushes worked overtime, stores and repair lists were drawn up, and shore-going clothes brought out of musty wardrobes to air on deck.

Meanwhile, half a world away, Germany signed a non-aggression pact with the Soviet Union and the end of two decades of uneasy peace in Europe drew near.

On Friday 1 September, German tanks rolled across the Polish frontier, and the die was cast. Two days later, at 11 am on the 3rd, when the *Olivegrove* was 350 miles north-west of Flores in the Azores, where Sir Richard Grenville had fought his last battle, Prime Minister Neville Chamberlain announced that Britain was at war with Germany. Within five minutes, the following radio signal went out from Wilhelmshaven to the U-boat fleet:

1105/3/9.39 FROM NAVAL HIGH COMMAND STOP TO COMMANDERS-IN-CHIEF AND COMMANDERS AFLOAT STOP GREAT BRITAIN AND FRANCE HAVE DECLARED WAR ON GERMANY STOP BATTLE STATIONS IMMEDIATE IN ACCORDANCE WITH BATTLE INSTRUCTIONS FOR THE NAVY ALREADY PROMULGATED.

At this time, U-33 was patrolling to the west of Ireland, and it was with a decided lack of enthusiasm that Hans-Wilhelm von Dresky opened his small safe and took out the sealed orders he had carried with him from Wilhelmshaven. He was instructed to move south to cover the south-western approaches to the English Channel and there attack and sink any British ships sighted.

The news of the outbreak of war was received philosophically on board the *Olivegrove*. The general consensus of opinion was that they would have little to fear from the Germans; the omnipotent Royal Navy would look after them. But there were those who said otherwise, and they spoke with the voice of authority and experience. Barnetson himself, his chief officer William Wilson and Chief Engineer Duncan Robb had lived through the other war and had no leanings towards complacency. The *Olivegrove* was immediately brought onto a war footing, with watches doubled, extra lookouts posted, and the ship darkened at night. That evening, her radio officer reported plaintive cries for help from the passenger ship *Athenia*, torpedoed without warning some 250 miles north-west of Ireland. For Britain's merchant fleet, the killing war had begun.

Noon sights on 7 September put the *Olivegrove* 420 miles to the west-south-west of Land's End. The weather remained fine, visibility was good, and she was making a respectable 9½ knots. When Captain Barnetson left Second Officer John Alexander in charge of the bridge and went below for his midday meal he was well pleased. Within twenty-four hours his ship would come under the protection of the Royal Navy's patrols, and the worst danger would be behind them.

His appetite curbed, Barnetson returned to the bridge less than an hour later. After a word with Alexander, he moved out into the port-side wing and began to pace up and down briskly, mindful of the extra portion of duff he had indulged in. He was on his fifth lap of the short wooden deck when a movement on the horizon to port caused him to halt in mid-stride. He raised his binoculars and, as the long grey shape, with its fin-like conning tower came into focus, he muttered a curse, not so much at the sight of the enemy – and he had no doubt that this *was* the enemy – but at the gross unfairness of his lot. He had brought his ship and her cargo 3,500 miles without incident, and was almost within reach of sanctuary. Now, it seemed that his efforts had been for nothing. The *Olivegrove* was unarmed, and therefore at the mercy of the approaching U-boat.

Frustration suddenly turned to anger, and Barnetson stormed into the wheel-house, ordered the helm hard to starboard, and gave a savage double ring on the engine-room telegraph calling for emergency full speed. Damn the Germans! He would make a run for it.

In the conning-tower of U-33, Hans-Wilhelm Dresky also felt a surge of anger as he saw the merchantman contemptuously offer him her squat stern. Having no wish to add to the furore caused by the sinking of the *Athenia,* he had been making his approach to the British ship strictly in accordance with the Prize regulations laid down by the Hague Convention. U-33 was on the surface, flying code flags ordering the merchant ship to heave to, and her signal lamp was flashing the same message. How typical of the British to complicate matters!

On the *Olivegrove*'s bridge, which was shaking violently as Chief Engineer Robb worked his engine up to maximum possible revolutions, Barnetson braced his shoulder against a stanchion and examined the U-boat through his binoculars. She was now about 5 miles off on the starboard quarter, and trimmed right down, so that much of her casing was awash. The flags she flew were too small to make out at the distance; nor could Barnetson read her signal lamp. The German signaller, who so obviously regarded merchant seamen of all nationalities as blind half-wits incapable of reading Morse Code was sending his message so slowly that it was impossible to string the dots and dashes together to make letters, let alone words. Nevertheless, the message behind the flashing lamp was unmistakeable.

The U-boat's deck gun now caught Barnetson's attention. It was manned and trained on his ship with obvious intent. As he watched, there was a flash from the muzzle of the gun, and a shell whined over his head. This was the final warning to heave to. Barnetson chewed his lip and considered the situation. The U-boat was making a good 5 or 6 knots more than the *Olivegrove,* so he had no real hope of running away. Given a gun, however small, he might have been tempted to make a fight of it. He had fought the sea all his life and never given a thought to surrender, whatever the odds he faced, but this time it was different. Pure seamanship would be of little avail. If he continued to run, sooner or later a hail of well-aimed shells or the silent torpedo must follow. The end result could only be grieving widows and fatherless children in Glasgow, Liverpool and Cardiff.

With a hopeless shrug, Captain Barnetson walked back into the wheel-house and rang the engine-room telegraph to stop. By this time Second Officer Alexander had succeeded in deciphering the U-boat's signals. As expected, the order was to stop and abandon ship. Nodding agreement, Barnetson instructed Alexander to pass the word for boat stations.

There was no panic in abandoning ship. With as little enthusiasm as they habitually showed at the fortnightly practise drill commonly referred to as 'Board of Trade Sports', the *Olivegrove*'s crew swung out their two lifeboats and lowered them to the water before boarding. It seemed like a bad dream from which they would soon awake. Equally unhurried, James Barnetson retrieved the ship's confidential books from the safe in his cabin, placed them in the weighted bag provided, and hurled it into the sea. He then gathered up the few papers he would need to conclude the voyage, and went to his boat.

The two loaded lifeboats pulled away from the *Olivegrove*'s side, leaving her stopped and rolling gently in the swell. Less than an hour previously she had been a homeward bound merchantman, hurrying north full of purpose; now she was a pathetic sight: a ship with a past, but no future. The U-boat lay 4 or 5 miles off her starboard beam, waiting like a hooded executioner.

As soon as the boats were clear of the *Olivegrove,* the enemy submarine moved in at full speed, submerging when she was within a mile of her. From the stern sheets of his boat Captain Barnetson watched and waited with a lump in his throat that threatened to choke him. He heard a dull thump and saw his ship shudder, and then throw up a great tall column of dirty water, steam and smoke as the torpedo blasted open her hull. She took only six minutes to die. There were tears in Barnetson's eyes as she slipped beneath the waves.

Meanwhile, the U-boat had re-surfaced, and was moving back towards the drifting lifeboats. Barnetson had seen photographs of German submarines in recognition books, and he judged this one to be of the largest class. As the long predatory shape glided near, he made mental notes of her appearance. Her grey-green paintwork looked new, and she mounted a short-barrelled 3-inch calibre gun just forward of her conning-tower; a formidable enemy.

The submarine stopped within 50 yards of the lifeboats, and a voice called for the Captain to come alongside. Barnetson, suspicious, yet curious to meet the man who had sunk his ship, hailed back, and ordered his men to pull for the U-boat.

As the lifeboat bumped alongside U-33, Barnetson noted that her hull was free of barnacles, but she had three-inch-long grass growing just below the waterline. In different circumstances, he might have been amused at his unconscious critical assessment of the other man's ship, but this was not the time. Grim-faced, he clambered aboard the U-boat clutching the few papers that were all that remained of his own command.

Hans-Wilhelm von Dresky did not volunteer his own name, but shook Barnetson by the hand, and in heavily accented English requested to see his papers. While the German commander studied the documents, Barnetson studied him. He was thirty-five to forty years old, tall and very thin, with sharp features and dark hair. His chin carried a good two weeks of growth, but he showed no signs of fatigue.

The German returned the papers, saying 'I am sorry I have to sink your ship, Captain. But why does your Mr Chamberlain want to make war on us? We do not want war.'

Somewhat taken aback by the other man's reasonableness, Barnetson shrugged and answered that he, personally, had no wish to make war on anyone.

They were now joined in the conning-tower by two other officers. Both were unshaven, in their mid or early thirties, and spoke good English. They were extremely polite and friendly. One, whom Barnetson took to be the engineer, was a golf fanatic, and having learned that Barnetson hailed from Leith, enthused about St. Andrews and the holidays he had spent there. The conversation, which was all of a general nature, went on for nearly two hours. The Germans showed no animosity towards Barnetson, and asked no compromising questions. In fact, they gave the British captain the distinct impression that they, and their commander in particular, were whole-heartedly opposed to the war with Britain.

As they stood shoulder to shoulder in the U-boat's conning-tower chatting genially like old friends in a pub, Barnetson began to feel a certain sympathy for these men. Like himself, they were seamen caught up in a war that was not of their making. He reached the point where the situation had become so unreal that he felt the need to pinch himself, when a younger officer joined them and gave the Nazi salute, inviting Barnetson to 'Heil Hitler!' Only then did it come home forcibly to the Scottish captain that these men had just sunk his ship, and would probably have killed him and his crew if necessary. When the U-boat commander shook his hand again, and said he was free to go, Barnetson wasted no time in returning to the lifeboat.

Back with his men, Barnetson conferred with Chief Officer Wilson, who was at the helm of the other boat, and it was agreed that they should make for the island of Fastnet, off the southern coast of Ireland. The distance to go was some 290 miles, and if the weather did not deteriorate, it was estimated that the boats would make a landfall in about three days. It was a long enough haul in open boats, but it seemed preferable to staying put to await a rescue ship which might never come. Hoisting sail, they set off to the north-east.

Unbeknown to the Olivegrove's survivors, their fate had been decided for them. Von Dresky was about to make recompense for sinking their ship. The German commander had contacted the American passenger liner Washington, and for the next nine hours U-33 circled the lifeboats at a discreet distance, keeping watch over them. When the Washington hove in sight at about 9.30 that night, von Dresky fired two Very lights before making off to the west. As he watched the U-boat motor away, Captain Barnetson was forced to conclude that he had received his first taste of the war at the hands of a gentleman. He wondered if it would be like that in the coming years.

All thirty-three of the Olivegrove's men were picked up by the Washington that night and landed in Cork twenty-four hours later.

The Olivegrove had been Hans-Wilhelm von Dresky's first victim. His subsequent war record was neither long nor impressive.

15

U-33 sank only ten more ships, six being mere fishing boats, before she was caught and sunk in the Firth of Clyde by HMS *Gleaner* on 12 February 1940. The owners of the *Olivegrove* fared little better, losing their entire fleet of seven vessels to the U-boats during the war.

Chapter Three

Ropner's Gunboats

On a sunless morning in October 1939 Swansea's King's Dock was not a sight to inspire men to poetry. Even the most sombre of Welsh bards would have been hard pressed to sing its praises. A leaden sky, hovering at mast-top height, deposited a steady curtain of drizzle into an atmosphere already dark with suspended coal dust. From the direction of the Bristol Channel, a south-westerly wind keened in over the breakwaters sending black-topped wavelets scudding across the dock, pushing before them fragments of rotting driftwood, clusters of empty beer bottles and an obscene fleet of discarded condoms.

Moored bow to stern under the towering coal-hoists, two of Sir Robert Ropner's best bared their hatches to the rumbling, cascading coal. On the quayside, clustered around the gangways of both ships, drums of paint, coils of rope, cases and cartons were piled in untidy heaps, indicating that the voyage stores had arrived – as always, when the ships were at their busiest and dirtiest.

The *Heronspool* and *Stonepool,* if not sister ships – for they were out of different yards – were certainly first cousins, and typical British tramps. Their box-like hulls, sparse superstructures and tall 'Woodbine' funnels stamped them as products of the bustling ship-yards of the north-east coast of England, designed to carry maximum cargo at minimum cost, with the end result of maximum profit for their owners. The *Stonepool* was the younger of the two by a year, having left her slipway in 1928. Both were registered at West Hartlepool and owned by the Pool Shipping Company, a

17

subsidiary of Sir Robert Ropner & Company Limited of Darlington.

The two ships were near to their marks and within hours of sailing. Commanded by Captain Sydney Batson, the 5,202-ton *Heronspool* was about to set off for Montreal with a full cargo of anthracite. The *Stonepool,* slightly smaller at 4,803 tons gross, commanded by Captain Albert White, had on board steam coal for the bunker station in the Cape Verde Islands.

Batson and White, friends of long standing and one-time ship-mates, had enjoyed the pleasure of each other's company while their ships occupied adjacent berths in Swansea, but now both were anxious to be on their way. October, as they well knew from past experience, is when autumn turns to winter in the North Atlantic, the time when that tempestuous ocean begins to unsheathe its claws in earnest. Of the two ships, the *Heronspool* faced the most arduous voyage by far. Her route to the Gulf of St. Lawrence would take her far to the north, across 2,400 miles of inhospitable sea where the additional danger of icebergs lurked. For her crew there would be no escape from the full rigours of the oncoming winter. The *Stonepool,* on the other hand, was southbound, and every turn of her screw would bring her nearer to the more gentle ways of the tropics. A month or so earlier, either voyage would have been routine for the tramps, but now there were the unknown hazards of war to face. Despite the Royal Navy's claim that the Germans had already lost half their ocean-going U-boats, thirty-three British merchant ships, totalling 164,205 tons, had already been sunk – a ship for every day of the war so far.

As a sure sign that the noose around Britain's sea lanes was about to tighten even further, during their stay in the Bristol Channel the Ropner ships had each been equipped with a World War I vintage 4-inch gun mounted on the stern, and a light machine gun to ward off attacking aircraft. In charge of the manning and maintenance of this formidable array of weaponry were two experienced gunlayers of the newly-formed DEMS (Defensively Equipped Merchant Ships) force. Able Seamen John Hayter and John Pearson, both Royal Navy pensioners recalled to active service for the duration of the war, while enjoying the relaxed atmosphere in the merchant ships, were already experiencing some misgivings

18

about their new roles. Pearson, sailing in the *Heronspool,* and Hayter, in the *Stonepool,* had been handed the unenviable task of forming guns' crews from among the merchant seamen manning the ships. It was quite obvious to both men that a great deal of training and motivation would be needed before these unruly civilian sailors were in a fit state to swap shells with the enemy. The Navy men had yet to be exposed to the astonishing adaptability of the 'Pound & Pint Sailors'.

The problems of the two gunlayers were insignificant compared with those faced by Captains Batson and White. They had been informed, somewhat peremptorily, by the Admiralty that their ships were to sail in convoy from Milford Haven to a point 400 miles out in the Atlantic, before proceeding independently. Like all men who commanded merchant ships, Batson and White had an intense dislike and distrust of the convoy system. They felt that it unfairly restricted their freedom of movement, and imposed an unnecessary extra burden on themselves and their crews. In the interest of good station keeping, watches would have to be doubled on the bridge and in the engine-room, and in ships already operating on the absolute minimum of manpower this would mean increased hours on duty and precious little sleep for those involved. It also seemed to them ludicrous to bunch together a lot of slow-moving merchantmen, so that if a U-boat found one, it would find all. Their judgement was that it was far better to allow the ships to go their own separate ways, and let the U-boats do the hunting. The open sea was a good place in which to get lost.

On Friday 6 October 1939, the *Heronspool* and *Stonepool,* down to their Winter North Atlantic marks, left Swansea within hours of each other. On the short, eight-hour passage around the Welsh coast hoses and brushes were broken out and the crews of both vessels tackled the thick layer of coal dust that covered every exposed inch of deck and superstructure. By the time they sailed into Milford Haven, one of the largest natural deep-water harbours in the world, the tramps were passably clean, and their crews were exhausted.

Fortuitously, the convoy was not yet fully assembled, and three days were passed at anchor in the shelter of the haven, during which Batson and White used every daylight hour in fully preparing their

19

ships for the voyage to come. The last of the ubiquitous coal dust was chased away, hastily loaded stores were consigned to their correct lockers, and the securing of derricks and hatch covers was double checked. It would not do to venture into the Western Ocean unprepared.

At 0700 on 10 October, the two Ropner ships hove up their anchors and, in company with seven other ships and escorted by a single destroyer, sailed from Milford Haven. It was a fresh autumn morning, with the whitecaps tumbling and the enticing smell of frying bacon in the air. As the ships rounded St. Ann's Head and, one by one, pointed their bows to the west, more than a few hearts beat faster in anticipation of the unknown. The proposed arrangement was to join forces off the Smalls with seven other ships, which had left Liverpool on the previous evening. Unfortunately, the most carefully laid plans often come to grief, and this one was no exception. Three hours later, the Bristol Channel ships were off the Smalls' lighthouse, which guards the south-western corner of Wales, but there was no sign of the others. To wait off the Smalls, in full view of prowling U-boats and aircraft, was out of the question. There was no alternative but to carry on out to sea.

At daybreak on the 11th, the convoy was 80 miles to the west of the Smalls when a low-flying Sunderland and tall columns of smoke on the horizon astern announced the belated arrival of the Liverpool ships. Due to the slow speed of one of their number, the Cardiff ship *Leeds City*, which was flying light, they had been over four hours late at the rendezvous off the Smalls.

Under the direction of the Convoy Commodore, sailing in the *Bolton Hall*, another West Hartlepool tramp, the fourteen merchantmen formed up in columns and, zig-zagging at 8½ knots, set off to the west. Escorting them, the destroyers *Imogen* and *Ilex*, their bow waves foaming, made broad sweeps ahead and astern, lookouts scanning the horizon and Asdics constantly probing the depths for signs of a hidden enemy. Overhead, the great four-engined Sunderland flying boat circled slowly, its guns and depth charges ready to ward off attack from above or below. Convoy OB 17 was operational, and in good hands.

At first, although this was one of the earliest organised convoys of the war, station keeping by the ships was good. But before many miles had been covered it became evident that the designated convoy speed was beyond the reach of some of its ageing participants. Within the hour half had become stragglers, among them the *Heronspool* and *Stonepool*. At 0930, the Commodore reduced speed to 8 knots, and ordered the stragglers to steam on straight courses in order to catch up with the main body of the convoy. A moderate swell was running in from the west and, although the two Ropner ships struggled valiantly to keep up, they dropped further and further astern of the others. Sydney Batson and Albert White began to regret the mistaken pride in their ships that had prompted them to declare top speeds of 9 knots when joining the convoy.

At 0645 on the 12th, when full daylight revealed the horizon, the *Heronspool* and *Stonepool* found they were alone on an empty sea. They were then 120 miles to the south-west of Fastnet, and 100 miles from the agreed dispersal point of OB 17. Realising the futility of continuing the charade of keeping station on a non-existent convoy, Batson and White decided to part company, and go their separate ways. After a brief exchange of goodbyes by signal lamp, the *Heronspool* continued to the west at a more leisurely pace, while the *Stonepool* altered course to the south.

Night was closing in when Captain Batson joined his chief officer, Charles Clifford, on the bridge of the *Heronspool*. The weather remained fair, but Batson was becoming increasingly concerned at the rising swell. To his experienced eye this indicated a heavy blow far out in the Atlantic. He was, in fact, correct, for 800 miles to the west the American liner *Matson* was reporting 'tremendous seas', as a result of which thirty of her passengers had been injured.

For a while, Batson and Clifford stood in the open wing of the bridge discussing ship's business and the voyage ahead. To them, it still seemed unlikely that the war would upset their routine to a great extent. In ten days, weather permitting, they would be in the Gulf of St. Lawrence, and beginning the 900-mile passage up the river to Montreal. Once there, and far removed from the shooting war, they would spend a pleasant, if busy week or so discharging the anthracite, then, if they were lucky, load a full cargo of wood pulp, returning home in time for Christmas. It was all very hypothetical and unlikely, but then, by nature of their calling, seamen are incurable optimists.

The dream vanished minutes later, wiped away by reality. As the stand-by man on the bridge struck four bells, indicating the end of the first dog watch, the lookout on the forecastle head reported a ship on the port bow. Batson and Clifford, instantly alert, raised their binoculars in unison. On the darkening horizon they sighted a large tanker at about 5 miles off, and apparently stopped.

Batson was about to instruct his chief officer to contact the tanker by lamp, when he became aware of the long, low outline of a submarine on the surface close to the other ship. The first flash of gunfire was enough to confirm that he had stumbled on the enemy in the act of savaging his prey.

For a brief moment, steeped in the ancient code of the sea that dictates that no seaman shall turn his back on another in distress, Sydney Batson was tempted to intervene, to open fire on the U-boat with his newly acquired 4-inch. But he was quick to realise the futility of such action. Although he had an experienced man in his gunlayer, Able Seaman John Pearson, the *Heronspool*'s scratch gun's crew were complete newcomers to the art of naval gunnery. They had, in fact, yet to fire their 4-inch. Batson shook his head, and ordered the helm hard to starboard. He must think of his own ship first, and run away before she too became a victim of the U-boat.

Batson's next, and instinctive, move was to order Chief Officer Clifford to sound the pre-arranged signal for action stations. This was a series of twelve short blasts on the steam whistle. Its sounding was to have dire consequences for the *Heronspool* and her crew.

Five miles away, in the conning tower of U-48, *Kapitänleutnant* Herbert Schultze peered into the gathering dusk and grunted with satisfaction as another 88 mm shell slammed into the helpless tanker. His victim, as he would later learn, was the 14,115-ton Frenchman *Emile Miguet*, which had sailed from Jamaica before the outbreak of war and was unarmed. Her crew had already taken to the boats, and she was burning fiercely. Soon she would slip beneath the waves in a cloud of steam and smoke to double the tonnage U-48 had sent to the bottom in these first few weeks of the war. Herbert Schultze was well on his way to becoming Germany's top-scoring U-boat ace.

The faint sound of the *Heronspool*'s steam whistle echoing across the water brought Schultze spinning around. He raised his binoculars, and a grim smile began to play around his lips as, on the blur of the horizon astern, he caught sight of the squat stern of the British tramp as she made off to the north-west. Schultze had good cause to smile, for U-48, a Type VII C boat, was capable of 17 knots on the surface. There was ample time to finish off the tanker before going after the latest victim to walk uninvited into his net.

Meanwhile, on board the *Heronspool*, unaware that he had unwittingly announced his presence to the enemy, Captain Batson was making every effort to save his ship. Gunlayer Pearson and his crew of eager amateurs were at their battle stations around the stern gun, while Chief Engineer Charles Dobson was below, coaxing every possible revolution out of the *Heronspool*'s hissing, thumping engine. Darkness was now almost complete and, as the moon had not yet risen, escape into the safety of the night seemed a good possibility.

An hour passed, then two, and Batson dared to entertain hopes that his plan had succeeded. The night was as black as the inside of a pit, the sky clear and star-studded, so the *Heronspool* seemed to be steaming along in a dark void. Only the phosphorescence rolling away from her bows revealed her presence as she zig-zagged away to the north-east.

At 2000, they went through the routine of changing watches, but although men moved aside to make way for their reliefs, there was no standing down. On the bridge, Batson and Clifford stood side by side staring silently astern, their faces showing the strain as they willed away the miles. Their hopes were high, but in their hearts they knew the U-boat must by now be in pursuit.

U-48 was a lot closer than either man anticipated. The sound of eight bells was still ringing in the air when there was the loud crack of a gun, and a column of water shot skywards close on the *Heronspool*'s starboard quarter. Herbert Schultze had arrived to claim his fifth victim of the war.

Uncertain of his attacker's position, Captain Batson could only press on at all speed, praying that the torpedo he feared would not come. Then, twenty minutes later, it was Schultze's turn to give himself away. Unsure of the *Heronspool*'s identity, and perhaps unwilling this early in the war to make the mistake of sinking an innocent neutral, he ordered his signalman to challenge the unknown ship by lamp.

Batson saw the challenging flash of the lamp and shortly afterwards was able to distinguish the dark outline of a surfaced submarine on his port quarter. He now had only two moves open to him. He could stop and order his crew into the boats, or run and fight. No one could have blamed him if he had taken the easy way out, for the submarine would have twice the speed of his ship and, unlike the *Heronspool*'s, her gun's crew would be trained to a peak of perfection. Yet it took the merchant captain only a few seconds to make up his mind. Crossing to the engine-room telegraph, he gave another double ring for extra speed and then passed the order for the 4-inch to open fire.

Crouching by their gun on the poop, where they had been at action stations for more than two hours, John Pearson and his 4-inch crew needed no urging. Within seconds of receiving the order to open fire, the first shell was in the breech and the U-boat in their sights. The ancient gun thundered and recoiled. Working swiftly and with remarkable cohesion, the crew cleared the breech, swabbed out, loaded and fired again. No fall of shot was observed, but the U-boat was seen to dive in a hurry. The first round was to the *Heronspool*.

On the bridge, Captain Batson gave the order to cease fire, and made another bid to escape. Hauling around to the west, he steamed at full speed, once again hoping to take cover in the darkness. In the engine-room, Charles Dobson, who had been torpedoed in the 1914–18 war, needed no incentive to push his already hard-pressed engine to its utmost limits.

Two more wearying hours passed with no further sign of the U-boat, and Batson, fearing an underwater attack, resumed zigzagging. He cursed roundly when, half an hour later, the enemy submarine was seen by the light of the stars to be on the surface again, and creeping up astern. Without waiting for orders, the *Heronspool*'s 4-inch opened fire and two shots were seen to fall close to the U-boat, which immediately dived again.

And so the running battle went on, with U-48 surfacing from time to time to swap shells with the stubborn little tramp that refused to surrender. Gunlayer Pearson, who had earlier entertained great doubts about the ability of his ragbag of a gun's crew, began visibly to glow with pride. These men – his men – were good. They fought with a careless precision that was perhaps born of countless battles in dockside pubs around the world. They had then, as they did now, stood shoulder to shoulder, sailors, firemen and stewards, defending the good name of their ship. Even the youngest member of the *Heronspool*'s crew, 14-year-old deckboy Frank Elders, demonstrated his contempt for the enemy by appearing on the gun platform with steaming mugs of tea during each lull in the firing.

But the fight was between a crack German war machine and a civilian ship pushed beyond normal limits, and armed with an ancient gun crewed by amateurs. There could be only one outcome. Shortly after midnight, U-48 landed a shell dangerously close on the *Heronspool*'s starboard side which sent her rolling on her beam ends. When she righted herself, Batson glanced at the wheelhouse clock. It was now Friday the 13th. Ominous.

The end came an hour later when, at 0100 the U-boat dived and almost immediately the *Heronspool* was rocked by a violent explosion that lifted her clean out of the water. Debris showered down on the bridge, and the ship took a heavy list to port. Schultze's torpedo had slammed into her forward hatch, blasting open her hull to the sea. Angry, and at the same time sad, Sydney Batson reached for the whistle lanyard to sound the signal for boat stations. His old ship had fought her first and last fight.

At the first urgent tug of the lanyard, the whistle jammed wide open, and its mournful shriek added to the confusion reigning in the stricken ship. On the poop, Pearson and his crew struggled to extricate themselves from the wreckage of the gun platform, which had collapsed under them when the torpedo struck. In the wireless-room, Radio Officer George Haresnape, resisting the temptation to run for the boats, bent over his key and began tapping out a plaintive call for help.

In spite of an increasing list, the blackness of the night, and the unnerving shrieking of the steam whistle, there was no visible panic. Having supervised the dumping overboard of the secret code and signal books, Captain Batson went to the boat deck, where Chief Officer Clifford was already preparing the two lifeboats for lowering. As the *Heronspool* was now well down by the head, Batson wasted no time in ordering his crew to abandon ship. Assisted by the stalwart Gunlayer Pearson and Able Seaman Brown, one of the gun's crew, he then lowered both boats to the water. Once the boats were clear of the ship, the three men, Batson, Pearson and Brown, followed by jumping overboard.

Fortunately, the sea was calm, and the boats were able to lie close to the sinking ship, waiting for the dawn, and the help their occupants hoped would come. The *Heronspool,* tough Tyne-built ship that she was, took a long time to die. She was still afloat when, shortly before dawn, the American passenger liner *President Harding* arrived on the scene. She had raced through the night in answer to George Haresnape's SOS.

The cold waters of the Atlantic finally closed over the *Heronspool* as her lifeboats reached the side of the brilliantly lit American ship. The old tramp had hung on until her men were in safe hands.

As Sydney Batson and his men clambered up the side of the *President Harding*, 90 miles to the south-west, the *Stonepool* was peacefully following her normal early-morning routine. Captain Albert White, sipping at a mug of hot, strong tea, was on the bridge waiting to see the sun over the horizon. Out in the wing, Chief Officer Peter Love busied himself with morning star sights. Neither man was then aware of the *Heronspool*'s fate.

The weather was surprisingly good, and the *Stonepool* was forging her way southwards at a steady, if not impressive, 8 knots and rolling easily in the long Atlantic swell. Yet Captain White was far from at ease. He was not normally a superstitious man, but it was Friday the 13th, and the ship was still in an area known to be the haunt of marauding U-boats.

The grey dawn became a promising sunrise. Peter Love finished working out his star sights, and plotted the ship's position on the chart. This put the *Stonepool* 430 miles due west of Ushant, with 1,942 miles to run to her destination, St. Vincent in the Cape Verde Islands.

Looking up from the position chit handed to him by Love, White allowed his gaze to wander around the deserted horizon. So far, so good. He walked out into the port wing of the bridge and leaned on the well-scrubbed taffrail, deep in thought. With an average day's run of only 190 miles, it was a long haul to St. Vincent, but there would be compensations. Within two days at the most they would be in warmer weather, and far enough away from the Western Approaches to be safe from attack by U-boats. There was always the possibility of a German surface raider being at large, but then the ocean was a big place . . .

White broke off from his reverie and reached for his binoculars. The early morning haze was lifting, and he had spotted what appeared to be the funnel of another ship hull-down on the horizon to port. A homeward-bounder heading for the Bristol Channel, White decided, not without a small pang of envy.

The distorting veil of mist suddenly lifted, and the funnel became the conning-tower of a submarine on the surface, and less than 3 miles off the *Stonepool*. White dived for the whistle lanyard just as the submarine's gun barked. U-42, commanded by *Kapitän-leutnant* Rolf Dau, as yet unblooded in this war, had found her first likely victim.

The U-boat's opening shell fell ahead of the *Stonepool,* Dau's gunners having over-estimated the slow-moving merchantman's speed. Without hesitation, White swung his ship hard to starboard, presenting her stern to the attacker. Like his old shipmate, Sydney Batson, Albert White had decided to fight and run.

Gunlayer John Hayter and his crew, which included Third Officer Leonard Corney and Chief Steward John Shipman, had reached their gun before the whistle finished sounding the alarm. By the time the *Stonepool*'s stern had swung through 90 degrees and the U-boat was in their sights, the 4-inch was loaded and ready. Within two minutes of U-42's first shell landing, the *Stonepool* fired back.

Over the next ten minutes, a fierce gun battle raged. White, facing aft on the bridge, his face grim with defiance, skilfully threw his ship from side to side, dodging the enemy's shells. Aft, on the poop, Hayter's gun's crew, whose sole battle experience was the firing of three practice shells, calmly returned shot for shot. In

27

the engine-room, Chief Engineer Richard Parsons screwed down his boiler safety valves and advanced the engine control lever hard up against the stops. The deep-loaded British tramp rattled and vibrated until it seemed that every rivet in her stout hull must pop. Abaft the bridge, in the tiny wireless cabin, the *Stonepool*'s radio officer, in the absence of orders from the bridge, took it upon himself to tap out a continuous SOS.

Soon, the more accurate shooting of U-42's 88 mm gun's crew began to take its toll.

The *Stonepool* was hit time and time again. Both her lifeboats were smashed, and with them went her crew's only hope of survival. Now they must continue to run and to fight.

But U-42 did not have it all her own way. The *Stonepool*'s part-time gunners had at last found the range, and 4-inch shells began to land uncomfortably close to the pursuing U-boat. In desperation, Rolf Dau fired a torpedo at the fleeing ship, but the canny Albert White was ready for this move. Watching the feathered track racing through the water towards the ship, he made a sharp alteration of course at the precise moment. The torpedo passed harmlessly down the starboard side and porpoised across the bows.

At the same time, one of Hayter's shells found its mark, and U-42 crash-dived in a cloud of spray and smoke.

Ten minutes later, the U-boat surfaced again and White ordered his gunners to recommence firing. The submarine did not return his fire. Puzzled, White took the ship's telescope from its rack and steadied it against an awning stanchion while he focused. When he lowered the telescope, he was smiling. The powerful glass had revealed that the U-boat's deck gun was pointing uselessly at the sky, its barrel smashed by one of the *Stonepool*'s 4-inch shells. White's smile broadened when it became evident that the U-boat was steering an erratic course, indicating either her steering gear was damaged, or she was holed below the waterline.

Deciding not to stretch his luck too far, White now broke off the action, and steamed away to the west at all possible speed. Half an hour later, with the enemy out of sight, he altered course to the south, resuming his interrupted voyage. Unfortunately, the *Stonepool* had taken more punishment than he realised. A quick inspection by Chief Officer Love revealed she had been hit five times, some of the U-boat's shells striking near or below the water-line. The bilges were sounded, and showed that she was taking water in both fore and after holds. When Love reported that both lifeboats had been damaged beyond use and the ship was notice-ably settling by the head, White had no real alternative but to reverse course and head back for the Bristol Channel.

About three hours later, at 1500, the destroyers *Imogen* and *Ilex* appeared on the horizon. The escorts had been on the point of turning for home after the dispersal of Convoy OB 17, when they picked up the *Stonepool*'s SOS. Racing to the position given by the *Stonepool*'s operator, they had found U-42 still on the surface, and obviously crippled. They moved swiftly in to attack, but Rolf Dau had no stomach left for the fight. He scuttled his boat, and he and his crew were taken prisoner by the destroyers. The career of U-42 had been short and unproductive. In her only action of the war she had made the mistake of underestimating the determina-tion and capability of the crew of a British tramp, and had paid the price.

As for the *Stonepool,* her ordeal was far from over. She was 450 miles from the nearest friendly port, badly knocked about, and with water rising in her holds. Captain Albert White's only consoling thought was that he had suffered no casualties in the engagement with the enemy.

After disposing of U-42, *Imogen* and *Ilex* took station on the limping *Stonepool,* and prepared to escort her back to port. However, she was not to enjoy the comforting presence of the destroyers for long. At 1700, when the setting sun was low in the west, the *Stonepool*'s masthead lookout reported a submarine on the surface off the port beam. They were being shadowed again.

This time there was no need for the battered merchantman to fight a desperate action. Her signal lamp winked out from the bridge wing, warning the escorting destroyers of the danger, and they peeled off to attack. The *Stonepool* was left to stagger home alone. She reached Barry on 16 October, and lived to sail and fight another day. Her end finally came in the icy waters off Greenland in September 1941, when she was caught up in the dreadful massacre of Convoy SC 42. In an action lasting three days and nights, a pack of ten U-boats, including U-432, commanded by the now legendary Herbert Schultze, the *Heronspool*'s executioner, sank sixteen merchantmen for the loss of only one of their number. Ironically, the U-boat lost, U-207 commanded by *Oberleutnant* Fritz Meyer, fell to the escorts' depth charges only a few hours after she had claimed her first, and only, victim of the war, the gallant little *Stonepool*.

Chapter Four

No Quarter Given

The island of Eleuthera, 100 miles long and 2 miles wide, is no more than the outer fringe of the Great Bahama Reef, which, by some quirk of nature, lies a few feet above sea level. A thin strip of fertile land runs the length of the island, and is fronted on the Atlantic side by a beach of fine, pinkish-coloured sand. On Wednesday 30 October 1940, a local farmer named Johnson was working in his field on the eastern side of the island, when he saw what appeared to be two turtles crawling up the beach below. In the Bahamas, the turtle is regarded as a great delicacy, and Johnson unsheathed his knife, and set out for the beach at a run. Turtle steaks were on the menu for his evening meal.

When Johnson reached the beach, he was amazed to see that the slow-moving terrapins were in fact two men. Dreadfully emaciated to the point where they resembled sun-burned skeletons, the men were dragging themselves up the beach from a small boat which had been thrown onto its side in the breaking surf. Taken into the shade and revived with sips of water, these men had a harrowing tale to tell. It began nearly three months earlier in the Bristol Channel port of Newport, Mon.

Summer was at its height when, on 6 August 1940, two tugs pulled the *Anglo Saxon* clear of the coal hoists in Newport docks, and pointed her towards the locks and the open sea. The 5,596-ton steamer, her wartime grey barely visible beneath a thick canopy of coal dust, was on her summer marks, heavy with a full cargo of best Welsh steaming coal destined for Bahia Blanca, Argentina.

Owned by the Lawson Latter Steamship Company of London and commanded by 53-year-old Captain Philip Flynn, the *Anglo Saxon* carried a crew of forty, many of them local men, all of whom had joined the ship only a few days earlier.

Making her way down the Bristol Channel overnight, the *Anglo Saxon* reached Milford Haven next morning, where she anchored, and Captain Flynn went ashore to receive his routing orders for the 6,000-mile voyage ahead. He returned with the news that they were to sail again the next day, and join the Liverpool-Halifax convoy OB 195 in the North Channel.

The passage around the north of Ireland in convoy was uneventful, but tiring of the irksome restrictions involved, it was with some relief that, late on the 13th, having reached longitude 15° West – then considered to be the western limit of U-boat activity – Flynn was able to signal his farewells to the Convoy Commodore, and break away to the south-west. From then on, with daily improving weather, and every revolution of the propeller taking them further away from the dangerous waters, it should be all plain sailing.

Unknown to Captain Flynn, while he may have been moving away from the danger posed by the U-boats, he was also on a collision course with another foe. More than 2,000 miles to the south-west, in mid-Atlantic, the German armed merchant raider *Widder* was making her way to the north-east.

The 7,851-ton *Widder*, originally the *Neumark* of the Hamburg Amerika Line, and commandeered by the German Navy in 1939, had come out of the Blohm & Voss yard on the Elbe in May 1940 armed with six 5.9-inch, one 75 mm, two 37 mm and four 20 mm guns. This considerable armament was backed-up by four torpedo tubes and two Heinkel 114 spotter planes. She was manned by a crew of 363 reservists, and commanded by 49-year-old *Korvettenkapitän* Helmuth von Ruckteschell, a U-boat commander of some notoriety in the First World War.

Disguised as the Swedish ship *Narvik*, the *Widder* had been operating off the West Indies, and since arriving in the area in early June had sunk seven ships totalling nearly 41,000 tons. Thanks to Von Ruckteschell's ruthless policy of overwhelming his unsuspecting victims with shells and machine-gun fire before they were able to get away an SOS, the *Widder*'s presence in the Atlantic was unknown to the Royal Navy, and consequently to Captain Philip Flynn of the *Anglo Saxon*.

As August progressed, and the hunting off the West Indies became less and less profitable, Von Ruckteschell decided to try his luck further to the east and north. And so the two ships, the Bristol Channel tramp armed with a single 4-inch gun and the powerful German raider, now under the neutral Spanish flag and renamed *El Neptuno*, were drawn inexorably together.

On board the *Anglo Saxon*, as the patent log ticked off the miles, and the grey, overcast skies gave way to a purest blue dotted with fair-weather cumulus, the constant fear of the unseen torpedo became only a bad memory. Lifejackets were put aside, and her crew settled into a relaxed routine of watchkeeping and ship maintenance. The war was a long way off. Noon sights on 21 August put the ship 750 miles south-west of the Azores, and just ten days' steaming from her destination, Bahia Blanca. She was under the influence of the last of the North-East Trades, the light following breeze matching her forward progress, so that the smoke from her tall funnel rose straight into the clear air like the smoke from a summer bonfire. The tall black column was visible for many miles around, a beacon guiding the *Widder* to her prey.

Helmuth von Ruckteschell patiently shadowed the merchant ship, remaining hidden below the horizon until darkness fell. He then closed the range to 1½ miles, and at 2020 opened fire.

The moon was still a few minutes to rising, and the night was very black. Third Officer Walter Pickford had the watch on the bridge, and Able Seaman Roy Widdecombe was at the wheel. Neither they nor the lookout man in the bows saw the *Widder* stealthily approaching. There was no challenge by lamp, no shot across the bows, the first indication they had that they were under attack was the flash of the *Widder*'s 5.9-inch guns lighting up the night. The crash of the salvo followed, then the whine of the German shells as they sped towards them.

Von Ruckteschell's gunners had aimed for the *Anglo Saxon*'s long-barrelled 4-inch gun mounted on her poop, and their aim was deadly accurate. Four shells crashed into the stern of the ship, wiping out the unmanned gun and setting off the shells in the ready-use magazine on the gun platform. Most of those in the crew's accommodation below the poop died without being aware that death was so close.

The *Widder* now closed to within 3 cables, and raked the helpless merchantman's decks with machine-gun fire, killing or injuring anyone not under cover. Captain Flynn had by now reached the bridge, and was in the act of hurling the ship's secret papers and books overboard, when he was hit in the chest and killed.

The raider's big guns crashed out again, and the *Anglo Saxon* was smothered by a hail of shells, one of which penetrated the engine space, bursting the main boiler. As the steam pressure fell, the engine slowed and ground to a halt, leaving the ship completely at the mercy of her attacker. With ruthless efficiency, the German gunners then proceeded to pour machine-gun and cannon fire into her, cutting down men as they struggled to launch the lifeboats, and wrecking the bridge and wireless room. First Radio Officer Michael O'Leary, tried in vain to get away an SOS. Both main and emergency transmitters had been destroyed by the raider's fire.

The *Anglo Saxon* was by this time a blazing wreck, a funeral pyre for those few of her crew still left alive. Chief Officer Barry Denny now took command, ordering the survivors to abandon ship. The ship carried four lifeboats, two large boats abreast the engine-room, and two 18ft gigs, or jolly boats, abreast the bridge, and a number of life-rafts on the main deck. The after boats were found to have been smashed by gunfire. There is no record of how many men were left alive, but it is known that the two jolly boats and two life-rafts were successfully launched.

Denny had the port jolly boat, and with him were Second Radio Officer Roy Pilcher, Third Engineer Lionel Hawks, Able Seaman Robert Tapscott, Able Seaman Roy Widdecombe, Assistant Cook Leslie Morgan and Marine Francis Penny, the DEMS gunlayer. Three of the survivors had been injured when the *Widder*'s machine-guns raked their ship: Pilcher's left foot was smashed; Morgan had been hit in his right foot; while Penny had bullet wounds in his right arm and right leg.

As the jolly boat pulled away from the burning ship, the *Widder* was seen to be lying half a mile off with her machine-guns firing tracer at the two life-rafts. There was no sign of life on either of them. The other jolly boat was nowhere to be seen, probably sunk by gunfire with all on board, Denny concluded. This was a very dangerous situation, for it seemed obvious that the raider was intent on leaving no witnesses to her action. While she was hastening the end of the *Anglo Saxon* by putting a torpedo into her, Denny prevailed upon his crew to put their backs to the oars and row away into the darkness. As they pulled away, they saw the *Anglo Saxon*, broken by the torpedo, sliding stern-first under the waves.

When he assumed they had put enough distance between themselves and the raider, Denny allowed his exhausted men to ship their oars, and with a sea anchor out, lay hove-to waiting for the dawn. Shortly after five o'clock there was sufficient light, and they searched around looking for others who might have survived. Most of the wreckage had dispersed, and there was no sign of life in the water, or of the other boat or the two rafts that were launched. It was as though someone had wiped the sea clean of all evidence of the sinking of the *Anglo Saxon*.

As the sun began to climb, Denny made an inventory of the boat's provisions and equipment. The food tanks contained one large tin of ship's biscuits, eleven tins of condensed milk and eighteen pounds of tinned mutton. The water breaker was almost full with about four gallons of water, while the boat locker contained a first aid kit, distress flares and matches. There was no navigational equipment, other than a compass.

Denny had taken star sights shortly before the German raider attacked them, so he had a good idea of their position, which gave him no comfort. The nearest land was the Azores, some 830 miles to the north-east, but it would be impossible to return that way with the wind and current against them. To the east, roughly the same distance, lay the Canary Islands, and beyond that the coast of Africa. Again, there would be little hope of a landfall there. The only feasible course open to them was to sail west to the West Indies. The distance was much greater – more than 2000 miles – but they would have the wind behind them, which is the only way in which a ship's lifeboat will make any speed, and the prevailing current in those waters ran westerly at 8 to 10 miles a day. Denny put it to the others, and as he was the only one on board with any knowledge of navigation, they could hardly disagree. Firstly, Denny attended to the injured men using the meagre resources of the first aid kit, then the boat's sail was hoisted, and course was set to the west. And so they began their voyage, in Barry Denny's words, 'Trusting to God's good grace to either finding a vessel en route or striking somewhere in the Caribbean Sea'. Knowing they were in for a long voyage, from the outset Denny set the daily ration per man at half a cup of water and half a biscuit, supplemented by an occasional issue of tinned mutton and condensed milk

The hopes of the survivors soared on the night of the 23rd, when a ship approached. She was showing no lights, and cruising around as though she might be searching for something. This was confirmed when she burned a white flare, and there was a clamour in the boat that they should try to attract her attention, but Denny sensed danger. He was of the opinion that she might be a German raider, either the one that had sunk their ship, or another one going about her murderous occupation. The other men accepted his judgement, and the unidentified ship was allowed to go on her way. Whether she was friend or foe they would never know.

Next day the wind freshened to force 4 from the north-west, and for the following forty-eight hours the boat bowled along at a speed which was estimated by Denny to be in excess of 4 knots. The morale of the seven men soared, and for the first time it seemed that the long voyage ahead was survivable. The entries in Chief Officer Denny's log for the next four days give an indication of conditions on board:-

AUGUST 26TH, MONDAY. *Bosun bird flew overhead. Sun rose at 6.25 am ATS. Becalmed occasional fitful gusts. Glaring sun's rays. Bale out 24 buckets daily. 6 am issued meat rations out from day previous wrapped in canvas, little taken, half a dipper of water per man, little drop of condensed milk, spirits of whole crew keen, no murmur from wounded men. Hoping to sight vessel soon but praying for squalls and a decent wind. During am medical treatment given by 3rd Engineer and myself. W/T operator's left foot, which is badly crushed, bathed with salt water for an hour and last linen bandage applied, well covered up but swelling badly. 2nd cook's right foot swollen badly, ankle badly strained with bullet wound just above the ankle, bathed with salt water and well bandaged. Gunlayer's right forearm washed first in fresh water, then iodine applied and bandaged. All day long blinding sun's rays and cloudless, becalmed. During afternoon First Officer, 3rd Engineer, Gunlayer, ABs Widdecombe and Tapscott dipped their bodies in water overside, taking care to keep their faces out of water, result greatly invigorating. Rations still half a dipper of water per man at 6 am and 6 pm, only eat half a biscuit per day, no need for more, and a little condensed milk. The boiled mutton kept in canvas still good and the fat is appreciated. Although the W/T is weak, everyone else in good spirits and very cheerful. Keeping two watches, one myself and other 3rd Engineer, two ABs, four on and four off. Having no nautical instruments or books on board can only rely on the compass and stars at night. Trusting to make a landfall in vicinity of Leeward Islands, with God's will and British determination. 10.30 pm, wind freshening from eastward, skimming along fine at about 5 knots.*

AUGUST 27TH, TUESDAY. *Wind ENE 3 to 4, partly cloudy. No rain yet. 6 am ration given, half a dipper of water, no one felt hungry. Managed to give each man a cigarette made out of newspaper and half a can of tobacco, but only 8 matches left so this luxury will soon be stopped. On port tack heading SW true making about 4 knots and throughout the night, held a lottery in the evening as to who gave the nearest date of being sighted or making landfall. Sun sets at 6.42 pm ATS.*

AUGUST 28TH, WEDNESDAY. *During afternoon Chief Officer, 3rd Engineer, Widdecombe and Tapscott had a dip over the side, felt greatly improved as body absorbed the water leaving salt on the skin, saliva came to the mouth which previously parched. Moderate to fresh ENE trade, heading SW true. Bosun bird and ordinary black seagull flying around.*

AUGUST 29TH, THURSDAY. *On our eighth day in the boat, crew's spirits extremely cheerful. W/T operator weak owing to left leg going dead. Ration still half a dipper of water per man 6 am and pm, noon half a biscuit with light condensed milk. Wind ENE 4, moderate sea and swell. Gig running free on port tack heading SW true. High hopes of picking up a ship or making landfall shortly, we are all putting our trust in God's hands, everyone is fit except a weakness in legs and of course great loss in weight. Do not feel particularly hungry but suffer from parched throat owing to low water ration, pity we have no lime juice or tins of fruit, which would ease matters considerably, but no one is complaining. All day long strong ENE wind with strong swell, shipping a little water everywhere.*

As August moved into September, the upbeat mood that had previously prevailed on board the tiny boat began to fade.

SEPTEMBER 1ST, SUNDAY. *During Saturday night crew felt very thirsty, boiled mutton could not be digested and some felt sick. Doubled the water issue that night. 6.15 am half a dipper of water per man and same in pm. Wind SSW 2, slight northerly swell, steering West true. W/T op failing slowly, hope to see something soon. 8 am W/T operator R.N. Pilcher passed peacefully away. Committed his body to the deep with a silent prayer.*

SEPTEMBER 2ND, MONDAY. *6.15 am issued half a dipper of water per man and same in evening with a little condensed milk diluted with it. Wind E 2, slight sea, steering W true. Crew now feeling rather low, unable to masticate hard biscuit owing to low ration of water.*

The writing in the log had grown steadily weaker, and this was the last entry made by Chief Officer Barry Denny, who up until now had been the tower of strength that held together the little band of survivors. Subsequent entries were in a different hand.

SEPT. 3RD, TUESDAY. *One dipper of water per man at 7 am and again in evening. Things going from bad to worse. 1st Mate*

38

who wrote this diary up to this point going fast. Good breezes from ESE.

SEPT. 4TH. *Everybody very much weaker. The Mate is going fast now. 1.30 pm Sunday, Penny very much weaker slipped overboard. From 10 pm tonight 14 days out, tried to make the Leeward Islands, Porto Rico, Hayti, but the German raider had given none the right to take a sextant, chronometer, extra water, tin fruit or bottled fruit, no rum or brandy for the wounded crew. Evidently intended to smash all lifeboat gear to kill all inquiry, but we got the small gig, seven of us, by wind somewhere in the vicinity of Leeward Islands.*

In fact, contrary to the belief of the five men remaining on board, they were nowhere near the Leeward Islands. Their boat was still in mid-ocean, with many, many miles to go before their ordeal came to an end, an end which most of them would never see. By 5 September, the drinking water was all gone, and on that day Chief Officer Barry Denny and Third Engineer Lionel Hawks died, and their bodies were lowered over the side. Four days later, Assistant Cook Leslie Morgan went mad, and also died. That left only the two seamen, 19-year-old Robert Tapscott and 21-year-old Roy Widdecombe. They had no water and only a limited amount of food left. Lesser men might have given up there and then, and followed their shipmates over the side.

For the next three days, Tapscott and Widdecombe, comforted by their belief that they were near to the land, stoically endured the heat of the sun which beat down on them from a cloudless sky, and the cold chill of the long nights. To the best of their ability, they kept the boat on a westerly course, but with only a rapidly dwindling supply of dry biscuits to hold off the pangs of hunger, and with no water to wet their parched lips, they grew steadily weaker and more despondent. Then their luck changed.

On Thursday 12 September, their twenty-second day adrift on this empty ocean, the two men lay in the bottom of the boat, slipping in and out of consciousness, their bodies shrunken, their tongues so swollen through lack of water that they were unable to talk. Then, in the middle of the afternoon, the sun was obscured by a towering cumulo-nimbus, and the heavens opened when a massive rain squall enveloped the boat. Roused from their stupor by the drenching rain, they slaked their raging thirsts, and filled every utensil they could find. When the rain finished, as abruptly as it had started, they had six days' supply of drinking water in their wooden breaker.

Over the next twelve days, Tapscott and Widdecombe were blessed with the occasional heavy shower that satisfied their thirst, but on the 24th the last remaining crumbs of their biscuits were eaten and the water was finished. There was no more rain, and from then on they existed in a shadowy world, hovering between life and death, sustained only by a few flying fish they caught and odd bits of seaweed they scooped up from the sea. By the time the boat was cast ashore on Eleuthera Island, they were on the point of slipping into their last sleep.

The survival of Robert Tapscott and Roy Widdecombe against such tremendous odds was one for the record book. They had endured seventy days in an open boat measuring 18 feet by 6 feet, much of the time without food and water, and had sailed 2,500 miles in a westerly direction. On the long voyage they had watched their five companions die in the most horrible way, and when they came ashore on Eleuthera, both men had lost half their body weight, were unable to speak, were blinded by the merciless sun, and suffering from serious vitamin deficiency, but in spite of their ordeal, had retained their sanity. They were the only survivors from the *Anglo Saxon*'s crew of forty.

The authorities in the Bahamas showed the utmost compassion for Tapscott and Widdecombe. Their removal from Eleuthera was personally supervised by the Chief Medical Officer for the islands, who flew them to hospital in Nassau, where with careful nursing they made a full recovery. They then went their separate ways, Tapscott to Canada, where he joined the Canadian Army, and Widdecombe to New York to cross the Atlantic again as one of the crew of the British ship *Siamese Prince*, which sailed in February 1941. On the 17th of that month, when she was 200 miles off the Outer Hebrides, the *Siamese Prince* was torpedoed by U-69, and sank with all hands. Roy Widdecombe, who had triumphed over so many adversities since that night in August 1940 when the

40

Widder came out of the darkness with her guns blazing, did not live to see his homeland again. After two years with the Canadian Army, Robert Tapscott rejoined the Merchant Navy, and served at sea until September 1963, when at the age of 42 he took his own life. So died the only remaining survivor of the sinking of the *Anglo Saxon*. The 18ft jolly boat that carried Tapscott and Widdecombe on their epic voyage is preserved for posterity in the Imperial War Museum at London.

After sinking the *Anglo Saxon,* the *Widder* moved out into mid-Atlantic, where she sank the British tanker *Cymbeline* and the Greek steamer *Chandris Piraeus*. Then, dogged by recurring engine breakdowns, Von Ruckteschell took her back to Brest, where she became a naval depot ship. On her only voyage as an armed merchant raider she had caused considerable disruption in the Atlantic, sinking ten Allied merchant ships totalling nearly 50,000 tons gross, some of them, including the *Anglo Saxon* under very questionable circumstances.

After a short spell ashore, Helmuth von Ruckteschell took command of another merchant raider, the *Michel*. When the war ended, he was arrested and tried for war crimes. Several charges of brutal behaviour on the high seas were brought against him, not least that he opened fire on the *Anglo Saxon* without regard to the safety of her crew, in evidence of which an entry in Chief Officer Denny's log was quoted which stated that the German captain 'opened fire within a mile, killing many, closed to 600 yards, and raked the deck with machine-guns, mowing the crew down as they went to the boats, then fired on two life-rafts in the water'. Von Ruckteschell was found guilty of the charges against him and sentenced to ten years in jail, later commuted to seven years. He died in Spandau Prison, aged fifty-eight, after a heart attack.

Chapter Five

The One That Got Away

In the autumn of 1940 the whole of Western Europe lay supine under the iron heel of Hitler's *Wermacht*. Britain alone stood fast, but she was in mortal danger. Only the thin line of weather-beaten ships stretching across the North Atlantic to the arsenals and store-houses of the Americas could save her. But that lifeline was perilously near to breaking point. In September alone, sixty ships of 291,679 tons had fallen to the enemy, and the toll was rising steadily.

The situation was so when, in the early evening of 5 October, four U-boats sailed from the Biscay port of Lorient, in occupied France, and turned their sleek grey hulls to meet the Atlantic swells rolling in from the west. Led by *Kapitänleutnant* Fritz Frauenheim in U-101, the four Type VII boats were the outriders of the first of Admiral Dönitz's 'wolf packs', whose allotted task was to finally and irrevocably cut Britain's Atlantic lifeline. On that same day, and within the hour, 2,360 miles to the west, Convoy SC 7 sailed from Sydney, Cape Breton, bound eastwards.

The majority of the thirty-five ships making up SC 7 were old, slow and, in some cases, woefully small. Many were plainly no match for the North Atlantic at the approach of winter, and would normally have made the crossing only in high summer, if at all. But Britain's immediate needs were so great that the rewards on offer far outweighed the risks.

Fortunately, the weather was fine and calm when SC 7 cleared the headlands of Sydney harbour and, with a great deal of black smoke and grumbling confusion, formed up in nine columns abreast, and set off at its designated speed of 7 knots. The convoy's meagre escort, consisting only of the 1,200-ton sloop HMS *Scarborough* and the Canadian armed yacht *Elk,* did not serve to inspire confidence in the breasts of the captains commanding the merchant ships. Resolute though they might be, the naval ships were too small and too lightly armed to be a serious deterrent to the U-boats now holding sway over the Atlantic sea lanes. If SC 7 was to arrive in Britain intact it would need the protection of the Lord, and the luck of the Devil.

Leading the third column in the convoy was the British cargo ship *Blairspey,* under the command of 54-year-old Captain James Walker of Glasgow. The *Blairspey,* a steamer of 4,155 tons, was owned by George Nisbet & Company of Glasgow, also known as the Clydesdale Navigation Company. Built in 1929, she was one of the younger and more agile members of SC 7, and for this reason Captain Walker had been appointed vice-commodore of the convoy. In addition to navigating his own ship, it fell to him to assist the Commodore, who flew his flag in the small Ellerman & Papayanni cargo liner *Assyrian,* to mould together the motley collection of eighteen British, six Norwegian, four Greek, three Swedish, two Dutch, one French and one Danish merchantmen, in the hope that they would cross the ocean in some semblance of order. It was therefore with an added sense of pride that James Walker trod the bridge of his ship as she stood out into the Atlantic.

In her holds, and on deck, the *Blairspey* carried a cargo of 1,798 standards of timber, loaded in Quebec and consigned to Grangemouth, on the Firth of Forth, which was much to the liking of her mainly Scottish crew of thirty-four. They also took great comfort from the fact that their cargo of timber offered a degree of protection against the attention of the enemy. Should the *Blairspey* be torpedoed, she would almost certainly stay afloat for some time, thereby giving her crew a chance to abandon ship in good order. It could not be said that the *Blairspey*'s armament offered any such comfort. Her 4-inch anti-submarine gun mounted aft was a museum piece, and her only defence against aircraft was a .45 Thompson machine carbine, a weapon as incongruous aboard a

British tramp as it was at home in the world of the Chicago gangsters of the 1920s.

The convoy's route, as laid down by the Admiralty, would take it into the northernmost reaches of the Atlantic, to within 250 miles of Iceland, before then curving to the south-east to approach Britain through the North Channel, which runs between Ireland and Scotland. In this way, it was hoped to keep well out of range of patrolling U-boats until the final leg of the 16-day passage, at which point it was planned to reinforce SC 7's escort substantially.

Two days out of Sydney, the armed yacht *Elk* turned back for Nova Scotia, having reached the limit of her range. Fortunately for this diminutive warship, the weather up to this point had remained unusually calm. But as SC 7 inched its way to the east with its sole escort HMS *Scarborough* bravely scouting ahead, the North Atlantic began to bare its teeth.

By the morning of the 11th, it was blowing a full gale from the north-west, which brought with it a heavy beam swell and rough, tumbling seas. Very soon, two of the smaller merchant ships, the 1,800-ton Great Lakes steamers *Trevisa* and *Eaglescliffe Hall*, were forced to drop out. It was indeed something of a miracle that these ships had progressed so far, for they were not built for ocean steaming.

As the day wore on and the weather worsened, the bigger ships began to go. The first to fall behind, wallowing helplessly in the troughs, was the 3,554-ton Greek vessel *Aenos*. She was soon joined by her compatriot, the 5,875-ton *Thalia*. Both ships had suffered engine breakdowns, their old and poorly maintained machinery unable to stand up to the strain imposed by the heavy rolling and pitching.

The gale, which was part of a huge equinoctial depression moving across the North Atlantic, blew fiercely and without let-up for the next four days. Throughout, the remaining ships, although in some disarray, moved doggedly north-eastwards, with the gallant little *Scarborough* rolling her rails under as she fought to maintain a modicum of cover for her thirty-one charges. On the afternoon of the 15th, the *Aenos* rejoined and, coincident with her reappearance, the barometer began to rise, bringing a dramatic improvement in the weather. As the convoy was now less than twenty-four hours steaming from the rendezvous point with the local escort heading out from the North Channel to join it, the prospects for a successful crossing began to look good.

The first intimation SC 7 had of approaching danger came in the darkest hours of the morning of the 16th, when distress calls were heard from the *Trevisa*. Straggling some 120 miles astern of the convoy, the small British steamer had been torpedoed by U-124, one of the quartet of outriders that had left Lorient eleven days earlier. She had missed the main convoy, and was casting about for a lone straggler when the *Trevisa* crossed her path.

Sunset was only forty minutes away when, that afternoon, SC 7's luck ran out. U-93, commanded by *Kapitänleutnant* Klaus Korth, was patrolling on the surface when she sighted several columns of smoke on the horizon to the east. Pressing ahead at full speed, Korth was soon able to confirm his hopes: he had fallen in with a large British convoy. He at once reported his find to U-boat Headquarters at Lorient.

Admiral Dönitz ordered Korth to shadow the convoy, and then set about laying a trap for the unsuspecting merchantmen. By midnight, a line of eight U-boats, led by the Admiral's top ace, *Korvettenkapitän* Otto Kretschmer in U-99, was stretched across the convoy's path.

Meanwhile, help was at hand for SC 7. During the afternoon, HMS *Scarborough* had been joined by the sloop *Fowey* and the Flower-class corvette *Bluebell,* the first of the local escort to arrive. Between them, the three warships still made up only a token show of force, but their mere presence indicated to the merchantmen that they were within striking distance of the safety of the North Channel. Morale on board the ships went up several notches.

On the bridge of the *Blairspey* that night the atmosphere was tense. Captain Walker and his officers were acutely aware that, if an attack was to be made on the convoy, it would come within the next twenty-four hours. There had been many times during the crossing when Walker had roundly cursed the foul Atlantic weather, but now, with the wind and sea falling, and a bright moon occasionally breaking through the clouds, he had an uneasy feeling in the pit of his stomach. Conditions for the U-boats could not have been better. Had Walker but known the extent of the danger, his uneasiness would have been more acute. Out in the darkness of the night the unseen shadower, Klaus Korth in U-93, had been joined by Heinrich Bleichrodt in U-48.

The first hammer blow fell at three o'clock on the morning of the 17th, when on the instructions of Lorient, Bleichrodt opened the attack. The 9,512-ton French tanker *Languedoc*, following close astern of the *Blairspey*, suddenly erupted in a sheet of flame. Seconds later, the 3,843-ton British cargo ship *Scoresby* sent distress rockets arcing skywards as she was hit and began to sink. Bleichrodt's third torpedo hit and severely damaged the *Haspenden*, a 4,678-ton British steamer. Walker had little time to reflect on the horror of the sinkings, as the Commodore had ordered a series of emergency turns, and he was fully occupied in trying to save his own ship.

Confusion reigned for a while, then there was an eerie quiet, and the rest of the night passed without incident. By dawn, hope was again rising in the ships as they zig-zagged towards British waters with a renewed sense of urgency. At 0700, the escort was further reinforced by the Grimsby-class sloop HMS *Leith*, while a Sunderland flying boat made a brief appearance overhead. Later in the day, another Flower-class corvette, HMS *Heartsease*, also joined. Even the sceptical Captain Walker, bleary-eyed and unshaven after so many long hours on the bridge of the *Blairspey*, began to see the odds on a safe arrival shortening. It was with mixed feelings, therefore, that he watched the weather improving as the day wore on. Fine weather allowed a faster rate of advance towards safety, but it also meant more exposure to the seeking eyes of the enemy.

By nightfall, the visibility was excellent, with the moon behind the clouds shedding a diffused light on the orderly columns of ships as they zig-zagged their way across a calm sea. The five escort vessels, three sloops and two corvettes, were spread out around the perimeter of the convoy, their lookouts searching the horizon with night glasses, their Asdics probing underwater. There was little else to be done but to wait and hope.

Shortly after 0100 on the 18th, U-38, commanded by *Kapitänleutnant* Heinrich Liebe, penetrated the thin defensive screen from astern, and sent a torpedo speeding towards the

3,670-ton British steamer *Carsbreck*, sailing in the outside column on the port side of the convoy. As the *Carsbreck*'s distress rockets flared, those on the bridge of the *Blairspey* caught sight of the track of another torpedo overtaking their ship on her port side. It was a near-miss, but Captain Walker did not take kindly to being shot at from behind. He felt doubly vulnerable.

The *Carsbreck* did not sink, but her speed dropped away, and she began to straggle astern. That she was still afloat was a stroke of good fortune for her crew, but it spelled disaster for the other ships of SC 7 when the corvette *Bluebell* was detached to stand by the stricken ship. In effect, Liebe had succeeded in reducing the convoy's escort force by a substantial twenty per cent at one stroke.

By 1900, the convoy had reached the furthest point north in its route, and was then 250 miles to the south of Iceland. The ships now altered course to the south-east, making for the entrance to the North Channel. The moon not being up, and with the darkness of the night complete, with a little more than forty-eight hours to go before they came abreast of the Outer Hebrides and within range of continuous air cover, there were once more grounds for optimism. Then, without warning, Dönitz sprung his trap.

The first blow was dealt by Karl-Heinz Möhle in U-123, when he torpedoed the *Shekatika*, a 5,458-ton timber carrier registered in Leith. She was badly holed, but her cargo of pit props kept her afloat. There was a lull of some forty minutes, then, just as it seemed the danger had receded, Engelbert Endrass in U-46 and Fritz Frauenheim in U-101 sank between them, in quick succession, the 4,885-ton Cardiff ship *Beatus*, the Swedish-flag *Convallaria*, and the 28-year-old *Creekirk* of London.

For a while, confusion reigned. Distress rockets soared skywards, ships' whistles wailed, and the escorts dashed blindly to meet an enemy they could not see. In the midst of all this, the Convoy Commodore, in the *Assyrian*, and his deputy Captain Walker, in the *Blairspey*, attempted to lead the ranks of nervous merchant ships through a series of violent emergency turns. By the grace of God and the instinctive seamanship of the merchantmen, there were no collisions, and by 2030 all was quiet again. The U-boats' score was now seven ships sunk and three damaged.

And the danger was not yet past, for Otto Kretschmer, in characteristic style, had manoeuvred U-99 into the middle of the convoy, and selecting the largest ship in the ranks, the 6,055-ton *Empire Miniver*, he sent her to the bottom with one well-aimed torpedo. Twenty minutes later, Endrass in U-46 sank the convoy's smallest ship, the 1,572-ton Swedish-flag *Gunborg*.

The *Gunborg* was only two ships astern of the *Blairspey*, and seeing her go Captain Walker wondered how much time his own ship had left. All around him ships were sinking or disabled, and it was plainly obvious to him the SC 7's escort force was powerless in the face of such a savage and determined enemy. The temptation to cut and run was very great, to steam away from this awful nightmare at all possible speed, in the hope that safety might be found under cover of the night. But James Walker was too experienced a master to fall for the easy option. He knew well that as soon as the *Blairspey* strayed from the protection of the convoy screen – poor though it may seem – the waiting wolves would pounce.

Even as Walker gave thought to his predicament, he heard from the starboard quarter the warning screech of another ship's whistle. He ran out into the starboard wing and was in time to see the track of a torpedo speeding down the side of his ship. It was a very near miss.

The convoy was now surrounded by U-boats, which appeared to be operating on the surface with impunity, for they outnumbered the hard-pressed escort ships of the Royal Navy by more than two to one. Circling the periphery and firing inwards were Heinrich Bleichrodt in U-48, Karl-Heinz Möhle in U-123, Englebert Endrass in U-46, Fritz Frauenheim in U-101, Wilhelm Schulz in U-124, Heinrich Liebe in U-38, Joachim Schepke in U-100 and Günter Kuhnke in U-28, while Otto Kretschmer cruised in the middle of the convoy firing outwards. Nine ships had gone, three others were damaged – and the slaughter was only just beginning.

An already serious situation worsened when the heavy cloud cover cleared away and the beleaguered convoy was bathed in the brilliant light of the full moon, then climbing high in the eastern sky. The gods were surely on the side of the U-boats that night.

A few minutes later, at 2230, the *Blairspey* moved into the sights of U-101, and Fritz Frauenheim gave the order to fire. Walker felt, rather than heard the dull thud of the torpedo striking home. There was no eruption of smoke or flame, and for a few brief seconds he dared to hope that some other ship close at hand had been hit. Then the *Blairspey* staggered, a deluge of water rained down on the bridge, and he knew the inevitable had happened.

Frauenheim's torpedo had hit the *Blairspey* in her No. 1 hold, about fifty feet from the bows. She took a slight list at first, but quickly straightened up again. Then, the air was suddenly filled with the roar of escaping high-pressure steam. The shock of the explosion had caused a blow-out of a joint in the main steam line in her engine-room. Robbed of their driving force, the gleaming pistons of the engine slowly ground to a halt.

Soon, the *Blairspey* was stopped and dead in the water, with the frightening cacophony of venting steam filling the night air around her. The rest of the convoy, intent on beating off its insistent attackers, was drawing slowly ahead. Walker felt very much alone and exposed. It was with some relief when, half an hour or so later, the senior escort ship, HMS *Leith*, appeared out of the darkness. The sloop circled the *Blairspey*, and then came in close to enquire the extent of her damage. At this stage, Captain Walker had no intention of abandoning his ship, and informed *Leith* that he hoped to raise steam again and limp along in the rear of the convoy in company with the other damaged ships. *Leith* wished him luck and, with a flurry of foam at her stern, swept away to rejoin the running battle for SC 7.

The *Blairspey*'s chief engineer, Alexander Henderson, now took his men back into the steam-filled engine-room they had been forced to abandon earlier. They were to spend the next two hours working without let-up to repack the blown steam joint.

Those on the bridge of the stationary ship, who could only wait and watch, suffered a subtle torture of the most fiendish kind. As the convoy drew ahead and out of sight, so the moon went behind the clouds again, and the darkness was complete. The uncanny silence was broken only by the slap of waves against the hull and the creak of derricks as they moved in their crutches with the roll of the ship. Each time the clang of a hammer rang out from deep in the engine-room, it was like the tolling of a funeral bell. Walker gritted his teeth, for he knew the job could not be done in silence.

For Henderson and his men, working by the light of flickering oil lamps twenty feet below the waterline, the tension was even greater. Each time steel rang on steel or the curses grew loud, glances strayed to the hull plates, beyond which, in the silence of the deep, the enemy might be listening. The great cathedral-like engine-space in which they worked with the sweat soaking into their boilersuits was the soft under-belly of the *Blairspey*. If a torpedo came crashing through those thin plates there would be no escape for them.

Having been involved in the fierce battle for SC 7 for forty-eight hours, Joachim Schepke was tired. It was inevitable that when, at 0100 on the 19th, he maneouvred U-100 into position to deliver the *coup de grâce* to the helpless *Blairspey*, his judgement was flawed. He aimed for her engine-room, but the torpedo struck between her No. 1 and No. 2 holds, which were packed tight with planks of Canadian timber.

The time had now come for Captain James Walker to make that decision that haunts all who bear the burden of command at sea. From the bridge, the effect of the second torpedo was much the same as that of the first. The explosion, the shudder, and the tall column of water and debris thrown into the air were frightening, but by no means fatal. While Walker was aware that the hull of his ship had been savagely ripped open, he was confident that her timber cargo would keep her afloat for many hours, perhaps days. However, he was a realist, and he knew in his heart that it was only a matter of time before the lurking U-boat put a torpedo into the engine-room of his helpless ship. This, the largest single compartment in the ship, would flood rapidly, and that would be the end of the *Blairspey* – or would it? The ring of a hammer came again from the bowels of the ship, and Walker was reminded of his duty to those men below. He gave the order to abandon ship.

As is customary in British merchant ships, Walker, as master, took charge of the starboard lifeboat, while Chief Officer John Glasgow had the port boat. Walker's boat, with twenty men on board, took to the water smoothly, and pulled clear. As Glasgow's boat was being lowered, Schepke put another torpedo into the

Blairspey, which exploded directly below the suspended boat.

Believing his chief officer and his boat's crew must have been killed, Walker took his own boat away from the *Blairspey* as fast as possible. A few minutes later, both U-101 and U-100 approached the lifeboat and asked for the name of the ship. The U-boats were cruising on the surface with complete disregard of any danger to themselves, which was not surprising, for the convoy and its escort were now out of sight over the horizon. The Germans, obviously believing the *Blairspey* would sink of her own accord, made no attempt to shell or torpedo her again.

Being of the same opinion as the U-boat commanders, Walker took one last lingering look at his ex-command, and prepared to sail for the Irish coast, which lay 100 miles to the south-west. As the sails were being hoisted, he was greatly relieved to see the other lifeboat appear out of the night. By some miracle, Glasgow and his crew had survived the torpedo uninjured, and without damage to their boat.

During what remained of the night, the wind freshened, bringing with it a choppy sea, and the two lifeboats became separated. Soon after dawn, Walker and his crew were picked up by the corvette *Bluebell,* which already had on board 150 survivors from various ships. John Glasgow and his men were not so fortunate. It was late afternoon before they were rescued by a salvage tug.

For Convoy SC 7 the one-sided fight had continued throughout the night. Before the grey light of dawn broke through on the 19th, another five ships had been lost. Only then did the U-boats withdraw, some to return in triumph to Lorient, others to attack Convoy HX 19, which was approaching from the west. There they would add another twelve ships to their score.

Early on the morning of the 20th, the Atlantic took a final spiteful swipe at SC 7, when a howling gale, accompanied by blinding rainstorms, scattered the tattered remnants of the convoy. Sanctuary was eventually found in the sheltered waters of the Firth of Clyde on 21 October, but of the thirty-five ships that set out from Canada sixteen days earlier, only fifteen remained.

So ended one of the bloodiest battles in recent maritime history. The U-boats, operating on the surface at night, had been able to run rings around the slow, lightly-armed escorts of SC 7. Confused and relatively defenceless, the merchant ships were picked off at will. In the space of seventy-two hours, twenty ships, totalling 79,646 tons went to the bottom, and with them went over 100,000 tons of precious cargo and several hundred merchant seamen. The heaviest slaughter took place on the night of 18/19 October, which thereafter became known amongst the U-boat men as 'The Night of the Long Knives'.

One of the great ironies of the battle of Convoy SC 7 was that the tiny *Eaglescliffe Hall,* which had dropped out of the convoy shortly after sailing from Sydney, found her way across the Atlantic alone and unprotected. On her way, she picked up twenty-five survivors from the torpedoed Greek steamer *Aenos,* thereby playing a vital role in the operation.

As for the *Blairspey,* in spite of the three torpedoes she had suffered, she lived to sail another day. When the shooting stopped, she was found still afloat, and towed into the Clyde by a deep-sea tug.

U-101 survived the war, and was surrendered to British forces in May 1945. U-100 did not have the same good fortune. On 17 March 1941, she was surprised on the surface while attacking Convoy HX 112, and rammed and sunk by the destroyer HMS *Vanoc.* Joachim Schepke and all but five of his crew went down with her.

Chapter Six

The Other Enemy

For the men of Britain's tramps, winter in the North Atlantic had never been anything but a season of acute discomfort and danger. To spend day after day and night after sleepless night hove-to with green seas sweeping the decks, cabins awash, and muscles aching through constant bracing against the roll and pitch of a ship in torment was accepted as an occupational hazard. Frequently, these slow and deeply laden ships limped into port with lifeboats reduced to matchwood, hatches leaking, and coal bunkers all but empty. Occasionally, one of their number would be lost without trace, simply overwhelmed by the awesome power of an angry sea that knew no bounds for a thousand miles in any direction. This too was accepted.

The winter of 1940 was said to be the worst ever recorded in the North Atlantic. It was a time when a never-ending series of deep depressions marched across that wide expanse of ocean, each following so close on the heels of the other that the barometer appeared to be stuck at an all-time low for months on end. Rarely did the wind drop below gale force, and often it rose to such a screaming crescendo that even the most hardened Western Ocean men felt butterflies stirring in their stomachs. The long Atlantic rollers became tall foam-topped mountains that sought to brush the low-hanging clouds, and hid dark valleys deep enough to swallow a 5,000-ton ship from truck to keel.

To all this, in 1940, was added the constant threat of the skulking U-boat, and the shadowy surface raider. The silent torpedo could break a ship's back like the punch of a sharp-fanged reef, and the whistling long-range shell make a bloody shambles of an unprotected bridge and its occupants. And now there was yet another enemy to face.

Following the fall of France in June 1940, and the subsequent availability of new bases on the Biscay coast, Hitler decided to strengthen the U-boat arm by the use of reconnaissance aircraft to seek out Allied shipping. For this role the four-engined Focke-Wulf Condor was chosen. The Condor had a range of over 2,000 miles and a top speed of 224 mph, carried a bomb-load of 4,626 lbs, and was armed with a formidable array of machine-guns and cannon. Flying from an operational base set up near Bordeaux, the Condors very quickly proved to be invaluable as the 'eyes' of the U-boats, and their progression to the attacking role was inevitable. Although this great, lumbering aircraft was too vulnerable to approach an escorted convoy, it proved remarkably effective against the lone merchantman.

On Saturday 26 October 1940, Convoy OB 235 sailed from the deep-water harbour of Milford Haven, and headed west into the St. George's Channel. The barometer was falling steadily and, under a lowering cloud base, the white horses had begun to gallop. At this stage, OB 235 consisted of only a handful of ships, and was lightly escorted. Later, off Liverpool, and later still off the Firth of Clyde, other ships would join, and the escort force would be reinforced before the completed convoy passed through the North Channel and out into the Atlantic.

In the ranks of the embryo OB 235 as it cleared the Welsh coast was the 5,702-ton *Starstone,* owned by the Alva Steamship Company of London. Commanded by 43-year-old Captain W.R. Thomas of Cardiff, the *Starstone* was a comparatively new ship, having been built by William Doxford & Sons at Sunderland only a year before the outbreak of war. However, like most tramps of her day, she was lamentably underpowered. On her trials, light ship and under ideal conditions, she had achieved a speed of 10 knots. Deep-loaded and with a perpetually dirty bottom through lack of dry-docking, her performance was, to say the least, unimpressive. On her current voyage she was, as usual, riding low in the water,

54

down to her marks with 8,500 tons of best Welsh steam coal, loaded at Barry for the River Plate.

In the less regimented days of peace, when merchant ships were free to go their own separate ways without interference from admirals and enemies, Captain Thomas would have taken a south-westerly course after leaving the Bristol Channel, and once clear of the Bay of Biscay some three days later, would have left the worst of the Atlantic weather behind him. Unfortunately, on this voyage the logical and time-honoured route to South America was not open to him. As a result of the capitulation of France, and the occu-pation of her long Atlantic coastline by German forces, the Admiralty had laid a huge minefield across the south-western approaches to Britain. The St. George's Channel and English Channel were completely sealed off, so that the only access to and from all ports lay to the north. The *Starstone* would be forced to go out through the North Channel, passing between Ireland and Scotland. Apart from adding 800 miles to her passage, this northern route took her directly into the path of the fiercest Atlantic gales for two days longer than necessary. Given that his ship was loaded very deep, with precious little freeboard, this gave Thomas grounds for concern.

With regard to the dangers presented by the enemy, Captain Thomas had rather more confidence in his ship. In addition to the usual 4-inch on the poop, she mounted a 12-pounder high/low angle gun aft, and a .303 Hotchkiss machine-gun on the bridge. As a morale booster more than anything else, Thomas also kept a .303 rifle handy in the wheelhouse. The *Starstone* carried only one DEMS gunner, Gunlayer Jackson of the Royal Navy, who had organised and trained guns' crews from the ship's officers and ratings. The only weak link in the *Starstone*'s defence, in the opinion of Captain Thomas, lay in her unprotected navigation bridge. At this stage of the war it was normal practice to shield the bridge, the vital control centre of a ship, with concrete armour to protect it from bullets and flying splinters. The *Starstone*'s bridge was still unprotected, despite Thomas's persistent lobbying at each recent port of call.

Thomas might also have been forgiven if he had anticipated crew problems on this voyage, for his men were certainly one of the most cosmopolitan assemblies ever to sail out of Britain in one ship. While the Captain and his chief engineer were Cardiff men, his chief officer hailed from County Durham, his second officer from Glasgow, his third officer from Norway, his chief radio officer from Swaziland, his fourth engineer from South Africa, and his chief steward, who bore the fairy-tale name of Hans Christian Olsen, was a native of Denmark. In the forecastle, the carpenter was Japanese, the deck crew were from Sierra Leone, the engine-room ratings from India, and the stewards were British. As subsequent events were to prove, no better prototype for the as yet unformed United Nations could have been found anywhere.

At noon on the 28th the convoy, having trailed its coat across the estuaries of the Mersey and Clyde, had swollen to thirty-three ships, and was passing the Mull of Kintyre, bound out through the North Channel. The naval escort consisted of the destroyers *Veteran, Verity, Chelsea* and *Witherton,* plus the Flower-class corvette *Gentian.* This seemingly generous protective screen was short-term however, as OB 235 was to disperse 300 miles to the west of Ireland, when the main danger from U-boats was considered to be astern.

The *Starstone* was the leading ship in the third column, and was, for the moment, comfortably maintaining the convoy's speed of 8 knots. The weather was fine, with only a slight sea running, and there was a crisp, exhilarating bite in the air which spoke of winter soon to come. On the bridge of the *Starstone,* Captain Thomas, glad of his heavy bridgecoat, regarded the weather with suspicion. Winter in the North Atlantic was all very well for some, but he would not rest easy until he felt the warm Portuguese Trades on his back, safe in the knowledge that it would be fair-weather sailing from then on.

On deck, Chief Officer H.L. Poulson's thoughts were also running ahead of the ship. At twenty-eight, Poulson was comparatively young to be in such a senior rank, but he had learned his trade well, and in a hard school. At the head of his long list of shipboard responsibilities was the care of the *Starstone*'s cargo of coal. To the uninitiated, the carriage of this dirty, and apparently inert, cargo might appear undemanding, but Poulson, through past experience, knew better.

The transportation of coal in ships is fraught with the twin dangers of fire and explosion, and over the years many a fine vessel has been lost as a result. Immediately after loading, coal emits an inflammable gas, which can explode with catastrophic results on contact with a spark or naked flame. Consequently, maximum ventilation is required during the early stages of the voyage, even to the extent of leaving open corner hatches, a practice that calls for a careful eye on the weather. The risk of fire is longer-term, and usually caused by spontaneous combustion taking place deep within the cargo when too much oxygen is absorbed from the air. In this case, excessive ventilation increases the risk. So, in caring for a cargo of coal at sea a thin tightrope must be walked. Insufficient ventilation may result in an explosion, whereas too much air flowing into the holds could well start and fuel a deep-seated fire which is almost impossible to extinguish at sea.

All the 'alarms and excursions' of war apart, Poulson had much to occupy his mind on the long passage to the River Plate.

Soon after the convoy rounded the north of Ireland, the wind began to freshen, and by the early hours of the morning of the 29th a full gale was blowing from the west. Before dawn, the *Starstone*'s Japanese carpenter, W. Wada, was on deck in oilskins and sea-boots hastily battening down the corner hatches. Chief Officer Poulson's careful attention to the ventilation of the cargo had come to naught. The sea was now presenting a far greater danger to the ship than pockets of marsh gas.

Throughout that morning, the wind continued to strengthen, and by noon it had reached storm force. The *Starstone*, sitting low in the water, found her decks being swept by angry green seas as she struggled valiantly to keep up with the convoy. But despite Chief Engineer Cusworth's careful nursing of his engine, she was soon down to 6 knots and falling astern of the other ships. When the davits of her port lifeboat were bent and her jollyboat smashed by the huge seas, Captain Thomas decided that enough was enough. Much to the relief of his harassed chief engineer, he called for reduced speed, and pulled the *Starstone* out of the convoy. Very soon, she was alone on the storm-swept sea.

For the next thirty-six hours, the *Starstone* was hove-to with the wind and sea on the bow, her engines just ticking over, so that she was able to hold up into the wind without incurring any damage. Her forward progress was negligible, and she was a sitting duck for any U-boat that might happen along, but this Thomas refused to contemplate. For the time being, his most dangerous enemy was the sea.

By dawn on the 21st, when the *Starstone* was 200 miles west of Ireland, the wind eased to gale force, and it was possible to increase speed to 5 knots. There was still a heavy sea running, and the cloud was low, but the visibility was beginning to improve, indicating that the depression was passing. Thomas saw little hope of rejoining the other ships, but feeling that the effort was required of him, he set a course calculated to intercept the convoy.

At 0915, when the cloud had lifted still further, an aircraft was sighted approaching from the south-west. Thomas was on the bridge with 29-year-old Third Officer Hansen, who had the watch. Both men lifted their binoculars at the lookout's warning shout, located and focused on the black dot showing low down on the horizon. Thomas was no expert at aircraft recognition, but he realised at once that this was no friendly Sunderland coming in to pay its respects. He ordered Hansen to sound action stations.

Before the alarm bells had stopped ringing, Gunlayer Jackson, with Chief Steward Olsen hot on his heels, was racing aft to the 12-pounder. Behind them, at a more sedate pace, came the Sierra Leonian seamen who made up the rest of the gun's crew.

On the bridge, Second Officer Joseph Kelly, who had just arrived to take his morning sun sight, put down his sextant and slammed a magazine into the Hotchkiss. He tested the gun with a quick burst to seaward.

In the wheelhouse, the Sierra Leonian helmsman, Able Seaman George Taylor, gripped the spokes of the wheel tightly and wondered how on earth he had allowed himself to get mixed up in this white man's war.

Bursting out through the galley door clutching a half-eaten bacon sandwich, 16-year-old cabin boy Ernest Webb rushed to the ship's side rail and gazed in awe at the approaching plane. On his first voyage to sea, Webb was determined not to miss a move in the unfolding drama.

Captain Thomas watched tight-lipped as the aircraft banked and flew down the port side of the ship at a distance of about 2 miles. He was unable to make out any markings, but the squarish wing tips, the gondola-like structure under the fuselage, and the irregular beat of the four engines were characteristics too ominous to ignore. He passed the word to the wireless-room to send out an 'AAAA' signal, indicating that the *Starstone* was under attack by enemy aircraft.

The plane flew on past the ship, then tipped its wings to port, and came around in a tight circle to end up head into the wind and right astern. For a while, it seemed to hover in the *Starstone*'s wake, as though the pilot was deliberating on how to begin the attack. By this time Thomas could see the black crosses on the underside of the plane's wings. He gave the order to open fire with the 12-pounder.

On the gun platform aft, Chief Steward Olsen set the fuse on the first shell to 1,250 yards and nodded confidently to Jackson. The breech clanged shut, and the gun barked. Seconds later, a puff of black smoke appeared close to the tail of the Focke-Wulf. Olsen shortened the next fuse to 750 yards, Jackson adjusted his sights, and the second round burst only feet away from the aircraft's nose. For a gun that had seen better days, manned by a largely untrained crew, this was excellent shooting.

But if the German pilot was at all worried by the *Starstone*'s spirited defence, he failed to show it. The Focke-Wulf roared down her starboard side at mast-top height with all its guns blazing.

Second Officer Kelly opened fire with his Hotchkiss as the plane came abreast of the bridge, but the gun jammed after a few rounds, and he was left cursing impotently as he tried to clear the fouled breech. Thomas, who was crouching in the wing of the bridge with his rifle, now jumped up and took aim. The loud roar of the plane's engines, the rattle of her machine-guns, the crack of the 12-pounder, all intermingled with the howling wind – the gale was still blowing – produced a frightening discord. But Thomas, furious at this unprovoked attack on his ship, and oblivious to the bullets thudding into the wooden deck beneath his feet, returned the enemy's fire as fast as he could work the bolt of the .303. So occupied was he that he failed to notice the helmsman, George Taylor, go down with a bullet in his eye.

The Focke-Wulf swept past the bridge with its rear turret opening up to add to the mad symphony. Thomas, who was busy reloading his rifle, saw an ominous shape fall away from under the plane's wing.

The bomb landed on the starboard side of the forecastle, bounced over the anchor cables, and exploded on the port side of the deck with a crash that shook the *Starstone* from stem to stern. When the smoke cleared, Thomas looked down from his bridge on a scene of complete devastation. The forward bulwarks were shattered, the windlass torn from its mounting, and black smoke poured from the paint locker.

With the helm unattended, the ship's head was now falling off, and there was a danger of her broaching-to in the heavy seas. At a word from Thomas, George Taylor, although blind in one eye and with blood running down his face, returned to the wheel and brought the ship back up into the wind.

The next attack came from ahead, the Focke-Wulf again flying down the starboard side of the ship. The 12-pounder opened up, Thomas crouched low with his rifle at the ready, but Kelly was still desperately trying to clear his jammed Hotchkiss.

This time the German pilot, possibly disconcerted by the fierce and unexpected opposition, miscalculated, and his second bomb fell into the sea off the *Starstone*'s starboard quarter. He circled and came in from astern, but again the bomb exploded harmlessly in the sea.

The plane now took a wide, deliberate sweep before returning to the attack for the fourth time, approaching from dead ahead. Now the Focke-Wulf's bomb aimer made no mistake. The bomb landed on the after deck abreast of No. 4 hatch, penetrating the steel deck before exploding. Hatchboards, beams and tarpaulins were hurled into the air, derricks and winches crumpled, and the *Starstone*'s mainmast slowly toppled and collapsed into the open hatchway. Within the space of a few moments, tongues of flame and billows of black smoke could be seen coming from the hold. The Focke-Wulf now withdrew, and began to circle well out of range.

Thomas lowered his smoking rifle and called for a damage report. This revealed that his ship was on fire fore and aft, and extensively damaged on deck. The wireless aerials had been shot

60

away, the main transmitter wrecked, and No. 4 hold was making water, indicating that the hull had been breached. Bearing in mind the inflammable nature of his cargo, and the fact that the fire aft was dangerously close to the ammunition lockers, Thomas reluctantly concluded that the *Starstone* might not have long to go. Fortunately, the weather was taking a turn for the better, so he ordered the one serviceable lifeboat to be lowered and sent away in charge of Second Officer Kelly with twenty of the older and less able crew. Seeing the boat going down, the Focke-Wulf, evidently satisfied that the *Starstone* was being abandoned, flew away to the south-east.

Those who stayed on board to tackle the fires were Captain Thomas, Chief Officer Poulson, Third Officer Hansen, Chief Engineer Cusworth, Second Engineer Riley, and the young cabin boy Ernest Webb. Hoses were rigged, and within an hour the ship was out of danger. The lifeboat was recalled, and Thomas prepared to get under way again, now making for the coast of Ireland, where he intended to beach the ship if she showed signs of sinking.

The defence the *Starstone* had put up against a vastly superior enemy spoke volumes for the courage and determination of Captain Thomas and his cosmopolitan crew. Throughout the action, although bullets, cannon shells and bombs rained down on them, not one man had flinched from his duty. The scratch gun's crew of the 12-pounder loaded and fired with a coolness and precision that had had a marked deterrent effect on the Focke-Wulf. It was unfortunate that the Hotchkiss jammed early in the attack, but Second Officer Kelly had never given up trying to clear the gun, even though he was under fire from the air. Captain Thomas, oblivious to danger, had defended his bridge with the .303 until the enemy came no more. Above all, there had been no sign of panic. It was as though the *Starstone*'s men – culled from the four corners of the earth, and many of them owing no real loyalty to the flag their ship flew – had regarded the attack as a very personal thing.

During the Focke-Wulf's first attack, Chief Steward Hans Christian Olsen, breech-worker on the 12-pounder, had taken a machine-gun bullet in the arm, but he stuck to his post. He was eventually persuaded to leave the gun to have his wound dressed, but was caught on deck when the plane swooped in again, and was shot through the neck. Olsen, a naturalised Briton who had lived in Cardiff for over thirty years, died with his face to the enemy responsible for the rape of the country of his birth.

Gunlayer Jackson, whose expertise with the 12-pounder was probably mainly responsible for the Focke-Wulf not pressing home its attacks with more determination, had ended the action with three enemy bullets in his body, but still at his post. George Taylor, far from his native Freetown, and with a bullet in his eye, had gone back to the wheel and stayed there until he collapsed from loss of blood. The Japanese carpenter, Wada, a man who knew no home but the *Starstone,* had been shot in the knee, and must have been in great agony, but did not complain. It was not until the day after the action that Thomas discovered that the Japanese was wounded. South African-born Fourth Engineer Peter Johnson, on his first trip to sea, had shown exceptional bravery in sticking to his post in the engine-room despite the bombs. Third Officer Hansen, in the opinion of Captain Thomas, had been a tower of strength throughout, not only physically, but inspirationally, to all on board. And there was the cabin boy, Ernest Webb, little more than a schoolboy, who in the space of a few short hours had moved into courageous manhood.

During the attack, three others had been injured, including 28-year-old Third Engineer Andrew Lloyd Smith, who was in a very serious condition.

The *Starstone* had been under way again for only a few hours when she was overtaken by the British armed merchant cruiser *Alcantara,* which had rushed to her aid on hearing her 'AAAA' signal. The AMC offered to escort the damaged steamer into port, but Captain Thomas refused the offer, insisting that his ship was capable of making her own way. He later admitted that his decision was influenced by reports he had received earlier of U-boats in the area. He was loath to put the 22,000-ton ex-Royal Mail liner and her large crew at risk while playing nursemaid to a limping tramp.

On the morning of 1 November, the *Starstone* was in the North Channel and heading for the Clyde at all possible speed. Thomas, tired and drawn, still paced her bridge, but there was a new confidence in his walk. It seemed that the long nightmare would soon be over. Then the drone of aircraft engines drifted across the water, and the adrenaline began to run again.

Before the plane could be identified as British, the 12-pounder gun's crew was in position, and ready to fire, with Second Officer Kelly acting as gunlayer in place of the injured Jackson. When the familiar roundels of the RAF were recognised, there was almost an air of anti-climax on the gun platform. On orders from the bridge, Kelly secured the 12-pounder, and the crew went forward to the accommodation, their shoulders drooping with fatigue, but with pride in their eyes. On their way forward, they met Gunlayer Jackson crawling along the deck towards his gun. Despite his wounds, the naval gunner had been determined to get to his post when the alarm bells sounded. It took four men to carry him, protesting vigorously, back to his cabin.

At 1400 on 1 November, in sight of the brooding island of Arran, which stands sentinel at the entrance to the Firth of Clyde, Third Engineer Andrew Lloyd Smith died of his wounds.

The battle-scarred *Starstone* arrived at Greenock later that afternoon. There were no cheering crowds or rousing brass bands to welcome her, only a doctor to tend the injured, and a bowler-hatted dockyard superintendent to survey her damage. When the repairs were discussed, the first priority on Captain Thomas's list went to the fitting of plastic armour to the bridge, and a shield to the 12-pounder. In view of the weight of evidence he now had to present, one must presume that this time he won his case.

Chapter Seven

The *Inishtrahull* and the Bomb

In peace or in war, life aboard a small collier is invariably hard, uncomfortable and unglamorous. The mechanised loading of coal makes for quick turn-arounds in port and, while passages between ports are also short, they are often nightmare battles against the hostile elements. And then there is the cargo. The carriage of coal is attended by a considerable risk, stemming from the presence of methane gas explosions and deep-seated fires caused by spontaneous combustion being quite common in a loaded collier. Added to this, the ever-present coal dust, disturbed during loading or discharging, deposits a black film on every exposed surface and, despite securely battened ports and doors, permeates into the very heart of a ship's accommodation. Everything a man touches, eats or drinks is contaminated by this gritty curse. Little wonder the men who crew the coastal colliers are a tough, resourceful breed.

The *Inishtrahull,* of 869 tons gross, was a typical small coal-carrier of her day. Built in 1935 by John Lewis Ltd of Queen's Quay, Belfast, she was a steamship 198 feet long and thirty-one feet in the beam, with a reputed top speed of 11 knots. Her engine-room and main accommodation were set right aft, leaving space on her foredeck for two large hatchways, through which her grimy cargo was worked. Separating the two hatchways was a small bridge-house, topped by a flimsy wooden wheelhouse. Her funnel was tall and thin, and she sported three raked masts, the forward two each supporting a single derrick served by a steam winch on deck.

In grudging acknowledgement of the dangers of war, the

Inishtrahull mounted a .303 Hotchkiss machine-gun in each wing of her bridge, and on her after deck she carried a Holman Projector, the only 'secret weapon' ever to be entrusted to British merchant seamen. The Holman Projector was in fact a crude form of mortar which used steam under pressure to fire hand-grenades at low-flying aircraft. Its performance was more spectacular than effective and, as the supply of deck steam in the average merchant ship was, to say the least, somewhat erratic, the grenades had a disturbing tendency to fall back on the deck after being fired from the projector. The operator of the Holman Projector therefore, in addition to possessing nerves of steel, was required to be fleet of foot. In the case of the *Inishtrahull,* the operator was Seaman Gunner William Gregg, the collier's sole DEMS rating.

Commanded by 42-year-old Captain Robert Gibson of County Antrim, and carrying a total crew of fourteen, the *Inishtrahull* left the port of Limerick, on the west coast of Ireland, on the evening of 12 March 1942, bound in ballast for Ayr, in the Firth of Clyde. Her route would take her around the north of Ireland and through the North Channel, a total distance to steam of 427 miles. Gibson planned to be alongside the coal berth in Ayr in time for the morning shift on the 14th.

The mouth of the River Shannon was cleared by midnight, and the *Inishtrahull* entered the open sea and settled down on a north-north-westerly course with the Irish coast on her starboard beam. It was a black night – the moon having not yet risen – but the wind was light and the sea relatively calm. While this would make for a comfortable passage, which would be welcomed by all on board, Captain Gibson could not help sniffing suspiciously at the air as he watched the twinkling lights of neutral Ireland passing to starboard. He was only too well aware from past experience that on this coast light winds and a nip in the air often meant that fog was not far away. In fact, he could already smell the unmistakeable salty dampness. By dawn, he estimated it would be as thick as a hedge, and likely to stay that way, turning the remainder of the passage around this treacherous, tide-swept coast into a navigator's nightmare. In common with most of her contemporaries, the collier's only navigational aids were a magnetic compass and a keen-eyed lookout.

But the rest of the night passed fine and clear, and the *Inishtrahull* pressed northwards at full speed. When the dawn came, she was off the coast of Connemara, and although it had turned hazy, Gibson's expectations of dense fog were not realised. On reflection, he would have felt more at ease if his gloomy forecast had proved right, for his small ship, alone on a neutral coast, was now dangerously exposed to the eyes of the enemy.

At 10 o'clock that morning, the *Inishtrahull* was 1½ miles to the south-west of Eagle Island, and less than a day's run from Ayr. After rounding the island, she would alter onto a north-easterly course to run across the broad sweep of Donegal Bay, picking up the coast again off Tory Island. From there it was a mere four hours' steaming to pass abeam of the island of Inishtrahull, for which the ship was named. She would then enter the North Channel, coming under the protective umbrella of the Royal Navy and Coastal Command, who patrolled this northern gateway to Britain with great assiduity.

When, at 1010, a large four-engined aircraft was sighted approaching the *Inishtrahull*'s starboard quarter from over the land, Captain Gibson assumed that the RAF had arrived on the scene earlier than usual. He focused his binoculars and examined the aircraft through the haze. She had the look of a Sunderland flying boat, and yet . . . The plane flew closer, crossing astern of the ship, and Gibson's stomach turned over. The visitor was a German Focke-Wulf Condor, the black crosses on her camouflaged fuselage now clearly visible. He reached for the whistle lanyard.

As would be expected in a ship with only fifteen crew and armed with two light machine-guns and a grenade thrower of doubtful effectiveness, 'action stations' in the *Inishtrahull* was an uncomplicated and expedient operation. Captain Gibson was immediately joined on the bridge by his two deck officers, First Mate Samuel Dalzell and Second Mate Wilfred Hosier; Chief Engineer William Roberts and Second Engineer Neale Mitchell went below, and Seaman Gunner Gregg sprinted aft to his Holman Projector. The rest of the crew took cover.

The Focke-Wulf banked steeply, and then approached from astern, flying at about 400 feet above the sea. Gibson instructed

Dalzell to take over the bridge, and then stationed himself at the Hotchkiss in the starboard wing. As was his prerogative and his nature, he intended to take a very active part in the defence of his ship. In the port wing, 37-year-old Hosier, as tenacious as his Liverpool birthplace, prepared to do the same. On the poop, Gregg carefully removed the safety pin from a hand-grenade and slipped the bomb into the cigarette-tin-like cylinder that would hold the firing handle in place until the missile was thrown into the air.

On Gibson's orders, fire was held until the enemy aircraft had closed to about 400 yards. Then he squeezed the trigger of his Hotchkiss, aiming at the nose of the Focke-Wulf. Hosier, in the port wing, joined in, but his gun jammed after half a dozen rounds had been fired. As the plane drew closer, its gun turrets spitting fire, Seaman Gunner Gregg dropped his grenade into the muzzle of the Holman Projector, took aim, and jerked the lever that released the high-pressure steam into the barrel. Much to his surprise, the crude gun functioned perfectly, hurling the grenade in its restraining tin high into the air right in the path of the approaching aircraft. Again, as per manual, the tin fell away at 300 feet, and the grenade continued its ascent for another three or four seconds before exploding. It was a hundred feet too high.

Unharmed, the Focke-Wulf roared in, its bomb doors gaping wide, and preceded by a swathe of bullets and cannon shells from its six gun positions, which sprayed the decks of the *Inishtrahull*, working from aft to forward. Wilfred Hosier, still struggling to clear his jammed gun, felt the wind of the 1,000 lb bomb as it sliced past. The bomb struck the bridge rail less than six feet away from him, but fortunately failed to explode, and shot harmlessly into the sea.

On the other side of the bridge, Gibson's Hotchkiss was working faultlessly, and as the great menacing shape roared overhead, its engines filling the air with the scream of a thousand angry demons, he poured a full belt of ammunition into its exposed underbelly.

The pilot of the Focke-Wulf, obviously shaken by the spirited defence put up by the little ship, flew on almost to the horizon, before banking, and then flying down the starboard side of the *Inishtrahull* well out of range of her guns. Once astern, he banked again, and dropped to 150 feet before beginning his second run-in.

Once again, Captain Gibson and his men stood to their guns, steeling themselves as the enemy's forward gun turrets rattled into action, striking fire from the decks of their ship. When the Focke-Wulf was within range, Gregg got off another grenade from his projector and Gibson and Hosier opened fire simultaneously. Hosier's gun again jammed after a few seconds, but Gibson continued firing. The captain watched with grim satisfaction as his tracers struck home in the fuselage of the attacking plane. Then his gun also jammed, but as the plane passed overhead he had the satisfaction of noting that its lower rear turret appeared to be out of action, possibly due to a hit during the first attack.

Gibson also saw the second bomb fall away from the Focke-Wulf's bomb-bay as the plane roared over, only a few feet clear of the collier's mainmast. He gave up his attempts to clear his gun, and watched transfixed as the bomb slammed into the *Inishtrahull*'s forecastle head, only fifty feet forward of the bridge. Miraculously, this bomb also failed to explode on impact, but Gibson's relief turned to fear when the bomb rolled slowly down the foredeck, smashed through the rails at the break of the forecastle head, and fell to the maindeck. To add to his present difficulties, Gibson now had an unexploded 1,000 lb bomb lying within spitting distance of his bridge. Better men might have panicked in such a situation.

There was no time for panic, or deliberation on the luck of the Irish, for the Focke-Wulf was once again coming in from astern. Both Gibson and Hosier had succeeded in clearing their guns, and kept up a continuous fire as the plane swooped in for its bombing run. Seaman Gunner Gregg painstakingly aimed and fired his projector, but again the grenade burst too high. However, the German pilot now seemed to have lost his nerve, for he dropped his bomb 150 feet short of the ship, and immediately sheered away, but not before the two Hotchkiss guns had raked the plane with a full belt apiece.

The bomb exploded on contact with the sea, sending up a tall column of dirty-grey water. The blast swept across the *Inishtrahull* like a localised hurricane, shaking the small ship, and sending loose equipment hurtling in all directions. Captain Gibson was hit by a flying cargo block, and was thrown from his gun.

By the time the Focke-Wulf had circled and embarked on its fourth attack, approaching from astern as before, Gibson, nursing a badly bruised arm, was back at his gun. He sprayed the plane with a full belt as it thundered in. Hosier was able to fire only fifteen rounds before his troublesome Hotchkiss again seized up, and Gregg experienced the recurring frustration of seeing his missile explode harmlessly above the attacking aircraft. The enemy pilot fared likewise, his bomb falling some 150 feet ahead of the *Inishtrahull,* shaking her, but causing no damage.

It seemed that there was to be no end to this one-sided battle, for the Focke-Wulf had tipped her wings, and was coming in to attack for the fifth time. The indefatigable Gregg fired his steam-powered mortar but, as on the previous occasion, the grenade burst in thin air. Gibson and Hosier held their fire until the plane was almost overhead, and both got off full belts, hosing the underside of the wings and fuselage with tracer. The Focke-Wulf replied with cannon and machine-guns, two shells bursting in the starboard wing of the collier's bridge, wounding Gibson in the chest and shoulders.

The bomb was a very near miss, falling only a hundred feet off the starboard bow, and exploding as it hit the water. Again, the *Inishtrahull* suffered no more harm than a thorough wetting. The Focke-Wulf then made as if to come in for a sixth attack, but at the last moment banked steeply to port, and flew off in a south-south-westerly direction. It would seem that she had had enough of this plucky little ship.

Robert Gibson stepped down from his gun with a sigh of relief as he watched the enemy plane dwindle to a tiny speck on the far horizon. There was no doubt in his mind that the Focke-Wulf had come off second best in the action. The plane had dropped five bombs, three of which missed, and two failed to explode. The *Inishtrahull* had been sprayed with bullets and cannon shells on each bombing run, with the result that much of her rigging had been shot away, her wheelhouse resembled a colander, and some rails and ladders had been demolished, but she was still a functioning ship. Apart from Gibson himself, whose wounds had been caused by splinters from the shattered wooden wheelhouse, there were no casualties. In return, the Focke-Wulf had received a thrashing her crew would remember for a long time. The underside of her fuselage and wings must have been in much the same state as the *Inishtrahull*'s wheelhouse, and it was probable that her lower rear gunner had been either wounded or killed.

There now remained the problem of the unexploded 1,000 lb bomb nestling with sinister intent on the collier's foredeck. While having his wounds dressed, Gibson was able to give the matter some thought. His first instinct was to put into Broadhaven, which lay around the next headland, and there call on the Irish Free State authorities to deal with the bomb. But he dismissed this idea quickly. He was suspicious of these so-called neutral Irish, fearing the possibility of internment. In any case, he had given his ETA Ayr as daylight on the 14th, and he had no intention of being late. He would deal with the bomb himself. Leaving Second Mate Hosier in charge of the bridge, Gibson, accompanied by First Mate Dalzell and Chief Engineer Roberts, walked forward to inspect the Focke-Wulf's unwanted gift.

The bomb lay in the gulley between the forecastle bulkhead and the coaming of the forward hatchway, a fat, grey-painted egg, full of menace, and rolling jerkily each time the *Inishtrahull*'s bows rose and fell with the swell. The fins had fallen off, but otherwise the bomb, which contained enough explosive to reduce the collier to a pile of smoking scrap, seemed intact. As it had been dropped from a height of 150 feet without exploding, it seemed reasonable to Gibson – and his senior officers agreed – that the bomb would stand up to some more rough handling. They would deal with it as they habitually dealt with any other rubbish that cluttered up the *Inishtrahull*'s decks, and that meant dumping it overboard.

When Gibson called the rest of his crew to the bridge to acquaint them of the situation, all thirteen volunteered to help tackle the bomb. It was then agreed that Gibson, who was partially incapacitated by his wounds, should take the helm, while Chief Engineer Roberts and one stoker looked after the engine-room. The rest, with the exception of the cook, who was considered rather too elderly for such strenuous work, collected crowbars, ropes and tackles, and made their way purposefully up the foredeck.

Second Engineer Neale Mitchell, a 27-year-old Belfast man, took charge, first reassuring his party that the bomb was 'probably a

70

bloody dud, anyway'. The laughs turned to worried frowns when it was realised that the derrick with which they had planned to lift the bomb was useless, all its running gear having been shot away. Five men crouched down by the bomb and tried to lift it, but it would not budge. A rope tackle was then rigged from the derrick boom, and a rope strop passed around the body of the bomb, but when the strain was taken on the tackle, it became obvious to Gibson, who was watching from the bridge, that the ropes would not take the weight. Not wishing to see the bomb dropped, perhaps wiping out most of his crew, he intervened.

Mitchell conferred with Gibson, and they decided to try a more devious approach. A wire strop was made up and passed around the bomb and, using the steam winch and a wire cargo runner led through the head block of the after derrick, the bomb was dragged along the deck until it was just forward of the bridge, and under the derrick head. Then, the strain was taken by the runner, and with the aid of crowbars, baulks of timber and a great deal of human sweat, the bomb was manhandled onto the hatch-top. Two skids were then laid from the hatch to the ship's side bulwark, and the 1,000 lb canister of high explosive was rolled to the ship's side, and unceremoniously committed to the deep.

When it was all over, Mitchell and his party found their hands were shaking so much that they had difficulty in downing the large tots of rum Captain Gibson saw fit to dispense. For many nights to come, they would relive in their dreams those awesome hours when ten men, straining and cursing, had manhandled half a ton of certain death along the deck and over the side.

The *Inishtrahull* reached the Scottish port of Ayr shortly after daylight on the 14th, less than an hour late on her ETA. She was battered, her crew were exhausted, but the loading of her cargo was not long delayed. Three days later, when she arrived back in her home port of Belfast, Captain Robert Gibson and his men found that their story had gone ahead of them, and they received a visit from no less a personage than the Flag Officer in Charge Belfast. The beribboned Rear-Admiral was lavish in his praise for the little company of men who had fought and won against the might of the *Luftwaffe*.

For his bravery in organising and leading the operation to

dispose of the bomb, Second Engineer Neale Mitchell was awarded the George Medal. Captain Robert Gibson, Second Officer Wilfred Hosier and Seaman Gunner William Gregg received a Commendation for their work at the guns. The *Inishtrahull*, having licked her wounds, returned to sea, and carried on her grimy, but essential work throughout the rest of the war.

Chapter Eight

The Hard Road to Russia

On 22 June 1812 the armies of Napoleon Bonaparte crossed the borders of Russia, marching towards what was to be a catastrophic defeat. One hundred and twenty-nine years later, to the day, Adolf Hitler set out to prove that he could succeed where Bonaparte had failed. On Sunday 22 June 1941, 164 divisions of the *Wehrmacht*, supported by 2,700 aircraft, advanced into the Soviet Union on a front extending from the Baltic to the Black Sea. In the first three months of the fighting, the Germans steam-rollered 300 miles deep into Soviet territory.

Although up until the time she was attacked the USSR had been openly supporting Germany morally and economically, and had turned her back on a Britain fighting alone, her immediate reaction was to vociferously demand all possible help from that country. Despite her own urgent needs at home and in the Middle East, Britain at once offered tanks, aircraft and guns. The first convoy carrying war materials set out from a British port for North Russia, sailing via Iceland, on 12 August 1941. Thereafter, a similar convoy sailed every ten or fourteen days, right up until the end of the war.

The dangers facing the ships and men who sailed in the Russian convoys were frightening. Tempestuous seas, fog and blizzard, temperatures down to 40° below zero, round-the-clock daylight in summer, and unending darkness in winter, all added to the misery of the 2,000-mile passage. At the same time, through every mile steamed, the ships were under constant attack from German U-boats, aircraft and surface ships. To sail the Russian convoys was to experience all the rigours of the cruel sea, aggravated by the horrors of war at their most extreme.

In winter, the port of Glasgow, with its twelve straggling miles of dreary quaysides and 400 acres of windswept docks and basins, is not the most desirable resting place for a ship. In late November 1941, made even more cheerless by the constraints of a war already two years old, and by a blanket of cold, persistent drizzle, the Scottish port can have held little charm for the men of the British ship *Harmatris*. That they were soon to face a voyage to Arctic Russia, and all that entailed, perhaps made it just that much more bearable. In fact, there were many aboard the *Harmatris* who would gladly have endured a lifetime of winters in Glasgow, rather than sail for Russia.

Born in 1932 at the Lithgow Shipyard, Port Glasgow, just a few miles downstream from her loading berth, the 5,395-ton *Harmatris* was strongly built on lines of stark practicality, and capable of carrying anything from anthracite nuts to railway engines. Her coal-fired steam reciprocating engine gave her an operating speed of 8 to 9 knots, at which she carried her various cargoes with maximum economy. Owned by J & C Harrison of London, she was commanded by 47-year-old Captain R.W. Brundle of Hull, who was supported by a crew of forty-six. They included seven DEMS gunners, who manned and maintained her armament of one 4-inch, one 20 mm Hispano cannon, five .303 Lewis machine-guns, and two twin .303 Marlins. As an additional defence against attacking aircraft, she also carried two PAC rocket-launchers and five kites.

The *Harmatris* completed loading and sailed from Glasgow on the morning of 27 November, having on board 8,000 tons of military stores, vehicles and ammunition consigned to Archangel on the White Sea. Her orders were to proceed independently to Reykjavik, and there to await a convoy for Russia.

The 825-mile passage to Iceland was trouble-free, and the *Harmatris* sailed for Archangel in convoy on 4 December. In view of the ever-present danger of attack by German aircraft and surface ships based in northern Norway, the convoy was routed as far north as the limits of the polar ice pack would allow. It was expected, therefore, that the passage would take at least ten days.

74

Given that Russian methods of discharging cargo were notoriously slow, Brundle and his men faced the prospect of spending Christmas and New Year in Archangel. This was not something they looked forward to.

Trouble came sooner than anticipated, but not from the enemy. Shortly after leaving Reykjavik, early on 6 December, the convoy ran into a strong south-westerly gale, which increased to storm-force as the eye of the depression passed over the ships. The wind then suddenly veered to the north-east, and the sea became very confused and high. The *Harmatris,* having a low centre of gravity due to a concentration of heavy cargo in her lower holds, began to roll violently. Within an hour she had fallen astern of the convoy, and was fighting a lonely battle against the angry elements in the grey half-light of the Arctic afternoon. As the day wore on, and the ever-lowering clouds turned the twilight into sombre darkness, mountainous seas began to break over the ship, flooding her well decks and tugging at the tightly wedged tarpaulins of her hatches. Captain Brundle, already deeply concerned for the safety of the vehicles stowed in the tween decks, was now faced with the possi-bility of having his hatches stove in. He had no alternative but to ride out the storm hove-to with the wind and sea on the bow. The *Harmatris* would make no progress towards her destination, but the damage to ship and cargo would be kept to a minimum.

At 2300, Brundle was still on the bridge, but the ship was riding more easily. He was tired, his tongue furred from too many cigarettes and cups of strong coffee, and he longed for a hot bath, followed by, perhaps, a few hours' sleep. At his side was 23-year-old Third Officer William Watson, officer of the watch. When midnight came, the watch would be taken over by the more ex-perienced Second Officer Young, and then Brundle hoped to be able to go below for a while. This was not to be.

The first hint that all was not well below decks came at 2330, when it was reported from aft that spray was evaporating into clouds of steam when hitting the deck plates alongside No.4 hatch. Brundle lost no time in ordering the hatch to be opened for investi-gation. His worst fears were confirmed when it was found that a lorry stowed in the tween decks was on fire, and had broken adrift. With every lurch of the ship, this blazing torch was slamming into the bales and cases stacked in the sides of the deck, spreading the fire and destruction in its wake.

Of all the dangers a seaman has to face in the course of his voyaging, there is none he fears more than fire at sea. For those on shore, fire is hazard enough, but can usually be swiftly dealt with by calling in the local fire brigade. At sea, in a merchant ship, there is no fire brigade to hand; the ship's crew largely untrained in the techniques of fire-fighting and inadequately equipped, have no alternative but to fight the blaze unaided. Should the fire prove impossible to contain, there is only the last resort of taking to the boats – always assuming the weather is kindly disposed towards such a move. In the case of the *Harmatris,* already fighting for her life against mountainous seas, this means of escape was out of the question. For her crew there would be no running away from the fire.

Nor was time on their side, for in her No. 4 hold, separated from the fire only by a floor of wooden hatchboards, the *Harmatris* carried ten tons of cordite and a large quantity of small-arms ammunition. Brundle knew that once the flames penetrated into the lower hold, his ship would be finished. Leaving Third Officer Watson in charge of the bridge, he went aft to assess the situation.

On the after deck, Brundle met Chief Officer G. Masterman and Chief Steward R. Peart, who with a team of crew members were rigging hoses preparatory to entering the hatch. As no heavy seas were breaking over the after deck, this could be done in comparative safety, but Brundle first instructed Masterman to flood the hold with steam in an attempt to smother the fire.

It is probable that the blaze was now too well established for the steam appeared to have little or no effect, and after a while it became clear that they must get the hoses down into the tween deck. The forward end of the hatch was opened, and Masterman, wearing a smoke helmet and safety line, climbed down into the deck, dragging a fire hose behind him.

The task the Chief Officer had undertaken was a daunting one, for the tween deck was full of choking black smoke and searing flames. Added to this was the danger presented by the rampaging lorry. The protection afforded by the smoke helmet (a primitive form of breathing apparatus fed with outside air by a bellows and hose) was minimal. But with great courage, Masterman, a 41-year-old West Hartlepool man, turned his hose on the blaze, and continued to fight the fire until he was overcome by fumes and smoke. Fortunately, the men on deck saw his plight, and hauled him out of the hatch before he lost consciousness.

There was no lack of volunteers to take Masterman's place. Chief Steward Peart, a South Walian in his early twenties, now donned the smoke helmet and spent thirty minutes below fighting the flames, before he too was forced to return to the deck. Fearing an explosion might rip the *Harmatris* open and send her to the bottom, Captain Brundle went forward to the bridge, where he instructed his radio officer to send out an SOS. The call for help was immediately answered by the 1,559-ton *Zaafaran*, a small British ship acting as rescue ship for the convoy. The *Zaafaran* reported she was proceeding towards the *Harmatris* at her maximum speed of 12 knots. Thus assured he had secured a chance of survival for his men, Brundle returned aft, and throughout the rest of the night he and Peart spelled each other in the smoke-filled tween deck in a desperate fight to quell the fire before it reached the explosives in the lower hold.

By 0730 on the 7th, the battle had been won. The fire was out, the runaway lorry secured, and Brundle was able to radio the *Zaafaran* that her services would not be needed.

Although the *Harmatris* was no longer in immediate danger, a brief examination of her hatches, where accessible, showed that the terrible battering she had received over the previous twenty-four hours had played havoc with her cargo. In the tween decks other vehicles had broken adrift, causing chaos in the cargo around them. It was not possible to gain access to the lower holds, but it seemed likely that the damage below would be of the same order. Brundle decided it was pointless to proceed further, and radioed the Convoy Commodore asking permission to return to Glasgow to have his cargo examined and restowed. This was approved, and the *Harmatris* was brought round onto a southerly course to run for the Clyde with the wind and sea astern.

Far on the other side of the world, where the sun had not yet risen, Japanese carrier-borne aircraft were warming up in preparation for their attack on the American fleet at Pearl Harbor. Before

77

the *Harmatris* reached the safety of the Clyde, the United States would be in the war.

Perhaps the only good to come out of the *Harmatris*'s abortive attempt to reach Russia was that Captain Brundle and his crew were able to spend Christmas tied up alongside in Glasgow. This was a small reward for men who had faced so much danger and who by their prompt action and unflinching courage had saved a valuable ship and her cargo from almost certain destruction. But the reward was more than they had asked for, and when, on the morning of the 26th, the *Harmatris* was again ready for sea, the tenuous links that had temporarily bound her to the shore were cut without hesitation. There was the business of an unfinished voyage to attend to.

The passage to Iceland in convoy was accomplished without incident, and in weather no worse than was to be expected in the North Atlantic in winter. On New Year's Day 1942, the *Harmatris* once again entered Reykjavik harbour. Seven days later, she sailed in Convoy PQ 8, bound for the North Russian port of Murmansk, which lies in the Kola Inlet, and near the border with Finland.

Convoy PQ 8 was made up of eight merchant ships escorted by two minesweepers. Once clear of Reykjavik, the merchantmen formed up in two columns of four, with the *Harmatris,* acting as commodore ship, leading one of the columns. For the first two days they experienced strong winds and rough seas, adding to the misery of the sub-zero temperatures and never-ending darkness. Fortunately, the elements relented late on the 10th, and the small convoy ran into fine, calm weather. Also, during that night the ocean escort joined, consisting of the cruiser HMS *Trinidad,* the destroyers *Matabele* and *Somali,* and the fleet minesweepers *Harrier* and *Speedwell*. This formidable array of strength was a most welcome sight, but the men in the merchant ships knew that it was also an indication of the many dangers ahead.

The convoy continued on a north-easterly course until, on the 11th, in latitude 73° 45' N, it met with the ice field and was forced to divert further to the south. Six more days passed quietly, with the ships making 8 knots in unbelievably calm weather with maximum visibility. Only the bone-chilling cold and the tedious darkness, relieved by an hour or two of pale daylight each side of noon, marred what might have been a pleasant voyage.

On Saturday 17 January, the convoy was deep into the Barents Sea and shaping a course for the Kola Inlet. It seemed that the worst dangers had been passed, for there were less than 60 miles to go to waters guarded by Soviet forces. At 1615, the ships were formed into line astern, with the *Harmatris,* as commodore ship, leading. The cruiser *Trinidad* was on her starboard bow, with HMS *Harrier* zig-zagging five cables ahead of *Trinidad.* The destroyers *Somali* and *Matabele* were stationed approximately 2,000 yards on the port and starboard beams respectively, while *Speedwell* brought up the rear. Of the local escort, scheduled to join within the next six hours, it had been reported that the fleet minesweepers *Britomart* and *Salamander* were fogbound in the Kola Inlet, where visibility was down to nil. Only HMS *Sharpshooter,* another fleet minesweeper, had managed to get under way and was proceeding seawards at all possible speed. However, the Senior Officer Escort, in HMS *Trinidad*, was not unduly worried. To the best of his knowledge, there were no reports of U-boats operating in the area, and the darkness would deter the enemy bombers. It was his opinion that, at this stage, the only real threat would come from mines. However, the SOE had not yet received a recent Admiralty signal warning of the presence of at least one enemy submarine known to be in the area. Ahead and to starboard of the convoy, U-454, commanded by *Kapitänleutnant* Burkhard Hackländer, lay waiting on the surface, hidden in the shadows of the long Arctic night.

At 1845, Captain Brundle, who had been on the bridge of the *Harmatris* so long that his feet seemed to have taken root in the deck, rasped the bristles of his chin and decided it was high time he went below for a shave. The weather was clear, and the experienced Masterman had the watch. Brundle walked out into the wing and took a quick look around the horizon. It was empty, except for the reassuring silhouettes of the escorting naval ships. The darkness was too complete to reveal the thin pencil of U-454's periscope breaking the surface on the starboard bow.

Brundle was in the act of drawing aside the curtain at the doorway of his day cabin when the torpedo struck the *Harmatris* on her starboard side, and exploded with a thunderous roar.

Half-deafened, Brundle clawed his way back up to the bridge, where he found that Masterman had already stopped the engines. The Chief Officer reported that the ship had been hit in No. 1 hold, whose hatches and derricks he had seen hurled skywards on the column of water thrown up by the explosion.

First giving orders for the crew to stand by the lifeboats, Brundle went forward with Masterman to assess the damage. He found the forecastle deck to be a smoking shambles, with No. 1 stripped of its hatches and tarpaulins, but there appeared to be no fire in the hold. The *Harmatris* was noticeably down by the head, and soundings taken of the bilges showed water in both forward holds, and rising rapidly. In spite of this, Brundle judged the ship was in no immediate danger of sinking.

The SOE, who had not yet received the Admiralty's U-boat warning, at first thought the *Harmatris* must have struck a mine, but when the destroyer *Matabele* reported hearing torpedo hydrophone effect, he was quick to take action. *Matabele* and *Somali* were ordered to carry out an anti-submarine search to seaward of the convoy, and *Speedwell* was told to stand guard over the crippled merchant ship.

Aboard the *Harmatris*, Captain Brundle and his senior officers were discussing the possibility of saving their ship when, at 1935, three-quarters of an hour after the first, another explosion occurred amidships on her port side. The ship shuddered violently, but there was no flash or column of water usually associated with a torpedo striking, and Brundle concluded that his ship must have suffered the additional indignity of striking a mine. He concluded wrongly, the *Harmatris* having been the recipient of Hackländer's second torpedo.

The damage caused by the second explosion appeared to be severe, and Brundle, fearing his lifeboats might be smashed in the next attack, decided it was time to get his men off. He signalled *Speedwell* and asked her to close in. The *Harmatris* was abandoned and all her crew were safely on board the minesweeper by 1945.

Although the *Harmatris* was so far down by the head that her propeller was out of the water, Brundle had ascertained before leaving her that her engine-room was still intact. Once aboard *Speedwell*, he discussed with her commander the possibility of

80

taking his ship in tow, so that she might be beached and her valuable cargo saved. After some deliberation, it was agreed that the minesweeper would attempt to tow the *Harmatris* towards Cape Teriberski, which lay only 15 miles to starboard. When Brundle called for volunteers to re-board the ship with him, every member of his crew stepped forward.

Within the hour, they were all back on board the *Harmatris,* and towing lines had been passed and made fast. *Speedwell* took the strain, but the damaged merchantman refused to move. With her funnel belching black smoke, the minesweeper pulled harder, but succeeded only in parting the tow wire. On investigation, it was found that the first torpedo had caused the *Harmatris*'s starboard anchor to run out and drag on the bottom. The ship had in fact been brought up to her anchor with 130 fathoms of cable out. As the windlass had been shattered by the explosion, there could be no question of raising the anchor. Brundle sent for hammers and punches, and his men set about splitting the cable.

While this work was going on, the convoy, which had scattered after the attack on the *Harmatris,* was being re-formed by the other escorts, the tanker *British Pride* taking over as commodore ship. By 2130, the seven remaining merchantmen had formed up in single file, and resumed their original course. This done, *Matabele* was instructed to drop back and assist *Speedwell* with her tow.

At 2145, HMS *Sharpshooter,* having succeeded in breaking out of the fog-bound Kola Inlet, joined and took up station on the starboard beam of the convoy. *Matabele,* finding her assistance was not required by *Speedwell,* rejoined at 2215, and also took up a position to starboard. Cape Teriberski was now abeam only 10 miles off, and at each flash of its powerful light the convoy and its escorts were sharply silhouetted against the night sky. This gave Burkhard Hackländer the chance he had been waiting for. His sights were trained on the tanker *British Pride,* but it was the zig-zagging *Matabele* that caught his fan of two torpedoes. The British destroyer disappeared in a sheet of flame as her magazine exploded. Only two ratings survived the sinking.

The operation to cut the *Harmatris*'s anchor cable was meanwhile proceeding with agonising slowness. The fact that the joining shackles had not been split in many a long year, combined with the darkness and the icy cold, was making a difficult job almost impossible. Following the sudden loss of the *Matabele*, *Speedwell*'s commander became anxious for the safety of both ships, and signalled Brundle advising that he and his men would be better off aboard the minesweeper for the time being. Captain Brundle was very loth to leave his ship again, but as the *Harmatris* was now so obviously a sitting target, he took the Navy man's advice. A hot meal and a few hours' sleep would not go amiss.

With Brundle and his men back on board, *Speedwell* circled the area throughout the rest of the night, and at 0600 put the merchant crew back on their ship. There, they were immediately confronted by a major problem. They discovered that the main steam had been inadvertently left on throughout the night, with the result that the boilers had run dry. As a consequence of this catastrophic mistake, the decks' steam pipes were frozen solid, and all winches therefore unusable. The task of splitting the cable and bringing aboard towlines was made more difficult, but with the help of a great deal of sweat and colourful language, both were accomplished. At 0800 on the 18th, HMS *Speedwell* commenced towing the *Harmatris* towards Murmansk at 5 knots. The rest of the convoy had long since disappeared over the horizon, and the two ships were sailing alone.

And still the torment was not yet over for the *Harmatris*. At around noon, in the short twilight that passes for daylight in the Arctic winter, a German aircraft suddenly appeared, roaring in at mast-top height and spraying the ship with cannon and machine-gun fire. Fortunately, the *Harmatris*'s DEMS gunners were already manning their guns, and returned fire with considerable accuracy. *Speedwell*'s guns joined in and arcs of tracer from both ships were seen to hit the attacking plane, which then headed for the shore trailing black smoke and losing height. An hour later, another enemy aircraft was sighted, but this one, no doubt aware of the fate of its predecessor, was more cautious. Maintaining a respectable height, it dropped a stick of bombs which fell harmlessly a mile away from the *Harmatris*. The aircraft then flew over the two ships without losing height, and fired its guns in a largely futile gesture of aggression. Both the *Harmatris* and *Speedwell* replied, but no hits were scored on either side. The plane flew off without attacking again.

1. 'A poem of the Empire's mercantile greatness'. Every dot represents the position of a British merchant ship on 24 November 1937. Photo: *Daily Express*.

2. SS *Inishtrahull* 869 grt. Photo: *Welsh Industrial & Maritime Museum.*

3. The British ship *Chulmleigh*. Lost off Spitzbergen in Operation "FB". Photo: *Welsh Industral & Maritime Museum.*

4. J & C Harrison's *Harmatris* in her peacetime livery.
Photo: *Welsh Industrial & Maritime Museum.*

5. SS *Heronspool* 5202 grt. Photo: *A. Duncan.*

6. U-boat makes a stealthy approach to a convoy on the surface.

Photo: *Source unknown.*

7. Winter in the North Atlantic

Photo: *Captain J. Thomson*

8. Survivors coming alongside rescue ship. Photo: *Reardon Smith.*

9. U-boat returning to port and a hero's welcome. Photo: *Johannes Vahlburch.*

10. Robert Tapscott poses with the lifeboat that carried him across the Atlantic.
Photo: *South Wales Argus.*

11. Roy Widdecombe, one of only two men to survive the sinking of the Anglo Saxon.
Photo: *South Wales Argus.*

12. A quiet moment in the middle watch. Photo: *Imperial War Museum*.

13. Chief Officer George Stronach, *Ocean Voyager*. Awarded George Cross and Lloyd's War Medal for Bravery at Sea. Photo: *Daily Telegraph*.

Ironically, at 1430, HMS *Speedwell*, having faithfully watched over her disabled charge for nearly twenty hours, suffered her first damage and casualties – but not at the hand of the enemy. A high-pressure steam pipe burst in her boiler-room, and three seamen were badly scalded. Her commander signalled for a Soviet tug, which arrived within the hour, and took over the tow. *Speedwell* then headed for Murmansk at full speed to land her injured men. Two additional tugs arrived alongside the *Harmatris* at 1700, and she continued on her slow way, berthing in Murmansk at 0800 on the 20th.

With his ship safely tied up in port, Captain Brundle was for the first time able to make a detailed examination of the damage she had sustained. The second torpedo, which had struck amidships on the port side, he found had inflicted very little damage, except for a severe buckling of the hull and deck plates in the area. On the other hand, U-454's first hit had caused chaos. The torpedo had torn a large hole in the hull on the starboard side forward, both the forepeak and forward watertight bulkheads were fractured, and No. 1 hold was three-quarters full of water. On deck, the locking bars of No. 1 hatch had been ripped off, and the wooden hatch-boards and tarpaulins were missing. The heavy steel hatch beams lay strewn around the decks, derricks were missing or bent double, and the shrouds and rigging of the foremast were draped with odds and ends of cargo blown out of the hold, giving the mast the appearance of a gigantic Christmas tree. Over all there lay a thick coating of ice and snow which, in a way, softened the horror of the mauling the ship had received.

From the time the *Harmatris* first set out from Glasgow on that grey November day in 1941, almost two months had elapsed. Two months during which her crew had faced up to, and survived, more perils than most men will meet in a lifetime. Yet never once did they seriously consider abandoning their appointed task, which was to deliver a desperately needed cargo to the Soviet Union. Whether their valiant efforts were appreciated by the recipients is a matter which will be debated for as long as those who served in the Russian convoys are alive.

The crippling of the *Harmatris* and the sinking of the *Matabele* with such fearful loss of life proved to be the pinnacle in the careers of Burkhard Hackländer and U-454. They sank no more ships, and on 1 August 1943 had the misfortune to be surprised on the surface in the Bay of Biscay by a Sunderland of Coastal Command. When the flying boat dived to attack, U-454's gunners put up such a fierce barrage that the aircraft crashed into the sea, but its bombs had been released at precisely the right moment, and the U-boat was hit and sunk. Hackländer and twelve other survivors from U-454 were picked up later by the Royal Navy. Thus were the *Harmatris* and *Matabele* revenged.

Chapter Nine

The Voyage of No Return

*We are preparing ten ships to sail individually during the
October dark. They are all British ships, for which the crews
will have to volunteer, the dangers being terrible, and their sole
hope if sunk far from help being Arctic clothing and such
heating arrangements as can be placed in their lifeboats.*
*Extract from telegram sent by Winston Churchill
to President Roosevelt 7 October 1942.*

In the autumn of 1942, apart from the North Atlantic, where the
U-boats were riding the crest of a bloody wave sending nearly a
hundred merchant ships to the bottom every month, the
momentum of war was beginning to slow. It might even be said
that slowly, very slowly, the tide was turning in favour of Britain
and her allies.

Although Japanese forces had finally reached the borders of
India, there were signs that they were at the absolute limits of their
long supply lines, and would be unable to move further west. In
the Pacific, their swift advance through the islands had been
halted and, as the first move in the long-awaited counter-attack,
American marines had landed on Guadalcanal. On the Russian
Front, the Germans appeared to have fought themselves to a
standstill. The siege of Stalingrad was crumbling, and it was plain
that the *Wehrmacht* would make no more progress before the
bitter cold of the Russian winter closed in around it. In the
Mediterranean, the situation, although still precarious, was even
more hopeful. Montgomery had taken over in the Western Desert
in August, and had already stopped Rommel dead in his tracks.

Preparations were now well in hand for a counter-attack designed to push the Germans back along the road to Tripoli. Coincident with this, it was planned that British and American forces would soon invade Morocco and Algeria in force from the sea.

Such momentous events meant little to the people of downtown Philadelphia as they stirred sluggishly to the rising sun on a morning in early October of that year. Compared with that other world across the Atlantic Ocean, where the cut and thrust of war were an exciting reality, life in Philadelphia was normal to the point of boredom. The trauma of Pearl Harbor had long since faded into history, the necessities of life were in abundance, there were no air raids, no threat of invasion, nothing in fact to quicken the pulses of those who had seen the coming of war as a great Hollywood adventure.

Down on the waterfront, where the morning mist still swirled over the Delaware, the mood was in sharp contrast. The wharves from Market Street to Greenwich Point were jammed with ocean-going ships, American and British, all painted overall in wartime grey. Even at this early hour, steam winches clattered and derrick blocks squealed as ton after ton of military equipment was whisked up off the dusty quays and lowered into the holds of the waiting ships. Philadelphia's longshoremen were caught up in Operation 'Torch', the projected Allied invasion of North Africa.

Only one ship lay idle at the wharves, her hatches battened down and her derricks lowered to rest. She was the British ship *Chumleigh*, already loaded to her hatch-tops with 5,000 tons of army stores, and due to sail before the sun set over the frowning Appalachians.

The 5,445-ton *Chumleigh*, registered in London, was owned by the Cardiff-based Tatem Steam Navigation Company, and had been built in 1938 by William Pickersgill of Sunderland. In outward appearance she was a typical South Wales tramp, but inwardly she differed radically from most of her miserable contemporaries. William James Tatem, Baron Glanely of St. Fagans, being a self-made man, had a penchant for the good things of life which had spilled over into the superior accommodation of his ships. The *Chumleigh*'s cabins, both for officers and crew, were spacious and well-furnished, her elegant dining saloon

86

was panelled in polished mahogany, and her captain's quarters would not have disgraced a first-class ocean liner.

The *Chumleigh* carried a total crew of fifty-eight, many of whom had already endured three years of war at sea, much of that period spent in the North Atlantic, where there was little respite from the marauding U-boats and Focke-Wulfs. It would not then be surprising to find that, to a man, they welcomed the prospect of a voyage to the Mediterranean, where the sun shone and the torpedoes and bombs were less abundant. As yet, the *Chumleigh* had been given no destination for her cargo, but it was obvious to all on board that she would be part of the North African invasion fleet. It was assumed she would be told to leave her berth during the day to anchor in Chesapeake Bay to await a convoy.

Chief Officer Ernest Fenn, having worked late into the previous night preparing the *Chumleigh*'s cargo papers, was on deck early with Boatswain Andrew Hardy checking on the ship's readiness for sea. No experienced seaman will ever venture out into the Atlantic unprepared for bad weather, and 45-year-old Fenn, well versed in the ways of the sea, was no exception. With Hardy at his side, he checked and double-checked hatch tarpaulins, derricks, ventilators, air pipes, anything on deck the sea could possibly make mischief with. It was the time of equinoctial gales in the North Atlantic, and within hours of clearing Cape Henlopen the *Chumleigh* might well be shipping green seas.

On the *Chumleigh*'s bridge, Second Officer James Starkey and Third Officer David Clark were likewise engaged in preparing for the forthcoming voyage. Starkey was in the chartroom making last-minute corrections to the Mediterranean charts, while Clark haunted the wheelhouse running a critical eye over code flags and signalling equipment.

Below decks, in the engine-room, 47-year-old Chief Engineer Richard Colvin was on his rounds accompanied by his second engineer, Richard Middlemiss. In deference to the start of a new voyage, both men wore clean white boilersuits as they ran practised hands and eyes over the gleaming engine and its auxiliaries, an occasional nod of satisfaction being their only communication. The *Chumleigh*'s triple expansion steam-engine, built by Richardsons, Westgarth & Company of Hartlepool, would set no speed records, but it was as solid and reliable as the men who looked after it.

Breakfast-time came around, and with it the inevitable ship's chandler and a late delivery of fresh stores. Chief Steward Islwyn Davies cursed the clause in Sod's Law that decrees the arrival of stores always coincides with the serving of a meal. Followed by his stewards and cooks, he marched purposefully down the gangway to tackle the small mountain of sacks of potatoes and carrots, nets of cabbages, boxes of eggs and cases of fruit, all to be brought aboard and stowed in their respective lockers.

In his cabin below the bridge, Captain Daniel Morley Williams caught the smell of frying bacon drifting up from the galley, checked his watch, and reached for his uniform jacket. He was leaving his cabin for the dining-saloon when he received a most unwelcome visitor.

The tight-lipped official brought orders from the Admiralty for the *Chumleigh* to sail at once, to proceed at all speed to Halifax, Nova Scotia, and there join a convoy bound eastwards across the Atlantic. Willams ate his breakfast bacon, cold and greasy, between two pieces of bread, while the tugs plucked the *Chumleigh* off her berth, and pointed her bows down-river.

Daniel Williams was on his first voyage in command, having previously served in the *Chumleigh* as chief officer. The promotion had come out of the blue when, in July that year, the ship returned to London after a particularly harrowing trip to Russia. The ageing Captain Priestly, weary of the knocks of war, had decided to retire on arrival, and Williams had found himself moving his belongings into the Master's cabin.

Those summer days spent in Surrey Commercial Docks while London basked in the sunshine, free of air raids for the time being, had been heady ones for Daniel Williams. His nerves were still raw from the horrors of the Archangel run, and he found blessed relief in the new responsibilities suddenly heaped on his shoulders.

At thirty-five, Williams was tall and lean, with a keen sense of humour and dark, curly hair betraying his Celtic origins. Born in the quiet Cardiganshire village of Llangranog, son of a farmer, he was a first-class seaman and navigator. He was a natural leader, a man with the rare ability to be both scrupulously fair and kind without being indulgent. Long before the *Chumleigh* reached Philadelphia, Captain Williams had earned the respect and loyalty of his crew.

When the *Chumleigh* entered the outer harbour at Halifax three days later, the grey waters of the bay were covered with ships as far as the eye could see. More than forty British and Allied merchant ships were assembled at anchor awaiting the word to sail eastwards. The word was not long in coming. Only a few hours after the *Chumleigh*'s arrival, the convoy was under way, and heading out into the Atlantic. For most of the ships this was to be just another routine crossing, a 2,400-mile slog through an ocean bedevilled by storms and infested with U-boats. Those who crewed the British ships, who had been through it so many times before, were content to bite the bullet and concentrate their thoughts on the welcome waiting on the other side – for the uninitiated, it was a voyage of adventure. Soon after leaving, Williams, who had been hustled ashore in Halifax for a briefing, had the unpleasant task of telling his crew that, for them, it would be different. The *Chumleigh* was going back to Russia.

In the spring of 1942, when Hitler came to realise that the conquest of the Soviet Union would not be the easy campaign he had envisaged, he turned his attention to those who were supplying the Soviets with arms and equipment. At that time, Allied convoys were going through to Murmansk and Archangel at the rate of two a month. Heavy units of the German Navy, including the *Tirpitz,* the *Hipper* and *Admiral Scheer,* were already operating against these convoys from the Norwegian fjords, but with little success. It was decided to send more U-boats and bombers north to rectify the situation. At that time of the year, the convoys were sailing in almost continuous daylight, and were particularly vulnerable. The losses began to mount, and had culminated in June in the slaughter of PQ 17, which lost twenty-four ships out of thirty-five. Over 130,000 tons of vital war supplies went to the bottom, and hundreds of Allied seamen died horribly in the icy waters beyond the Arctic Circle.

Following this debacle, despite insistent Soviet cries for ever more cargoes, it was decided to suspend all deliveries to Russia until the Arctic winter brought the cover of darkness twenty-four hours a day. Even then, the wisdom of sending large, heavily escorted convoys was questioned. As an experiment, it was thought best to first send through ten ships sailing independently and unescorted. Tatem's *Chumleigh* was to be one of the chosen ten.

The passage across the North Atlantic was arduous, but uneventful. Seven days out of Halifax, the *Chumleigh* broke away from the convoy, and headed north-east for Iceland. Less than an hour later, she was alone, with only the long, heaving swells in sight from horizon to horizon. Captain Williams was well aware of the dangers of being in the North Atlantic without the protection of the Royal Navy, and as the *Chumleigh* made her lonely way to the north-east, lookouts were doubled and guns manned around the clock.

For a supposedly non-combatant merchant ship, the *Chumleigh* was more than adequately armed. She mounted, in addition to the customary 4-inch on the poop, a quick-firing Bofors, four 20 mm Oerlikons, two Marlin machine-guns, and the usual array of PAC and FAM rockets for defence against low-flying aircraft. These guns were maintained and manned by a force of eighteen DEMS gunners, nine of whom were seconded from the Royal Navy, and nine from the Maritime Anti-Aircraft Regiment. In the event of an attack coming from the surface of the sea or from the air, the *Chumleigh* was capable of a credible defence: against underwater attack she was, like all merchant ships, completely defenceless.

As luck would have it, the *Chumleigh* was not called upon to use her guns, and she arrived at the Icelandic port of Hvalfjord on time, and unharmed. A few days later, at 1700 on 31 October, in company with nine other ships, four British and five American, she sailed out into the uninviting darkness of a bitterly cold night. Once clear of the harbour, the ships split up to go their own several ways. Operation 'FB' had begun.

After rounding the north of Iceland, Williams was instructed to make first for a position 250 miles north of Jan Mayen Island, thence to pass 30 miles south of Spitzbergen, and then in a south-easterly direction towards the White Sea and Archangel. The total distance was no more than 2,500 miles, but it was a passage that would take the *Chumleigh* through some of the most inhospitable

90

waters in the world. The strain of sailing in constant darkness would be aggravated by dense fog, blinding snowstorms and temperatures falling to as much as eighty degrees below freezing. To add to all this was the threat of a powerful and unseen enemy lying in wait along the way.

For Daniel Williams, as yet only a few months into command, the passage promised to be the ultimate test of his ability and courage. The *Chumleigh*, in common with most British merchant ships of her day, was equipped with the minimum requirement of navigational aids. Her owner's generosity, revealed in her above-average accommodation, had stopped short of the bridge, where the old rule of 'lead, log and lookout' still prevailed. Her only modern aid to navigation was a radio direction finder, an instrument that would be of little use to her on the passage to Archangel, as there were no shore radio beacons operating that far north. With the prospect of continually overcast skies and poor visibility, she would have to rely almost exclusively on dead reckoning. At the Admiralty briefing prior to sailing from Hvalfjord, Williams had drawn attention to this, but the Senior Naval Officer could only offer his sympathies. He pointed out that the supplies they were carrying to Russia were so urgently needed that all risks were justifiable. He urged the ships to press on at all possible speed, for ice was already reported forming at the approaches to Archangel, and before long the port would be closed.

It was as Williams had feared. Rounding the north point of Iceland, the *Chumleigh* ran into heavily overcast skies, with hazy visibility, and frequent blinding snow storms. Accurate navigation was out of the question. According to dead reckoning, the position off Jan Mayen was reached in the early hours of 3 November, and course was then altered to pass 30 miles clear of the southern point of Spitzbergen. There had been no improvement in the weather, and by that time Williams was becoming concerned about the accuracy of his magnetic compasses, which he was aware were unreliable in those high latitudes. When a momentary break in the overcast sky later that day enabled a quick azimuth to be taken of a bright star, both compasses were found to be eight degrees in error.

Late that night, the *Chumleigh*'s wireless operator listened in to

91

a series of distress messages. Some 350 miles to the south, several of the other ships taking part in Operation 'FB' were under attack by German long-range bombers. For the first time, Williams began to bless the protective mantle of fog and driving snow through which his ship was sailing.

At 0100 on the 5th, a radio message was received from the Admiralty instructing the *Chumleigh* to steer north to latitude 77 degrees, before shaping her course to pass south of Spitzbergen. In view of the attacks on the other ships to the south, two of which had been sunk, it had been decided to keep the *Chumleigh* well out of harm's way. The order was well intentioned, but misguided. Williams had had no further opportunity to check his compasses since the morning of the 3rd, and in his opinion another change of course might serve to make the ship's true position even more doubtful. In the hope that the cloud cover might break to allow star sights, he postponed the alteration until 0500. It was a decision he was to regret, for at 1100, during the brief period of twilight, a German reconnaissance seaplane dived out of the cloud, and began to circle the ship, taking care to keep out of range of her guns.

The aircraft made no move to attack, and soon flew off, but Williams knew that his position was already being reported to the bomber bases 400 miles to the south. The JU-88s would not be long in coming. An hour later, when the DR plot showed the *Chumleigh* to be in approximately 77° North, course was altered to return to the original route.

Throughout the remainder of the day, the atmosphere on board the *Chumleigh* was tense as she steamed southwards with the threat of air attack hanging over her. Captain Williams unwilling to leave the bridge, paced up and down, a worried man. The bombs and torpedoes of the enemy he had learned to live with, but the nagging uncertainty of not knowing exactly where his ship was in relation to the land weighed heavily on his mind. For far too long he had been steaming blind in unfamiliar waters, altering course on positions based on nothing more than educated guesses. He had no means of ascertaining his ship's exact speed, and he was unsure of the error on his compasses. This was an extremely dangerous situation, and he feared the outcome.

By evening, things had got worse, with great white flakes of snow falling, seriously reducing the visibility. There was a freshening breeze, and a moderate swell was running. At 2300, Williams checked his calculations on the chart for the last time and, having established to the best of his ability that the ship was clear of the southern point of Spitzbergen, gave the order to alter course to the east. He then walked out into the wing of the bridge and stood peering into the blinding snow, wondering if he had made the right decision.

Half an hour later, the *Chumleigh* ran headlong onto a reef off Spitzbergen's South Cape. She was 20 miles to the north of her intended course.

When the initial shock of the sudden grounding had faded, it became apparent that the *Chumleigh* had ridden up over the reef, and was firmly held amidships. Her bows sloped downwards so that the foredeck was awash, while her stern was out of the water. Thus balanced, Williams feared that his ship would soon break her back.

But the *Chumleigh*, built in one of the finest shipyards on Britain's north-east coast, was made of sterner stuff. She was still intact nearly two hours later, and Williams decided there might still be a chance of saving her. First he deemed it prudent to put most of his crew into the lifeboats to lay off the ship, in case she did break up without warning. He would stay on board with Chief Officer Ernest Fenn and Second Engineer Middlemiss, a 37-year-old Edinburgh Scot.

After the long ordeal the men of the *Chumleigh* had been through, culminating in the grounding of their ship on an unseen reef in a cold and inhospitable sea, it can be appreciated that their morale was now at a very low ebb. It was not surprising, therefore, that when Captain Williams gave the order to take to the boats, a certain amount of panic set in. By the time Third Officer David Clark made his way down from the bridge to take charge of his lifeboat, he found that its crew had already started to lower away. In the darkness and the heat of the moment, the after fall was accidentally cast off, and the boat plummeted to the water stern first, throwing out the two men on board. The boat was swamped, and the unfortunate men disappeared in the icy water.

93

Clark, a 22-year-old, soft-spoken Devon man, calmed his men, and distributed them amongst the other boats.

In spite of the heavy swell running, the three remaining boats were launched successfully, and taken away from the ship's side. Meanwhile, Williams, Fenn and Middlemiss remained on the bridge, Williams being occupied with dumping overboard all confidential papers and books in their weighted bags.

Having discharged his last duty to the Admiralty, Captain Williams was returning to the wheelhouse, when he heard a faint cry for help coming from below. He ran down to the main deck, and shining his torch overside, saw two men struggling in the water. They were the seamen who had been thrown out of the lifeboat when it up-ended. Realising that the men could not last much longer in the freezing water, Williams called to one of the boats lying off to go to their rescue. Unfortunately, the boat's crew, possibly still numb with shock at their predicament, made no move to carry out his orders. Daniel Williams, normally slow to anger, saw red, clambered down into the boat and physically forced its crew into action. With the help of Boatswain Hardy and one of the *Chumleigh*'s young apprentices, Williams hauled one of the drowning men out of the water. The man was rigid with cold and very near to death, but he revived when brandy was poured down his throat. The other man was not so fortunate. By the time the boat reached him, he was dead.

Williams now returned on board the *Chumleigh*, but so exhausted was he by his exertions, that he collapsed on reaching the deck. He recovered quickly, and was soon discussing with Fenn and Middlemiss the possibility of refloating the ship. At 0230, the lifeboats were called back alongside, and Williams asked for volunteers to assist with the operation. It was also in his mind that his men would be safer, and certainly warmer, on board the ship, but the men in the boats were of a different mind. It was only after some persuasion that two firemen agreed to reboard to help Second Engineer Middlemiss raise steam on the engine.

As soon as the engines were ready, Williams made an attempt to back the ship off the reef, but after running full astern for half an hour, he was forced to admit defeat. In fact, his efforts resulted only in settling the ship more firmly on the reef. Her bow and stern were now sagging dangerously, and fearful she was about to break her back, Williams rang the engines off and called Middlemiss and his men up on deck. There was nothing more to be done to save the *Chumleigh*.

In what he knew to be a futile gesture, but one that for the sake of protocol he must make, Captain Williams now brought one of the radio officers back on board to send a message informing all ships that the *Chumleigh* was being abandoned. At 0400, four and a half hours after she struck the reef, Williams took a last sad look around the deserted deck of his ship, swung his leg over the bulwarks, and climbed down into the waiting lifeboat.

As the three boats pulled away from the *Chumleigh*, the driving snow began to ease, and it was only then that Williams was able to see the awful danger into which he had unwittingly steamed. The ship was trapped into a horseshoe-shaped lagoon with angry breakers on all sides. There seemed to be no escape for the lifeboats, and Williams decided to take them back alongside the *Chumleigh* until the short Arctic twilight gave him the opportunity to assess the situation carefully.

Five or six hours later, when there was sufficient light, an opening was sighted in the reefs, and the boats once again left the shelter of the ship's side and pulled for the open sea. They were not a moment too soon. Low down on the horizon, five aircraft were seen heading in towards the ship. As the planes drew nearer, Williams recognised them as JU-88s, which were no doubt responding to the sighting sent in by the seaplane that had haunted them briefly twenty-four hours earlier.

The bombers began to circle the lifeboats ominously, and the survivors, who had recently been through so much, thought they were about to be machine-gunned for good measure. But the planes sheered off and directed their attack on the stranded *Chumleigh*. A number of bombs were dropped on the captive target from mast-top height, at least two of which scored direct hits. When the enemy aircraft flew away, a column of black smoke was seen to be rising from the ship.

Having been forced to watch his ship suffer this further indignity, Daniel Williams, tired and miserable though he was, now set his mind to the survival of his men. Although the southern coast of Spitzbergen was in sight, he knew it was pointless to attempt to land there. The Admiralty pilot book described it as coast of sheer ice cliffs and wandering glaciers, completely devoid of vegetation, and uninhabited except for polar bears and Arctic foxes. To put the boats ashore here – if that was indeed possible – would only add to their problems. The nearest habitation lay 150 miles to the north, at the Soviet mining settlement of Barentsburg, and it was for there that they must make. He gave the order to hoist sails.

The weather had now improved, and at first the boats made good progress. However, the smallest of the three soon started to drop astern of the others, and Williams decided it would be better to abandon this boat and redistribute its crew amongst the other two. When this was done, they set off again, hugging the coast and sailing smartly before a fresh breeze. The Captain's boat, with Third Officer Clark at the helm, had on board a total of twenty-eight men, while Chief Officer Fenn's boat carried twenty-nine. Both boats were overcrowded, but in the bitterly cold conditions prevailing this proved to be an advantage.

During the night that followed, the two boats became separated, but Williams continued on course, confident that Fenn would join up with him later. But on the morning of the 7th the weather suddenly changed. The wind fell right away, and the boat was becalmed for most of the day. Next day brought with it a full gale, and with it a short, heavy sea. The crowded boat was in danger of being swamped, and Williams was forced to stream the sea anchor and heave to. Throughout that day, and the following night, they drifted with the angry seas breaking clean over the boat. The survivors were cold, wet, and thoroughly demoralised, and it was only the indomitable Williams, by bullying them into bailing the waterlogged boat, who kept them alive.

On the morning of the 9th, the weather eased, but they found they had drifted out of sight of the land. The boat was equipped with a small engine and a limited supply of fuel that Williams was saving for such an emergency as now faced them – if they lost touch with the land completely, there was no hope for their survival. The engine was started, and they steered back to the east. After running under full power for about two hours, it was with great relief that they sighted not only the land, but the other lifeboat. The two boats came together again, and Williams and Fenn discussed the situation. They calculated that they were no more than 80 miles south of Barentsburg, and it was mutually agreed that Williams should push on ahead, using his engine to reach port and bring help for the others. This providential meeting of the two boats acted on their crews like a tonic, and when they parted company again, both crews were in high spirits.

Using both engine and sails, William estimated he would reach Barentsburg in fourteen or fifteen hours, a gruelling passage, but endurable. However, Lady Luck was no longer smiling on them. During the night, the wind rose and the temperature plummeted. The boat began to ship water, and soon the bottom boards were awash. A thick layer of ice formed on the gunwales, and the sails froze hard. Fortunately, the water in the bottom of the boat did not freeze, and the men were able to keep it at a reasonable level with continuous bailing. But later, to add to their misery, their clothes froze to their bodies. It now seemed that these men were condemned to die where they sat, their feet in icy water, their upper bodies buffeted by a cruel wind, and the relentless cold eating into their bones. Only the sheer force of Daniel Williams's personality stopped them from giving up there and then.

The first to slip away was the chief steward Islwyn Davies. In the small, lonely hours of the 10th, 30-year-old Davies, despite the efforts of his companions, fell into a delirium, and died as quietly as he had lived. As he committed the body of his fellow Welshman to the deep, Captain Williams reflected on the cruelty of a war that had brought this man all the way from the gentle hills of his native Ceredigion to die in the desolate wastes of the Barents Sea.

Pushing on through the rest of the night, under sail only to preserve his dwindling supply of fuel, Williams restarted the engine at the first hint of light. His calculations, if they were correct, put the boat very close to Icefjord, the large ice-free fjord at whose mouth Barentsburg lay. A few hours later, in the last of the short twilight, Prince Charles Foreland, at the entrance to the fjord, was sighted, and with rising hope Williams altered towards the headland. At that moment, the boat's engine spluttered and died. All attempts to restart it failed.

The morale of the men in the boat now fell to a new low. They were all desperately weak, and although it was not then apparent to them, suffering from frostbite in varying degrees. Huddled together for warmth, they had lost the will to eat, and were experiencing excruciating pangs of thirst, which the boat's meagre supply of water could not hope to assuage. At least one man, the ship's donkeyman, was delirious. The most grievous blow of all fell when Captain Williams, worn out by five days of constant mental and physical strain, collapsed and lapsed into unconsciousness. Robbed of their gallant leader, there now seemed to be no hope for any of them.

In the blackness of the freezing night, alone on the heaving ocean, the tiny lifeboat became an island of despair. This might well have been the point at which the story ended but, as in all walks of life, when one leader falls, another rises to take his place. In this case it was 22-year-old Third Officer David Clark.

The ink was barely dry on Clark's second mate's certificate, but what he lacked in experience he made up for in determination. Although his hands and feet were so frostbitten that he had no feeling in either, he immediately took command of the boat when Williams lost consciousness.

The task facing David Clark would have daunted many men twice his age. He found himself in charge of a partially waterlogged boat containing twenty-seven men, two of whom seemed to be dying. The others were cold, wet, thirsty and without hope. The boat's engine had failed, and they were drifting within sight of an unknown shore. Clark decided to wait until there was some light in the sky before committing himself to a course of action.

When the sky finally lightened, shortly before noon on the 11th, the land was no longer in sight. Clark drove the men to hoist sail, which proved to be a great effort, as the canvas was frozen hard, and they were all very weak. An hour later, the land was once again visible, and Clark began to search for a landing place. He had hoped to make Barentsburg, but as the cold was so intense, and his men so exhausted, he realised that unless they reached the shore and found shelter quickly, they would all die.

As the boat slowly closed the land, breakers were sighted, and it soon became evident that they were confronted by a line of reefs that ran parallel to the coast for many miles in either direction.

The air of disappointment in the boat was great, and was soon to be compounded by a gale force wind that sprang up, bringing rough seas that broke over the gunwales. Clark altered course to the south, and sailed along the outside of the reef, searching for a way in. It was time to end the awful nightmare.

All too soon complete darkness came down, but as it did flickering lights were seen on shore. This sign that they were not after all alone in this dark, frozen world raised a weak cheer from half a dozen pairs of cracked lips. Clark was quick to take advantage of this temporary upsurge in morale, and decided to tackle the reef. The sails were lowered, oars shipped, and they altered boldly towards the shore.

A number of times during the next few hours Clark thought he had found a break in the reef, but each time was forced to pull back when the opening proved to be no more than an illusion, a momentary slackening in the surge of the sea. Then, just before 0200 on the morning of the 12th, when Clark was on the point of giving up and heading back out to sea, the gods took pity on them. A huge ground swell lifted the heavily-laden lifeboat, carried it across the reef, and threw it onto the beach. Battered and bruised, cold and wet, the *Chumleigh*'s men had landed.

Half in and half out of the grounded boat, Clark disentangled himself from the jumble of bodies and crawled a few yards up the shingle beach on his hands and knees. When he got unsteadily to his feet, he found it hard to believe the sight that met his eyes. Twenty yards further up the beach stood a group of wooden huts. If David Clark had had the strength to cheer, he would have done so then.

But the night of suffering was not yet over. Many of the survivors were so weak that the twenty-yard crawl to shelter was beyond them. For three of the small band the shock of the heavy landing on the beach had been too much. They died where they lay, gasping out their last breaths on a cold and unknown alien shore.

It took the remainder of the night for Clark and the few others who were capable to drag, carry and cajole the rest up the short stretch of beach and into the huts. Captain Williams had by that time regained consciousness, but was very weak.

The huts, as Clark had anticipated, were peopled only by the ghosts of whalers of another age, but they were dry and afforded shelter from the biting wind. Without bothering to strip off their sodden clothing, the survivors lay down, and were asleep within minutes.

Next morning, as soon as there was light enough to investigate further, it was found that one hut contained a small wood-burning stove, a supply of wood, matches, and some tinned food, including coffee beans. No castaway has ever been confronted by a more welcome sight. Refreshed by their night's sleep, the survivors moved into this hut, and set about making themselves comfortable. The stove was lit, and when it was roaring, snow was melted to make coffee. The hot drink, the first they had tasted for eight days, breathed new life into them, and they began to look to the future. The more active members of the party, led by Clark, rummaged the other huts, and returned in triumph with tins of biscuits and corned beef. When the remaining lifeboat rations were retrieved and added to the store, and it was discovered that there was no shortage of driftwood to burn, life took on a new perspective.

After a few days in the warmth of the hut, Captain Williams recovered sufficiently to take command of the party again. Most of his men, he found, were in very poor physical condition, having frostbite in their hands and dreadfully swollen feet. They were suffering from 'immersion foot', a painful and dangerous inflammation caused by the long immersion of their feet in the icy water in the bottom of the lifeboat. David Clark, whose superhuman efforts had sustained them and brought them to the land while Williams lay unconscious, was particularly affected. Only the four Army gunners in the party seemed to be in reasonable physical shape. One of them, 20-year-old Gunner Reginald Whiteside, four feet eleven in his boots, and an ex-Liverpool docker, showed no more signs of the long ordeal than if he had been on a routine training exercise. Whiteside's toughness and cheery manner were to be an inspiration to all in the days to come.

But again it was Daniel Williams's determined and effective leadership and exercise of discipline under the most difficult circumstances that were to hold the men together. From the outset, he created and fostered the belief that it would only be a matter of days before rescue arrived. It was perhaps just as well that he was not aware that the SOS sent out before they abandoned the *Chumleigh* had been received by no one, except, it must be assumed, the hostile ears of the German bomber base in Norway. He was also not to know that the lifeboat containing Chief Officer Fenn and twenty-eight others had disappeared from the face of the sea, never to be seen again. As far as the outside world was concerned, the *Chumleigh* was missing, believed sunk with all hands, and no rescue operation would be mounted. Williams and his men were alone in a land of ice and snow, a land where no tree or bush grew, and where only the glowering, frozen mountains looked down on them in the short half-light of the Arctic day.

Inevitably, although the survivors now had shelter, warmth and a supply of food, the grievous hardships they had suffered began to take their toll. In the first four days, thirteen died from gangrene, brought on by frostbite and immersion foot. With no medical supplies to hand, Williams could do nothing for them, other than comfort them and see to their burial when they were gone. In this he was assisted by his only fit men, the Army gunners, led by 23-year-old Lance-Sergeant Richard Peyer. In addition to nursing the sick, the gunners took over the running of the camp, foraging for food and fuel in the time-honoured tradition of the British Army.

The first organised attempts to reach civilisation were made by Third Officer Clark and Lance-Sergeant Peyer, who twice set off in the direction in which it was thought Barentsburg must lie. Without skis or proper warm clothing, their attempts were doomed from the start, for the ground they had to cover resembled a frozen moonscape, with jagged rocks underfoot, deep ravines, and vast empty areas of snow and ice. Twice Clark and Peyer set out, and twice they came back, beaten by the cruel terrain.

As November moved into December, winter came in earnest, with increased cold and blizzards reducing visibility to a few yards. The short twilight they had so looked forward to in breaking the awful monotony of the almost total darkness shrank

101

to just a momentary greying of the sky around noon, and the men's spirits sank proportionately. The diet of biscuits and corned beef, supplemented by Horlicks tablets from the lifeboat, was enough for bare subsistence, but dull and unappetising. As is often the case under such circumstances, the survivors spent many hours discussing food, savouring over and over again meals they had eaten in the past, and planning sumptuous banquets they would indulge in when they reached civilisation. However, imagination is a poor substitute for protein, and although their gastric juices flowed, they grew steadily weaker.

Williams was acutely conscious that lack of hope would kill them quicker than lack of sustenance, and fought all the time to keep the flame of confidence alive. He persuaded those who were fit enough to take at least two hours' exercise a day and, so far as the visibility would allow, encouraged exploration in the vicinity of the camp. When a disused lighthouse was discovered on a nearby cape, it was thought that signals for help could be sent. Unfortunately, all the essential parts of the light had been removed.

In the first week of December, Lance-Sergeant Peyer, Gunner Whiteside and Gunner James Burnett volunteered to make another sortie in search of help. Setting off up the fjord in a north-easterly direction, they marched for several hours across the frozen, rocky wilderness, before they were forced to turn back. But their attempt did not go unrewarded. On the return journey, they came upon a small, isolated hut which contained a sack of flour and some tins of corned beef and cocoa. These they carried back in triumph to the camp.

This latest find came at an opportune time, for the lifeboat rations and original stock of food were running out. For the next month the survivors lived on small cakes made of flour and water. It was a far cry from *haute cuisine*, but with hot drinks – a choice of coffee or cocoa served three times a day – life was bearable for a while. When the coffee and cocoa ran out, they drank hot water. When the flour had gone the same way, they ate whale blubber, a few tins of which had been found during the foraging.

In mid-December, Williams, who was beginning to find strength in desperation, set out with Whiteside to make yet

102

another strike in the direction of Barentsburg. As before, they were beaten by the elements and the terrain, and forced to return to camp without any message of hope. No more food was found, and the survivors were reduced to drinking the boiled oil in which the whale blubber had been stored. Even for men on the verge of starvation, this rank, glutinous mess proved nauseous in the extreme.

As Christmas drew near, with nothing but the ever-present snow to remind them of a season they once knew as festive, the situation in the hut grew worse day by day. Clark and the boatswain, Hardy, were in a very weak condition, suffering from gangrene in their hands and feet. Several others also had gangrenous limbs oozing pus. The stench in the hut was unbearable.

Christmas Eve saw the death of another man, and Williams decided he must make one final effort to get help, or – and he knew this was a distinct possibility – die in the attempt. He took Peyer and Whiteside with him and set off up the fjord, forcing the pace as much as he dared. When they had covered what Williams estimated to be about half the distance to Barentsburg, the tough little ex-docker, Whiteside, at last broke down, and could go no further. Peyer was also near to collapse, so Williams had no alternative but to turn back.

The first day of 1943 was welcomed in an air of abject misery. There was no more food left in the hut, and the nine remaining men were sustained only by melted snow water and the warmth of the stove, in which they were now burning planks torn from the other huts. On the morning of 2 January, Reginald Whiteside – one of the few men still able to move – went outside to fetch more fuel for the stove. A few minutes later he threw open the door of the hut, his eyes wide, his speech incoherent.

Believing the gunner had gone mad, Williams struggled to his feet and tried to calm him. But he could make no sense of Whiteside's hysterical raving. It then occurred to the captain that the hut was about to be attacked by bears, for several had been recently seen in the vicinity of the camp. Cautiously, he went outside, and there he saw two white-suited figures skiing towards the hut. As suddenly as it had begun on that dark, storm-filled night off South Cape fifty-eight days before, the nightmare was over.

The newcomers, two Norwegian soldiers on a routine patrol from Barentsburg, were appalled by the sight that met them in the hut. The nine survivors, gaunt, hollow-eyed, their clothes in rags, and with evil-smelling pus soaking through the makeshift bandages on their hands and feet, simply stared back in disbelief.

Quickly sizing up the situation, the Norwegians handed over all the food and cigarettes they carried in their rucksacks, and immediately set off to return to Barentsburg to bring help. With them went Gunners Whiteside and Burnett, determined to reach the outside world on their own two feet, and with their heads held high. The indomitable Reginald Whiteside did just that, but James Burnett, who had used up his last reserves of strength, had to submit to being half-carried on the final stages of the journey.

Early next day, two sledge parties arrived at the hut, bringing with them food, clothing, and a doctor. Clark and Hardy, by then seriously ill, were taken back to Barentsburg at once. The doctor and two men stayed with Williams and the four other survivors until more men and sledges arrived next day. At 2000 on 3 January, they finally reached the goal that had eluded them for fifty-three days. It was no comfort to them to learn that all through those long, anguishing days and nights of suffering, Barentsburg had lain only twelve miles away.

All nine survivors were hospitalised in Barentsburg, where they were nursed back to health, a process which took over two months. Another two months were to pass before the cruisers HMS *Belfast* and HMS *Cumberland* arrived in Icefjord, and Daniel Williams and the only eight men of his crew to survive the wreck of the *Chumleigh* were returned to Britain. They landed in Thurso in northern Scotland on 15 June 1943, more than seven months after the loss of their ship. For six of those months they had been officially reported as missing, believed lost at sea. Captain Daniel Morley Williams arrived home in his native village of Llangranog six months too late to attend a memorial service held to commemorate his passing. For his outstanding courage and leadership under the most extreme conditions he was later awarded the OBE. Lance-Sergeant Richard Peyer, Gunner Reginald Whiteside and Gunner James Burnett received the MBE in recognition of their services.

Sadly, the *Chumleigh* was not allowed to rest in peace while her men were fighting to stay alive on a barren shore. Eleven days after she was abandoned, she was torpedoed by U-625, and again bombed by JU-88s. Her broken bones still lie rusting off the southern point of Spitzbergen, a grim monument to the fifty-one members of her crew who died a lonely death in their attempt to bring help to the Soviet Union.

Chapter Ten

In the Darkest Hour

On 8 June 1943, the Supplement to the London Gazette announced the award of the George Medal to Captain George Marmion Duff, the OBE to Chief Engineer John Bell Parker, the MBE to Chief Officer Glyn Roberts, Second Officer Francis Charles Hender and Second Engineer Dugald Charles Kinleyside, and the MBE to Carpenter Harry Shakeshaft and Storekeeper Frank Simmons. In a war when decorations were only sparingly handed out to 'non-combatant' merchant seamen, the award of seven medals to one ship was without precedent. The story behind the awards began in the ancient Egyptian port of Alexandria in October 1942.

At that time, Alexandria's West Harbour was in a frenzy of activity, its berths packed with ships discharging supplies for Montgomery's Eighth Army, then massing for the decisive battle of El Alamein soon to be fought. Amongst this vast armada of merchantmen was the 7,006-ton *Empire Glade*. Built in 1941 at Barclay Curle's yard in Glasgow, unusually for a wartime replacement, which were by-and-large very basic steamers, she was a well-equipped refrigerated motor vessel. Managed by the Blue Star Line for the Ministry of War Transport, the *Empire Glade* was commanded by Captain George Duff, and carried a crew of forty-three, supplemented by six DEMS gunners. Her four-cylinder Doxford engine gave her a top speed of 12½ knots, and she was armed with a 4-inch gun and a 12-pounder HA/LA mounted aft, two Marlin, two Hotchkiss and two Lewis machine-guns on her boat deck and bridge, with the usual rockets and kites to deter low-flying aircraft, plus three depth charges which, it was hoped, could be used against submarines. Although flying the Red Ensign, the *Empire Glade* was, for the duration at least, a warship in her own right. Come the peace, she would land her guns and fit nicely into Blue Star's South American meat trade.

Unlike the other ships berthed in Alexandria, the *Empire Glade* was to play no part in the North African war. She sailed from the port on 17 October with her holds empty and her ballast tanks full, under orders to proceed to Charleston and New York, via Cape Town and Trinidad, to load a cargo for the United Kingdom. The long passage south to the Cape was uneventful, and she reached Cape Town, where she was to take bunkers and stores, on 5 November. Twenty-four hours later, she sailed out of Table Bay into the Atlantic, and headed north again, leaving the comparative peace of the Indian Ocean behind her, and entering waters where the sea war was being fought in deadly earnest.

Soon after America entered the war, in December 1941, Admiral Dönitz sent five long-range U-boats out from Biscay to attack merchant shipping sailing between the Gulf of St. Lawrence and Cape Hatteras. What they found there was the stuff of every U-boat commander's dreams. Operation *Paukenschlag* (Roll on the Kettle Drums), as Germany's opening attack on American shipping was designated, proved to be an overwhelming success, and became known amongst the U-boat crews as 'the happy time'. America was totally unprepared for the war to be brought so near to home, and little was done to protect ships on or near the coast. They went about their business as though nothing had changed, as though the war was something that concerned only those on the other side of the Atlantic. Ships were not blacked out at night, sailing with all navigation and accommodation lights blazing, as they had done in peacetime. Meanwhile, all shore lights, lighthouses, buoys and beacons were on full power, and the lights of towns along the coast shone so brightly that they silhouetted passing ships against the skyline. To complete the farce, radio silence – a fundamental precaution in wartime – was not being kept, all ships, including US Navy ships, broadcasting in plain language day and night, passing vital information such as positions, destinations and ETAs, all of which was listened into by the delighted U-boat commanders.

By the end of January 1942, the five U-boats taking part in *Paukenschlag* had accounted for twenty-three Allied merchant ships, totalling 142,320 tons. This was particularly galling for the Royal Navy, as many of the ships lost were those they had so carefully guarded on the Atlantic crossing. Admiral Dönitz, on the other hand, was well-pleased, and sending every U-boat he could spare from the North Atlantic convoy routes and the Mediterranean hurrying westwards to take advantage of the American turkey shoot. And still the US Navy delayed instituting convoys on the coast, refusing to believe that U-boats were in their waters, and putting the sinkings down to mines laid off the coast by the enemy. Over the months that followed, the number of U-boats operating in American waters increased to thirty-seven, including a number of 1,600-ton U-tankers. By June, they were sinking ships at the rate of three a day, and in that month alone nearly 400,000 tons of precious merchant shipping fell to Dönitz's modern-day buccaneers. One of their first British victims was the 8,032-ton tanker *Empire Mica*, managed for the MOWT by the Anglo-American Oil Company of London.

Sailing under the command of 70-year-old Captain Hugh Bentley, called out of retirement to fill a gap in the thinning ranks of shipmasters, the *Empire Mica* crossed the Atlantic, and in the first half of 1942 was engaged in carrying cargoes between ports in the Gulf of Mexico. At the end of June, she loaded 11,200 tons of kerosene in Baytown, Texas, for Key West, Florida, sailing on 26 June. This was a short, three-day passage in normal times. But the times were far from normal, and Captain Bentley thought it prudent to hug the coast, sailing in daylight only, and anchoring offshore at night.

Bentley had planned to anchor in the lee of Cape San Blas on the evening of the 28th, but found the water too shallow, and decided to carry on to the south. The night was fine and clear with a full moon, the sea calm, and Bentley, in common with others on the coast, had probably not yet grasped the full extent of the dangers threatening. At 0100 on the morning of the 29th, he was making his last visit to the bridge before turning in, when a shout from the lookout warned of a U-boat surfacing half a mile off the port beam. U-67, under the command of *Kapitänleutnant* Günther Müller-Stöckheim, was about to add to her score.

Bentley, unable to comprehend that the enemy had penetrated so deep into the Gulf without coming up against the might of the US Navy, was still fumbling with his binoculars when the torpedo struck the *Empire Mica* abaft the bridge.

There was a violent explosion, and the whole of the after part of the tanker burst into flames. Many of the crew, off watch and asleep, died in the flames, others lost their lives when the rope falls of two of the lifeboats caught fire, and the boats plunged bow-first to the sea below. Out of a total crew of forty-seven, only fourteen men succeeded in abandoning ship, and were picked up by a passing yacht. The *Empire Mica*, her flames visible for many miles along the coast, burned for more than twenty-four hours, before sinking.

Only when the news filtered through that the *Empire Mica* had met her fate at the hands of an enemy submarine did the United States Navy finally take a leaf out of the Royal Navy's book and begin sailing ships in organised convoys. The introduction of convoys brought about an immediate fall in sinkings, and as the American escorts, supplemented by a number of British corvettes sent over to help, became more experienced, Dönitz was forced to withdraw most of his U-boats back into the Atlantic, leaving only a few small groups to harass shipping in the Caribbean.

In the second half of 1942, U-boats hunting independently had considerable success against ships sailing unescorted in the Caribbean, particularly in the Windward Passage between Cuba and Haiti. Inevitably, their attacks led to the introduction of a convoy system in those waters, and as the US Navy became more proficient in defending the merchantmen, the U-boats were once again forced to pull out. However, eight boats, among them Günther Müller-Stöckheim's U-67, began operating in the waters around Trinidad, lying in wait for ships sailing alone on the long haul between North America and the Cape of Good Hope. In the closing months of the year they were sinking 30,000 tons a week.

U-67, commissioned in Bremen in January 1941, was a long-range Type IX C boat of 1,540 tons. When 28-year-old Günther Müller-Stöckheim assumed command in July 1941, she embarked on a successful career, which included sinking thirteen Allied ships of 72,028 tons, and damaging five others. Her eighteenth victim was the 4,697-ton Norwegian-flag *Tortugas*, commanded by Captain Rolf Endresen, and sailing from Calcutta to the Clyde via Cape Town and Trinidad with a cargo of 2,200 tons of manganese ore, 1,000 tons of jute and 14,000 chests of tea, a priceless load in these troubled times.

The *Tortugas* was to the east of Barbados when she sailed into Müller-Stöckheim's ambush on 18 November. First Mate Agnar Hansen had the watch on the bridge and Ordinary Seaman Jacob Karlsen was at the wheel, neither man having the slightest inkling of danger, when Müller-Stöckheim's torpedo struck the ship on her port side between Nos. 4 and 5 holds. The *Tortugas* went down like the proverbial stone in a few minutes, but thanks to the lack of panic and their ability to handle boats, all thirty-eight crew, including Captain Endresen's wife safely abandoned ship in four lifeboats.

When she motored away from the scene of her latest sinking, having taken prisoner Captain Endresen and Chief Engineer Trygve Jensen, U-67 had been nine weeks at sea since leaving Lorient, and was running low on fuel and stores. It was time, Müller-Stöckheim decided, to head for home, but before she reached Biscay U-67 had one more appointment to keep.

Before she went down, the *Tortugas*'s British wireless operator Harold Clay succeeded in transmitting an SOS. This was picked up by a shore radio station, with the result that a signal went out to the *Empire Glade*, then deep in the South Atlantic, rerouting her to pass inside the islands, rather than outside them. This would have taken her away from the danger presented by U-67's torpedoes. Unfortunately, for reasons unknown, this order was rescinded on the night of the 27th, and Captain Duff resumed his original course for Charleston, passing outside the islands, and so committing his ship to a rendezvous with the enemy.

Meanwhile, the *Tortugas*'s lifeboats were already making good progress towards the land. At first, the motor boat, with First Mate Agnar Hansen at the helm, took the other three boats in tow, but when a favourable wind blew up next day, all boats went under sail. Over the next four days, the boats kept close together, with Hansen passing the tow line to the others whenever the wind dropped. Then they became separated, but the occupants of three boats were picked up by passing ships, while Agnar Hansen brought his boat ashore in a remote spot on the southern side of the island. With the exception of Captain Rolf Endresen and Chief Engineer Trygve Jensen, who ended up in a German prisoner of war camp, all survivors from the *Tortugas* were ashore on Trinidad by the 28th.

At 0445 on that same day, 28th November 1942, the *Empire Glade* was 650 miles to the east of the island of Barbados, and carving out a zig-zag wake through the dying night at a speed in excess of 12 knots. The moon was still up, but obscured by a partial overcast, and although there were a few passing showers, the visibility was fair. A light E'ly wind ruffled the sea, and a slight swell gave the ship an easy roll. Chief Officer Glyn Roberts was on watch on the bridge, and with the dawn only an hour away, was preparing for his morning star sights. In the darkened wheelhouse, the helmsman's face was just visible in the light of the compass binnacle, as he eased the wheel a spoke either way to keep the ship on course. Right forward, in the bows, the shadowy figure of the lookout man paced the gratings, his keen eyes scanning the horizon for any sign of life. Aft, on the poop gun platform, the two DEMS gunners on watch huddled in the shadow of their long-barrelled 4-inch and conversed in hushed tones. It was a peaceful scene such as might be found in any merchant ship around the world in this darkest hour before the dawn, except that in the case of the *Empire Glade*, the idyll was about to be shattered.

In the deep shadows, several hundred yards off the unsuspecting merchantman's starboard bow, *Kapitänleutnant* Müller-Stöckheim, who had been stalking her for most of the night, had brought U-67 to the surface. On his way back to Lorient with all his torpedoes expended, Müller-Stöckheim was unable to resist striking one last blow against the enemy – but this time it would have to be done with the submarine's 105 mm gun.

Captain Duff was dozing in an armchair in his day cabin, when the crash of gunfire brought him out of his fitful sleep. He rushed to the bridge just in time to see the flash of U-67's gun as she fired her second shot. As with the first, the shell went wide, but seconds later another flash in the darkness to starboard indicated that the hidden enemy had fired again. This time, Müller-Stöckheim's gunners found their target, their third shell striking home with devastating results. By some cruel twist of fate, the shell burst on a wooden liferaft stowed in the *Empire Glade*'s forward rigging on the starboard side, and ignited the container of red distress flares carried in the raft's locker. The result was spectacular, the whole ship being bathed in an incandescent red glow that must have been visible for many miles all round the horizon. To complete the disaster, the blast from the exploding shell brought down the main wireless aerial.

With his ship made an easy target by the burning flares, Duff decided that the only course open to him was to attempt to ram his attacker. He put the flash of the 105 mm right ahead, and rang for full emergency speed. The *Empire Glade* surged forward, but ran into a hail of shells as U-67's gunners found their mark, scoring hit after hit above and below the waterline. To make a bad situation infinitely worse, one shell struck the port side of the bridge, wrecking Duff's day room and severing electric wiring to the bridge which passed through the cabin, thereby causing the all-round signal lamp on the upper bridge to flash continuously.

Accepting that he had no hope of closing the enemy while his ship was so brilliantly lit up, Captain Duff put the helm hard over, and executed a tight turn to present his stern to the enemy. At the same time, he passed word aft for the gunners, who were closed up on the 4-inch, to open fire. Second Officer Francis Hender, the ship's gunnery officer, with nothing to pin-point his target but the enemy's gun flashes, was working under a severe handicap, but he directed his gun like a true professional. Meanwhile, Captain Duff and Chief Officer Roberts were dumping overboard all secret papers and books, along with the two bags of Consular mail taken on board in Cape Town.

At a few minutes after five o'clock, with his ship taking heavy punishment from U-67's gun, which was firing at the rate of five or six shells a minute, Duff reluctantly came to the conclusion that the time had come to look to the welfare of his crew. He rang the engine-room telegraph to stop, and instructed Chief Officer Roberts to make the boats ready for lowering. The *Empire Glade* was now drifting, her engine stopped, but an inspection of her damage showed that she was neither disabled, nor in danger of sinking. As the unidentified attacker had ceased fire – probably accepting that her victim was about to be abandoned – Duff decided to reverse his decision and fight on. At 0508, he rang for full speed ahead. By this time the engine-room had been evacuated, but when the bridge telegraph rang, Chief Engineer John Parker and Second Engineer Dugald Kinleyside, immediately went below. Under the circumstances prevailing, this was an extremely brave action on the part of both men, particularly so in the case of Kinleyside, who had been on watch when a shell burst in the engine-room early on in the action, and was slightly wounded by the blast. Under normal circumstances, when a motor vessel is stopped, it takes some time to warm the engine through before it can be restarted, but Parker and Kinleyside – no doubt driven by the very abnormal circumstances – worked a small miracle. The *Empire Glade* was under way and up to full speed in only seven minutes.

Seeing the merchantman under way again, Müller-Stöckheim ordered his gun's crew to continue firing. In reply, Second Officer Hender fired back, and for the next half an hour a running battle ensued, with the *Empire Glade*, her stern to the enemy, swopping shell for shell. During the action, U-67's deck gun fired between twenty and thirty shells, eight of which hit the fleeing ship. She was holed, above and below the waterline five times, and three shells struck her upperworks. Throughout, the *Empire Glade*'s gunners were firing at an unseen assailant, aiming only at his gun flashes. Whether or not they scored any hits on U-67 is not on record.

The sky to the east was now paling with the coming of the new dawn, and the *Empire Glade*'s engine, under the expert hand of Chief Engineer John Parker, was driving the ship at a speed her builders never dared dream of. But it could only be a matter of time before Müller-Stöckheim, with 17 knots at his disposal, caught up with her and, in full daylight, allowed his trained gunners to use her for target practice. And that is the way it might have gone, had it not been for the quick thinking of the DEMS gunlayer, Able Seaman Turner, who put two smoke floats over the side. With the wind slightly before the port beam, the floats formed an effective screen, behind which the *Empire Glade* was able to make good her escape.

After running at maximum speed for more than an hour on an east-south-easterly course, and with no enemy in sight, Captain Duff was at last able to say the day was won. Now came the reckoning. Sadly, it was learned that the youngest on board, 16-year-old cabin boy Leonard Prestidge, had been killed by a shell splinter, but only five others were slightly injured. The ship, however, was badly holed below the waterline, and taking on a considerable amount of water, and it was only through the untiring efforts of Carpenter Harry Shakeshaft and Engine-Room Storekeeper Frank Simmons, who worked day and night to plug the leaks, that she reached Charlestown nine days later.

That the *Empire Glade* had survived her clash with the enemy was no doubt largely due to U-67 having expended all her torpedoes. If this had not been the case, Müller-Stöckheim would surely have crept up on the unsuspecting merchantman during the night, and blown her out of the water. Instead, the German commander found himself engaged in a gunfight with a very determined adversary that might well have gone the wrong way. Just one of the *Empire Glade*'s 4-inch shells piercing her pressure hull would have been sufficient to send U-67 spiralling to the bottom.

The *Empire Glade* came through the war, and sailed on for many years afterwards, transferring to the Greek flag in 1962, and finally ending her days at the hands of a Turkish shipbreaker ten years later.

Kapitänleutnant Müller-Stöckheim brought U-67 safely into Lorient harbour on 21 December, so ending a patrol lasting thirteen weeks, in which he had sunk four ships of 20,467 tons, and damaged two others. This put Müller-Stöckheim's total score at thirteen ships sunk of 72,138 tons, in recognition of which he was awarded the Knight's Cross. From then on, however, his fortunes changed. In March 1943 he took U-67 back to the West Indies, but by then the 'happy time' for the U-boats was over, the Americans having extended their convoy system to the area. After six frustrating weeks, during which he found no opportunity to use his torpedoes, Müller-Stöckheim returned to Lorient empty-handed. On her eighth consecutive patrol, again attempting to attack shipping off the West Indies, U-67 finally met her end. While crossing the Sargasso Sea on 16 July she was caught on the surface by an Avenger aircraft from the escort carrier USS *Core,* and sent to the bottom. Only three of her crew of fifty-one survived. Günther Müller-Stöckheim, by then promoted to *korvettenkapitän,* went down with his command.

Chapter Eleven

All Roads Lead to St. Pauls

The British ship *Teesbank* cleared the breakwaters of Port Elizabeth, 400 miles east of the Cape of Good Hope, on the morning of 17 November 1942 just as the sun was lifting off the eastern horizon into a blue summer sky. At the first push of the long Southern Ocean swell the grey-painted merchantman gave a lazy roll that brought groans of protest from her riveted plates and sent unattended crockery crashing to the deck in her saloon pantry. On her bridge, Captain William Lorains grunted at the arrogant flexing of the sea's muscles and turned to take a last look at the slowly awaking city they were leaving astern. After the rigours of a war-ravaged Britain and the long weeks of running the gauntlet of the U-boats on the outward voyage, South Africa had seemed like a taste of Paradise. The memory of the bright lights, the shops crammed with half-forgotten luxuries, and the lavish hospitality of the South Africans would stay with him for a long time to come. The return to the serious business of seafaring in wartime was not a prospect he relished, but it was reality. He shrugged, and turned to face the open sea, sniffing at the clean, salt air. At least, it was a good day to go sailing.

The *Teesbank,* owned by the world-wide traders Andrew Weir & Company of London – familiarly known as Bank Line – was a 5,136-ton motor vessel built at Doxford's yard at Sunderland in 1937. In her short pre-war career, she had worked the charter markets of the world, and was as much at home in the China Sea as she was off this southern tip of Africa. On her current voyage, she was bound in ballast for Demerara, British Guiana, which lay 5,500 miles to the north-west. After rounding the Cape of Good Hope, her route would take her across the broad reaches of the South Atlantic, a largely benign ocean ruffled only by the warm South-East Trades, once the motive power of the windjammers of a bygone age. From the weather aspect, the passage promised to be an easy one.

As he set a course to pass clear of Cape Recife, the tall black-and-white painted lighthouse on which was now visible to the west, 41-year-old Captain Lorains's thoughts were not only for the weather ahead. Before sailing from Port Elizabeth, Naval Control had warned him to be on the lookout for U-boats while off the South African coast. It was known that a group of Type IX C long-range boats, accompanied by a U-tanker, had penetrated into the South Atlantic as early as mid-September, and were creating havoc amongst unescorted merchantmen in the vicinity of the Cape. In the space of six weeks, twenty-four ships, totalling 103,164 tons gross, had been sent to the bottom, and pending the arrival of escort vessels from Britain, the slaughter seemed set to continue. The Cape of Good Hope had ceased to live up to its name.

The *Teesbank*, which carried a crew of sixty-two, including a party of DEMS gunners, was armed with the usual 4-inch and 12-pounder guns, two 20 mm Oerlikons, two .303 Vickers machine-guns and two Marlins. In a gun-fight with a surfaced U-boat she stood to give a good account of herself, but she was unlikely to be given the opportunity. The news of Müller-Stöckheim's brush with the *Empire Glade* had spread, and few U-boat commanders were prepared to do battle on the surface. An attack, if it came, would be unseen, and from beneath the sea.

The weather held fine, and the *Teesbank*, taking advantage of the west-flowing Agulhas Current, was abeam of the Cape of Good Hope by the evening of the 18th. As yet, there had been no sight of the enemy, and it was with some confidence that Lorains set out to cross the Atlantic. For the next eighteen days, until she closed the coast of South America, the *Teesbank* would be sailing in waters reputedly free from U-boats.

Unknown to Lorains – or indeed to the Admiralty – the U-boats thought to be off the Cape had long since withdrawn into the South

Atlantic. They were all running short of fuel and food, and many of them were down to their last torpedo. In late November 1942, seven of these Type IX Cs were in mid-Atlantic, clustered around a U-tanker that had been lying in wait to attend to their needs. Among the idling flotilla were U-128, commanded by *Korvetten-kapitän* Ulrich Heyse, and U-159, commanded by *Kapitänleutnant* Helmut Witte. Heyse, an ex-merchant seaman, and Witte were old friends, and they had a great deal to discuss as they lolled on the surface waiting their turn to go alongside the tanker. The talk was not all of Berlin and *bierkellers*. Witte had recently sunk eight ships of 47,233 tons off the Cape, and was well pleased with U-159 and his crew. Heyse, on the other hand, had drawn a blank in that area and had been forced to cast his net further north. Off the Cape Verde Islands, a point of convergence for heavily-laden ships bound for Britain from the Cape, West Africa and South America, he met with only marginally better luck. Three ships totalling 15,571 tons was a disappointing score for such a long and arduous patrol.

With their stores and fuel replenished, U-128 and U-159 went their separate ways. Both boats were due to return to base soon, and were anxious to increase their scores before the recall signal came, particularly U-128. A week later they had moved north, and were patrolling, out of sight of each other, in the region of St. Paul's Rocks.

Penedo de São Pedro, or St. Paul's Rocks, lie 55 miles north of the Equator, and 525 miles off the coast of Brazil. Completely devoid of vegetation, and streaked white with the droppings of the sea birds which inhabit them, the 64-feet-high rocks are an awesome sight on an otherwise empty ocean. In the days of sail they sat square in the path of the windjammers bound to and from Cape Horn and the Cape of Good Hope, and claimed many an un-suspecting victim. With the coming of steam, and the ability of ships to choose their routes without conforming to the whims of the fickle wind, St. Paul's Rocks slipped back into a world of splendid isolation, the tumbling breakers on their blackened feet rarely sighted by the new breed of seamen. The advent of war in 1939, and the necessity for cargo ships to keep clear of coastal waters, had brought the rocks back into the path of hurrying civlisation. The giant frigate birds which circle endlessly above St. Paul's now witnessed unfamiliar plumes of smoke on the horizon as steamers passed by on their errands of war.

At noon on 4 December, the *Teesbank* was abeam to the north-west of St. Paul's Rocks, with only 1,500 miles to go to her destination. As would be expected near the Equator and on the extreme edge of the South-East Trades, the weather was idyllic – blue skies, light winds, and the sea like a sheet of rippled glass. Given this continuing fair weather, Captain Lorains estimated the *Teesbank* would be off Demerara on the night of the 10th, probably berthing on the morning of the 11th. With a full cargo to be loaded, it seemed more than likely that the ship would stay over Christmas in the port. This was a prospect eagerly looked forward to by Lorains and his men who, lulled by pleasant memories of South Africa and a passage which, so far, had been blissful, were having some difficulty in associating themselves with the war. They were in another world.

The *Teesbank*'s luck was about to change. Two hundred and forty miles north of St. Paul's Rocks U-128 lay stopped on the surface, rolling gently in the long swell. Her off-duty men were on deck enjoying the unaccustomed warmth of the sun on their naked bodies, while in the conning-tower Ulrich Heyse, sweat staining the back of his thin tropical shirt, was contemplating the empty horizon. He was bitterly disappointed, for since leaving the rendezvous with the U-tanker, U-128 had still not improved on her score of only three ships sunk. Soon – probably within a few days, her time in the Atlantic would be up, and she must return home. Heyse was desperately in need of a substantial target.

At ten minutes to three on the morning of the 5th, the bridge of the *Teesbank* was as quiet as a graveyard. The only sound to disturb the stillness of the night was the measured thump of the four-cylinder Doxford engine as it drove the empty ship through the water at almost 13 knots. In the starboard wing, the Officer of the Watch, with the last hour of his watch approaching, paced the wooden deck with light footsteps, as though reluctant to disturb the slumbering magic of this tropical night. In the outboard corner of each wing of the bridge, where the slim barrels of the 20 mm Oerlikons silhouetted against the star-filled night sky were a grim reminder of the war, a heavy-eyed DEMS gunner scanned the horizon with a marked lack of enthusiasm. In the darkened wheel-house, his face dimly illuminated by the soft glow of the compass binnacle, the Indian quartermaster might well have passed for a sleeping statue, were it not for the occasional quarter turn he gave the wheel to hold the ship on course.

The tranquillity of the night was destroyed at precisely 0252, when Ulrich Heyse's torpedo tore into the *Teesbank*'s after cargo hold, and exploded with devastating effect. Captain Lorains was out of his bunk and racing for the bridge ladder almost before the sound of the explosion had died. As he went up the ladder at a run, he heard the beat of the engines quicken and accelerate into a fren-zied tattoo. Then, just as suddenly, it ground to a sudden halt. Lorains needed no engineer to explain to him that the propeller shaft, which passed through the after hold, had been smashed by the explosion, severing all connection between the engine and propeller.

By the time he reached the wheelhouse, the ship was already settling by the stern, and Lorains did not hesitate to give the order to abandon ship. Quickly, and with the minimum of panic, the *Teesbank*'s four lifeboats were lowered to the water and boarded. Lorains and his senior officers stayed with the ship, but a few minutes after the boats had pulled away Heyse put his second torpedo into the *Teesbank*. She began to go down, and there was no alternative but to abandon her altogether.

At 0341, the *Teesbank* went to her last resting place in 2,000 fathoms, leaving her crew adrift 700 miles from the nearest land. Providentially, the sea was calm, but there the good fortune of the survivors ended. Two men had been injured by the second torpedo, one of them seriously. The same explosion had damaged one of the boats so badly that it had to be abandoned, its occupants being distributed amongst the other boats. It also came to light that the first torpedo had brought down both main and emergency aerials, and it had not been possible to transmit an SOS. The demise of the *Teesbank* went unannounced to the world over the horizon. No search for survivors would be set in motion until long after she was found to be overdue at Demerara.

Having watched his ship go down, William Lorains took stock of the situation. The nearest land, the coast of Brazil in the region of

Fortaleza, lay 720 miles to the south-west. The three lifeboats were well provisioned, and with the south-easterly breeze, light though it was, likely to hold steady, Lorains calculated they could possibly reach the coast in twelve or fourteen days. It was a considerable voyage to undertake in open boats, but there was no alternative.

Dawn was breaking when the boats hoisted sail and set off to the south-west, running with the wind slightly abaft the beam. All went well for most of that day, but as evening was drawing in the lifeboat in charge of 20-year-old Third Officer John Milton began to drop astern. During the night, Lorains held the other boats back as much as he could, but when daylight came on the 6th Milton's boat was out of sight. Lorains decided to press on, hoping to reach land first, and then send help for Milton.

Three days later, the two boats keeping company, containing between them forty-three men, had covered over 200 miles, at an average speed of 3 knots. For awkward, heavily-laden boats built for stability rather than speed, this was fair progress. Unfortunately, the day started with tragedy, when one of the injured men, an Indian deckhand, died, and Lorains had the sad task of burying him at sea. Later in the day, when the sun was high, the boats were intercepted by U-461, which was returning from a special mission off the North America coast. *Korvettenkapitän* Steibler, after questioning the survivors, handed over some food, but in return took Captain Lorains prisoner. When the U-boat had gone on its way, the boats, with 30-year-old Chief Officer I. McLean now in command, again hoisted their sails, and continued to the south-west. The double blow they had suffered that day did nothing to raise the morale of the remaining survivors.

As William Lorains stepped into captivity aboard U-461, some 1,700 miles to the west-north-west the Cardiff-registered steamer *East Wales* was 40 miles out of Port of Spain, Trinidad, and steaming eastwards in convoy. It was a warm, cloudless day, an auspicious start to a voyage of nearly 11,000 miles which would take the ship across two oceans to the farthest reaches of another continent, where a long, hard-fought war was reaching a climax.

On the battlefields of North Africa, German and Italian forces under the command of General Erwin Rommel reeled under a two-pronged assault, the size and ferocity of which threatened to sweep them into the sea. General Montgomery's Eighth Army, having finally broken out of the stalemate of El Alamein, had rolled forward 1,500 miles, and was hammering at the gates of Tripoli. On the morning of 8 November, 290,000 British and American troops had landed on beachheads stretching from Casablanca to Algiers. In less than two weeks, they had established sovereignty over the whole of that coastline, and were pushing eastwards to the Tunisian frontier. Overall, close on half a million Allied troops were engaged in the fast-moving struggle, and the task of keeping this huge army supplied fell, in the main, to British merchant ships, the *East Wales* among them.

Built in 1925 by Dobsons of Newcastle, the 4,358-ton *East Wales* was owned by Gibbs & Company of Newport, Mon., and registered at Cardiff. Much of her life had been spent carrying coal out of the South Wales ports to the far corners of the earth, returning laden with grain or ores after long months in the cross-trades of the Empire. Commanded by Captain Stephen Rowland of Newport, Mon., she carried a crew of forty-five, including seven DEMS gunners. Her defensive armament consisted of a 4-inch anti-submarine gun, two 20 mm Oerlikons, and four Marlin machine-guns.

The *East Wales* had loaded a cargo of 7,000 tons of military stores in New York, and after calling at Port of Spain to receive routing orders from the Admiralty, was on her way to Alexandria, via Durban and the Suez Canal. For the first 400 miles out into the Atlantic, she was to enjoy the protection of a small convoy, but from then on she would be left to make her own way. On her long passage south, and then north again, she must run the gamut of German, Italian and Japanese submarines, as well as the odd surface raider that might cross her chosen path.

When the convoy dispersed on the morning of 11 December, Captain Rowland set an east-south-easterly course in accordance with Admiralty instructions. This would take the *East Wales* to a point 100 miles to the west of St. Paul's Rocks, from whence she would head south-east to the Cape. The weather was set fine, with a light south-easterly breeze taking some of the heat out of the sun. At an average speed of 8½ knots Rowland expected to round the Cape about 4 January, and reach Durban, where he would call for bunkers, some four days later. It was a long haul, and would include Christmas celebrated deep in the South Atlantic in the region of the lonely island of St. Helena. Rowland hoped that, for his ship at least, the season of goodwill would extend well either side of Christmas.

The next forty-eight hours of the passage passed quietly, the *East Wales* bowling along at a speed well in excess of 8 knots, and trailing her thick plume of smoke across a clear blue sky. Except for one hour of zig-zagging around dawn and dusk – this again on Admiralty instructions, there was little to remind her crew of the potential dangers they faced. Then, on 13 December, Radio Officer Sydney Riley picked up faint cries for help from the Swedish cargo ship *Scania*, under attack by a U-boat near St. Paul's Rocks, almost 1,000 miles to the south-east. This was followed closely by a message from the Admiralty advising the *East Wales* to make a diversion to the north. The war was back on her doorstep.

Twenty-four hours later, nearly 400 miles to the south-east, the *Teesbank*'s two lifeboats, under Chief Officer McLean, were sighted by the American freighter *West Maximus*. When the forty-one tired and hungry men were picked up, they had been in their boats for nine days, and had sailed 645 miles. No trace could be found of the *Teesbank*'s third lifeboat, and it was feared that Third Officer John Milton and his crew might have perished.

Milton and his men were, however, still very much alive, but a long way to the east. Light winds and the poor sailing qualities of their boat had slowed their progress to a mere 1½ knots, and in the nine days since the sinking of their ship they had covered only 330 miles. Fortunately, the nineteen survivors were in good shape, except for the Fourth Engineer, who had a broken collar bone, and they had still not given up hope of reaching the land.

By the afternoon of the 15th, the boat having made 30 miles or so to the west, John Milton was despondent. They were still nearly 400 miles from the land, and at their present rate of progress that meant at least eleven days sailing. Would their food and – more importantly – water, last that long? Who would be the first to go mad? Who would be the first to die? For a man only just out of his teens, Milton was carrying an awesome responsibility, and as he sat at the tiller of the boat the weight of this was heavy upon his shoulders.

When Milton first saw the thin pencil of smoke on the horizon to starboard, he thought his eyes were playing tricks. Then, when a hoarse shout went up from the man in the bow, he jerked himself and his men into action. Oars were shipped, and they put all their remaining strength into rowing towards the masts and funnel which followed the smoke over the horizon. They might only get one chance like this. Milton broke out a smoke float.

The last hour of his watch on the bridge of the *East Wales* had passed agonisingly slowly for Second Officer Andrew Dunn. The afternoon was hot and sultry and the sea around him empty. At fifteen minutes to four he took a last look around the horizon before writing up the log. As before, the sharp line between sea and sky was completely devoid of movement. He was about to enter the wheelhouse when the crow's nest telephone rang. It was the masthead lookout reporting a smudge of orange smoke on the horizon dead ahead. Dunn reached for his binoculars, and suddenly the day took on a new meaning. The smoke dissipated as quickly as it had arisen, but a few minutes later the distinctive red sail of a ship's lifeboat was visible. Dunn immediately called Captain Rowland to the bridge, and the wheels of rescue were set in motion. Before the sun set the *Teesbank* survivors were safely on board the *East Wales*, and John Milton was recounting the story of their eleven-day voyage.

The rescue of the *Teesbank* survivors brought home forcibly to Rowland the very real threat from the U-boats that existed in the area, and he wasted no time in getting his ship under way again. Before doing so, however, he took the precaution of having the empty lifeboat hoisted on board and re-stocked with food and water. As it turned out, he might just as well not have made the effort.

Throughout that night, and all next day, the *East Wales* steamed south-eastwards, zig-zagging around her mean course in order to spoil the aim of any stalking U-boat. Weather conditions were perfect, fine and clear, with a light south-easterly wind and slight sea, and marred only by a heavy swell, which gave the ship a slow, uncomfortable roll.

Helmut Witte, patrolling in U-159 about 120 miles to the west-south-west of St. Paul's Rocks, was anxiously awaiting the long overdue recall signal from Lorient. He was able to look back on what had been an arduous, but at times immensely satisfying cruise. The 6,000-mile passage from Biscay to the Cape of Good Hope had proved to be a harrowing game of hide and seek with the Allied anti-submarine patrols, but had been more than compensated for by the five action-packed weeks that followed in South African waters, U-159 having accounted for 47,000 tons of enemy shipping. The previous four weeks, however, had been spent in a tedious and largely unfruitful sweeping of the area in the vicinity of St. Paul's Rocks. Since the meeting with the other boats at the refuelling point, she had sunk only two more ships, and now the sea around her was as empty as the Alster on a wet Sunday. Witte and his crew were more than ready to go home. Then, an hour before sunset on the 16th, the *East Wales* hove in sight, her funnel belching black smoke as Stephen Rowland urged her on through the danger zone.

No one on board the *East Wales* saw the track of the torpedo that tore into her engine-room at precisely 1725 and exploded with a deafening crash. The ship stopped dead in the water.

Andrew Dunn was in the mess-room taking an early dinner, as was the custom of those who kept the middle watch. When he reached the deck, his ears ringing and the stench of burnt cordite in his nostrils, the *East Wales* was already settling by the stern, clouds of black smoke issuing from her engine-room skylight. Her funnel and both topmasts had fallen, littering her decks with a jumble of broken rigging and debris. Even as Dunn watched, the sea began to wash over the deck.

Clambering up onto the boat deck, Dunn looked around for Captain Rowland and Chief Officer Cecil London, but neither was in evidence. He assumed they must be too busy on the bridge, in which case he took charge of lowering the boats. It was then that he discovered that the *Teesbank*'s lifeboat, so carefully brought on board and re-provisioned in case of such a catastrophe, had been reduced to matchwood by the explosion. There remained only one lifeboat and two jollyboats –these little bigger than dinghies – and two life-rafts to carry away sixty-four men, assuming they were all still alive.

The lifeboat went down smoothly, fully manned, then Dunn, assisted by Chief Engineer Edwin Lloyd, turned his attention to the jollyboats. Fifteen men were crammed into one, which was again lowered without mishap. Lloyd and two able seamen then cleared away the other, lowered it to the water, and piled down the scrambling net. Dunn was about to follow, when it occurred to him that the boats were woefully ill-prepared to meet the challenge awaiting them once clear of the ship. The nearest inhabited land, the coast of Brazil, lay over 400 miles away, and to have any reasonable chance of reaching it they would need a sextant and a set of tables. Although it was now obvious that the *East Wales* was on the point of sinking, Dunn called to Lloyd to hold the boat alongside, and made a dash for the bridge.

Lying conveniently on the chartroom settee – probably left by Chief Officer London, who would have been about to take star sights when the torpedo hit – Dunn found a sextant, a nautical almanac, and a set of Nories Tables. He gathered them up, and was about to return to the boat deck, when he heard the staccato sound of morse coming from the wireless-room. Flinging open the door, he found Chief Radio Officer Sydney Riley bent over the morse key calmly transmitting a distress call. This was a brave action, but pointless. Riley was not aware that the explosion had brought down the wireless aerials. Dunn shouted to Riley to abandon ship. He could already feel the deck beginning to slide under him.

Confident the radio officer was following him, Dunn returned to the boat deck, lowered the sextant and books into the waiting boat, and then went hand-over-hand down the boat falls. He was suspended in mid-air, when the *East Wales* gave a lurch, and he was thrown against the ship's side. Momentarily stunned, he lost his grip on the falls, and fell into the sea.

Fortunately for Andrew Dunn, the men in the boat acted swiftly, and he was hauled aboard before he drifted away. His first action when he regained his senses was to look around for the radio officer. He was nowhere to be seen.

There was now nothing more to be done, but to get the boat clear of the ship before she took her final plunge and swamped them. The heavy swell and the crew's unfamiliarity with the oars made it a difficult pull, but a helpful wave gave the boat a push, and they were out of danger. It was then that Sydney Riley who, true to the tradition of wireless operators down the years, had stuck to his post to the last, appeared on deck – a forlorn figure alone on a doomed ship.

Dunn's first instinct was to take the boat back alongside, but he dismissed this as a foolish risk which could cost the lives of all on board. He called to Riley to jump, but the radio man, possibly because he was unable to swim, shook his head.

The other jollyboat, which was also lying off, now pulled towards the ship, its crew signalling wildly for Riley to take his chance with the sea. As the boat drew near, Riley summoned up his last reserves of courage, and vaulted over the rail, and into the sea. The mortally wounded *East Wales* chose that moment to break her back.

Gripping the tiller of his boat, Andrew Dunn watched in horror as, with a terrible grating of steel on steel, the forward half of the ship broke away and rolled to port before sinking. The after section followed seconds later, going down stern first. The port jollyboat, which was then close in, was caught by the wreckage and dragged under. Neither the brave Sydney Riley, nor the men who had sought to rescue him, were ever seen again.

From the time she was torpedoed until she went down, the *East Wales* had stayed afloat for a little over three minutes – albeit a long three minutes for those involved. When she was gone, swallowed up by the element she had fought and lived by for seventeen honourable years, she left wallowing in the flotsam-covered swell one lifeboat containing twenty-eight men, a jollyboat with thirteen on board, and two life-rafts carrying six survivors between them. Ironically, all nineteen who had escaped from the *Teesbank* had survived this their second brush with death in eleven days. But of the men of the *East Wales*, Captain Stephen Rowland, Chief Officer Cecil London, Third Officer John Grogan, Third Engineer Leslie Appleton, Chief Radio Officer Sydney Riley and twelve others were missing. Thus Second Officer Andrew Dunn found himself in command of the survivors of two sunken ships.

There was no time for the 31-year-old Yorkshireman to wrestle with the enormity of the task facing him, for U-159 had come to the surface, and was motoring slowly towards the boats. In the submarine's conning-tower eight men could be plainly seen, four of whom were manning machine-guns trained on the pathetic flotilla of boats and rafts. It appeared to Andrew Dunn that they were about to be shot down like dogs, but surprisingly he felt no fear, only sadness that he was to die so ignominiously after having survived thus far.

Dunn need not have feared for his life. In approaching with guns trained, *Kapitänleutnant* Witte was merely taking a precaution against the possibility of hand-grenades being hurled at his submarine. The U-boat men regarded British merchant seamen with a healthy respect, even when they were in lifeboats.

When the U-boat was within hailing distance, Witte, who spoke fluent English, asked for the ship's captain and navigating officers to declare themselves. Dunn, who had no wish to be whisked off into captivity, made himself as inconspicuous as possible. Third Officer Milton, of the *Teesbank,* the only other surviving navigator, did likewise. The remainder, realising that their lives would depend on skilful navigation from there on, chorused in ragged unison that the captain and all the navigating officers had gone down with the ship. Although Witte must have realised that they were not telling the full truth, he seemed content to take them at their word. He compromised by asking for details of the ship, her cargo, and destination. He received some very imaginative answers, none of them true, but again he seemed satisfied.

The two lifeboats drifted alongside the U-boat, and Dunn took the opportunity to examine her closely. She was about 700 tons, and seemed freshly painted above the waterline. Her undersides, which she revealed each time she rolled in the swell, were covered in barnacles and sea grass. She had been a long time out of dock.

After enquiring if there were any wounded, and being told there were some minor injuries, Witte sent bandages down to the boats. This done, he said with the ghost of a smile on his face, 'As you unfortunately have no navigating officer, you had better steer south-west for 420 miles, until you come to Brazil.' As the U-boat prepared to depart, he called across, 'Merry Christmas!' adding, 'The name of your ship is the *East Wales,* and you were bound from New York to the Middle East with a cargo of war supplies – am I right?' No one in the boats answered, but the looks on their faces spoke volumes. Under such circumstances, to be wished the compliments of the season was bad enough, but to learn that someone, somewhere, had betrayed their ship seemed like a last gross insult to those who had just given their lives.

The U-boat remained on the surface close by for some hours. Dunn assumed she must be recharging her batteries, but in fact Witte was preparing his boat for the long passage back to Biscay. U-159, with 59,372 tons of Allied shipping now to her credit, had received the long-awaited recall to base.

When the submarine did finally motor away, Dunn collected the lifeboats and rafts together. There was a choppy sea running, and those on the rafts, most of whom were violently seasick, were suffering. Dunn transferred the four worst affected to the larger boat, and then took the tiller of that boat himself. The lifeboats and rafts were then lashed together and sea anchors streamed. Dunn's plan was to remain in the vicinity of the sinking until daylight, as there was a possibility, however remote, that Riley had been able to get away an SOS before he died, and a nearby ship might then be racing to rescue them.

By dawn on the 17th, the two men remaining on the rafts were in such a wretched state that Dunn had no alternative but to make room for them in his boat. All stores and water were then removed from the rafts and distributed between the two boats. The rafts were then cut adrift, and with the lifeboat towing the jollyboat, they set sail for Brazil. Dunn had thirty-six in his boat, while the jollyboat, with Able Seaman Owens at the tiller, carried eleven. Both boats were uncomfortably crowded, and with little freeboard. Fortunately, although the swell was heavy, the sea decreased as the day wore on, enabling the boats to sail well, running free with a gentle south-south-easterly breeze abaft the beam.

The *East Wales* had been sunk in position 00° 24'N 31° 27'W, the nearest land, Capo de São Roque, on the north-east coast of Brazil, being, as Helmut Witte had correctly stated, 420 miles to the south-west. Assuming the south-easterly breeze held steady, Dunn estimated they should reach the coast in nine or ten days. The boats were well supplied with water, biscuits, pemmican, Horlicks tablets and chocolate. In addition, by some curious chance, they also had on board fifteen bottles of the finest West Indian rum. The voyage ahead of them would be tedious and uncomfortable, but the survivors were unlikely to die from the want of food and drink.

However, from the start Dunn prudently set the twice-daily ration at three ounces of water, one biscuit, four pieces of chocolate, four Horlicks tablets, and one teaspoonful of pemmican per man. The rum he put aside for emergency use.

On the second day under sail, Chief Engineer Edwin Lloyd, who was in the jollyboat, became desperately ill with seasickness, and it was necessary to transfer him to the bigger boat, which rode the swells more easily. That left Dunn with thirty-seven men crammed into his boat, and the extra weight soon began to tell. From time to time, the lighter jollyboat surged ahead on its towrope, over-taking the lifeboat. Both boats being very low in the water, a collision was likely to end in disaster for one of them, probably the smaller boat. On the morning of 19 December, the danger of colli-sion had become so acute, that the towline was slipped. Dunn instructed Owens to do his best to remain in sight.

The men's diet was also to cause Dunn trouble. As had been discovered before by so many who found themselves in lifeboats, the Horlicks tablets were sickly and thirst-provoking, while the pemmican was a vile concoction the likes of which only the Board of Trade could have contrived to inflict on shipwrecked seamen. As a small compensation for the inadequacies of their diet, Dunn began issuing a tot of rum to each man in the evenings, but was soon obliged to discontinue this. Although the spirit had a transi-tory uplifting effect on the men, it greatly aggravated their thirst.

The light south-easterlies stayed with them for the next twenty-four hours, and the boats made good a speed of almost 2 knots. But, on the afternoon of the 20th, the wind increased to force 4, kicking up a rough sea. The jollyboat began to fall astern, and by nightfall, having twice lost sight of the smaller boat, Dunn brought the towline back into use. Sun sights taken that day had shown they were no more than five days from the land, and Dunn felt confi-dent enough to increase the rations enough to give an extra meal at noon. To those safe at home in Britain, some of whom never ceased to grumble at the severity of the food rationing, a dry biscuit smeared with sour-tasting beef extract would not have seemed a very exciting prospect, but to the forty-seven survivors of the *Teesbank* and *East Wales*, crowded into two small boats and adrift on an increasingly hostile sea, the additional meal, however frugal and unappetising, was like a shaft of sunlight breaking through the dark clouds.

At 0830 on 21 December, smoke was sighted on the horizon, and a fever of excitement swept through the boats. Orange smoke floats were set off, but it soon became apparent that they had not been seen by the passing ship. However, the disappointment that followed quickly dissipated when, later that day, heavy rain fell. Dunn led the way by stripping off, and the others followed. Soon, all the survivors were revelling in the cool, clean rain as it sluiced down their naked bodies, washing away the dirt and salt of five days. As a tonic, the rain proved to be a far greater success than the rum.

Sails were used as rain catchers, and sufficient water was collected to fill the fresh water tanks of both boats. They were now, by Dunn's caculations, less than 200 miles from the coast, and crossing the track of shipping steaming between the Cape and the Caribbean. This was confirmed next morning, when another column of smoke was sighted on the horizon. Again, smoke floats were set off, but, as before, they were not seen by the distant ship.

They continued sailing in a south-westerly direction, and when night closed in on them for the sixth time, their spirits were flagging. It was then that the miracle they had been praying for happened. At 1940, bright lights were seen to starboard at an estimated distance of 8 miles. Dunn had no intention of being ignored for the third time, and shinned up the mast of his boat to light two red hand flares. These must have been seen at once by the approaching ship, as she signalled back with her morse lamp. In less than an hour the survivors were being helped aboard the Swedish cargo liner *Glimarren*. They had been in the boats for six days and two hours, in which they had sailed 240 miles.

Twenty-four hours later, the *Glimarren* landed Andrew Dunn and his men at the Brazilian port of Natal, close southward of Capo de São Roque. The exhausted, but happy band of men spent a Christmas Day in Natal's Grand Hotel that none of them would ever forget. Next day, US Army planes flew them to New York to await a ship home.

Following their encounter with U-461, when Captain William Lorains was taken prisoner, the other *Teesbank* survivors, led by

Chief Officer McLean, were to spend six days in their boats, before being picked up on 14 December by the *West Maximus* when only 90 miles from the land. They were put ashore in Rio de Janeiro eight days later.

The subsequent careers of U-128 and U-159 were short and largely unfruitful. The *Teesbank* was U-128's last victim, for she herself was sunk off the Brazilian coast on 17 May 1943 in a combined attack by the US Navy destroyers *Moffett* and *Jouett* and aircraft of US Squadron No. 74. On her way back to Biscay, U-159 sank the British cargo ship *Lagosian* off the coast of Spanish Sahara. She was lost on her next patrol, being sunk in the Caribbean by aircraft of US Navy Patrol Squadron No. 32.

Chapter Twelve

Caribbean Ambush

In the autumn of 1942 Axis naval planners estimated that in order to dry up the flow of food and war materials into Britain they would need to sink in excess of 700,000 tons of Allied merchant shipping a month, every month, over a prolonged period. By the end of October, this target was beginning to look obtainable, ninety-three ships of more than 600,000 tons having been destroyed in that month. In November, this increased to 109 ships of 729,160 tons, with the result that, although the enemy may not have been aware of it, he was sinking ships faster than American and British shipyards could build them.

The situation was critical, and made even more serious by the closure of the Mediterranean and the need to sail ships around the Cape of Good Hope. This added some 8,000 miles to the round voyage to the East, and required a greater number of ships. Furthermore, on the long passage through the South Atlantic, where few naval escorts were available, these ships sailed alone, and were exposed to frightful dangers, not least the long-range Type IX U-boats, now at large in those lonely waters.

It was against such a background that the 4,692-ton *Treworlas* sailed from Cape Town on the morning of 30 November, bound for Trinidad with 3,000 tons of manganese ore from India. The *Treworlas*, which had a top speed of 9 knots, and that in favourable weather, seemed a likely candidate for the attention of the marauding Type IXs.

Built in 1922 by Redhead & Sons at South Shields, the *Treworlas* was owned by the Hain Steamship Company of London. Like all her sisters, she was registered in the tiny Cornish port of St. Ives, which would have been hard-pressed to accommodate one of her lifeboats. This idiosyncrasy dated back to the founding of the company by Captain Edward Hain of St. Ives in the days of sail.

Although designed exclusively for world-wide tramping, the *Treworlas* had elegant lines, being flush-decked, with tall masts and funnel, and a clipper stern. In her heyday, painted in the distinctive black and white Hain colours, she had been able to hold her own with any smart cargo liner in appearance. In her drab wartime grey, streaked with rust, she now had about her the look of an ageing, genteel lady fallen on hard times. Her crew of forty-seven included seven DEMS gunners, and she was armed with a 4-inch, a 12-pounder, one Oerlikon 20 mm cannon, and eight light machine-guns.

The sun was well up over Table Bay when the *Treworlas* steamed out into the South Atlantic on that November morning in 1942. On her lower bridge, 21-year-old Second Radio Officer Richard Webb rested his elbows on the bulwark rail and gazed with some apprehension at the long swells marching in from the horizon, glassy smooth, but swollen with latent power. Despite the warmth of the sun on his back, Webb gave an involuntary shiver. The swells, he knew, would subside as they drew away from the land, but there were other dangers hidden beyond that distant horizon.

One deck above, in the wheelhouse, Captain Thomas Stanbury, 51 years old, and vastly more experienced in the ways of the sea, cast a less jaundiced eye at the horizon. Summer in the South Atlantic would make for a pleasant passage, with light following winds, slight seas, and untroubled blue skies. 'Flying fish weather', they called it. Stanbury's only real cause for concern was for the great weight of ore the *Treworlas* carried stowed low down in her holds. Beam-on to the prevalent south-easterly swell, she would roll her way across the ocean like a Saturday night drunk. But, after a few days, with everything movable safely lashed down, the roll would be bearable. As to the enemy, Stanbury had met him before, and was prepared to meet him again.

The *Treworlas* was 1,000 miles north-west of Cape Town when, in the small hours of the morning of 5 December, the *Teesbank* was torpedoed off St. Paul's Rocks by U-128. Captain Stanbury was not aware of her fate, but three days later he received an urgent message from the Admiralty warning him of increased U-boat activity ahead, and advising a change of course.

Days, then weeks, passed without incident, and all the while the *Treworlas* steamed north-west, flushing out silvery shoals of flying fish with her bow-wave, while the inevitable lone albatross untiringly criss-crossed her wake like a silent guardian angel. Day after day the horizon remained empty of both friend and foe, and gradually a sense of well-being crept over the ship. The sun shone, and all was right with the world.

On the 16th, the *Treworlas* was two days south of the Equator when, almost 800 miles to the north, the *East Wales* met her untimely end. At the same time, in the stormy waters of the North Atlantic, the ships of Convoy ON 153, bound from the UK to New York, were fighting a losing battle against a pack of six U-boats led by *Korvettenkapitän* Johann Mohr in U-124.

When the running fight was over, and ON 153 cut to ribbons, Mohr left the pack to try his luck further to the south. U-124, a Type IXB, had unwittingly taken on contaminated diesel oil at her last refuelling, and ever since had been dogged by a series of engine breakdowns. Mohr hoped that in the calmer waters of the Caribbean he might be able to solve his persistent problems.

French Guiana was abeam with less than 600 miles to go to Port of Spain when, on 25 December, the officers of the *Treworlas* gathered in their dining saloon, raised their glasses in the traditional Yuletide toasts. They were on their roast South African turkey, when the radio officer on watch entered the saloon, and handed Captain Stanbury a buff envelope, Stanbury tore open the envelope, and suppressed a smile as he read the radio message. The Admiralty sent their Christmas wishes to all on board, and took the opportunity to warn again of increased U-boat activity in the path of the *Treworlas*. When dinner was over, Stanbury took his chief officer on one side and quietly instructed him to ensure that the ship's life-saving appliances were in a high state of readiness.

During the course of his watch on the evening of the 27th, Radio Officer Richard Webb received two more Admiralty signals regarding U-boats sighted in the area. The warnings were ominous. An invisible net was closing around the *Treworlas*.

At midnight, having handed over the watch, Webb went to his cabin with thoughts of the danger the ship was running into uppermost in his mind. The night was hot and humid, and he knew he would get little sleep, but he stripped off and lay down on his narrow bunk. For a while he lay wide-awake, his mind racing ahead.

The *Treworlas* was then nearing the coast of Trinidad, having steamed 5,200 miles since leaving Cape Town. Thus far, she had come through unscathed, with no sight or sound of the enemy, other than the recurring warnings coming over the ether. In a little more than twelve hours she was due to reach Port of Spain, but first she must pass through the islands. It was likely that any attack would come there – just before dawn, perhaps? Richard Webb checked that his lifejacket was lying handy to the bunk, and fell into a troubled sleep.

There was no sleep that night for Johann Mohr. U-124 was on the surface and patrolling the 25-mile-wide channel between Trinidad and Tobago. It was a bright, moonlit night, with a calm sea and a light cooling breeze. In more peaceful times, Mohr would have been happy to lean on the conning tower rail drinking in the sheer beauty of the warm tropical night, but now the brilliant moonlight served only to make him uneasy. U-124, although only a dark shadow on the water, was far too conspicuous running on the surface, but there was a pressing need to take risks. The curse of the contaminated fuel was still upon his boat, and through this she had already missed a number of easy targets. Mohr fretted. He desperately needed to increase his score before returning to Lorient.

With little more than an hour to go before the coming of dawn would oblige U-124 to submerge, Mohr was jerked out of his reverie by an excited shout from one of the lookouts. Following the man's outstretched arm, he lifted his binoculars, nerve ends tingling as the adrenaline began to run. There, clearly visible in the light of the moon was a large ocean-going ship approaching from the east. Mohr was smiling broadly as he slammed the diving alarm with the palm of his hand. This one would not get away.

The crash of the exploding torpedo brought Richard Webb

tumbling from his sweat-soaked bunk wide awake. Without stopping to gather up his clothes, he made a lunge for the door, and as he did so, the ship gave a heavy lurch to starboard, catapulting him out into the alleyway.

The *Treworlas* went over twenty degrees to starboard, and stayed there, but Webb, ignoring the fact that he was still naked and without his lifejacket, clawed his way along the outboard alleyway to the wireless room. As he struggled to open the heavy teakwood door, the ship gave a convulsive shudder and sank under him. Webb was drawn down with her into the depths, until his lungs were on the point of bursting. Fortunately, he was a strong swimmer, and was able to break free from the grip of the sinking ship and shoot to the surface.

At that moment, Johann Mohr, who had sunk the heavily-laden *Treworlas* with just one well-aimed torpedo fired from his stern tubes, brought U-124 to the surface. He was anxious to secure details of his victim and be clear of the shallow water before daylight came.

First man through the conning tower hatch, Mohr looked around him, but the *Treworlas* had already gone, dragged down in less than a minute by the sheer deadweight of the ore in her holds. All that remained to be seen was a scattering of wreckage and a single life-raft, to which one man was clinging. Mohr started his diesels and headed for the raft. The lone survivor, thinking his frail craft was about to be rammed, hurled himself into the sea and swam for his life.

Had Mohr but known it, Second Radio Officer Richard Webb was treading water only six feet away from the U-boat when he brought her to the surface. Webb was still dazed by the events of the previous few minutes, but his mind automatically noted details of his enemy. The submarine appeared to be about 350 feet long, and had two guns on deck, but it was the insignia on her conning tower that set alarm bells ringing in the young radio officer's head. In the half-light, he mistook Mohr's edelweiss emblem for the Rising Sun of Japan, and having heard stories of the Japanese machine-gunning survivors in the water, he was not anxious to put them to the test. He let himself sink, and swam away under water.

When Webb re-surfaced, the submarine was out of sight, Mohr

having given up hope of finding a survivor to question. Treading water, the radio officer looked around him, but could see no sign of other life. It then occurred to him that he was in waters normally teeming with sharks, and that the sooner he found something to take refuge on the better. He had been swimming for about half an hour when, just as the sky was lightening in the east, he came across three other men clinging to a large piece of wreckage. He joined them, relieved to find that if he had to die, at least he would not die alone.

The four survivors drifted for another two hours, while the sun lifted over the horizon, and began to climb in the sky. The sea around them remained devoid of other life, and although no word was spoken, their greatest fear was that the cruising sharks would soon find them. Their joy was great when, at last, they saw a wooden life-raft drifting past. They struck out towards it, and scrambled aboard, none of them aware that they owed their great fortune to the *Treworlas*'s chief officer. On Christmas Day, after being warned of the growing threat from U-boats by Captain Stanbury, he had cast off the ropes securing the rafts to the ship, so allowing them to float off when the ship sank.

A short while later, two more survivors were seen in the water and hauled on board the raft. Although the raft was only nine feet by six, a rectangular wooden framework built around galvanised steel buoyancy tanks, it accommodated the six men in reasonable comfort, but offered no protection from the sun or weather. With Richard Webb on the raft were 20-year-old Apprentice Edward Beyer, who had abandoned the raft in such a hurry on the approach of U-124, DEMS gunner Marshall Burdett, Able Seaman Joseph McCrae, and two other ratings, a Palestinian and a Jamaican. Of the six, only Burdett, who had been on watch on the gun platform when the torpedo struck, was fully clothed. The others were naked.

Although, as second radio officer, Webb had not figured in the hierarchy on board ship, he was the only officer on the raft, and it fell to him to take charge. His first action was to institute a search for other survivors. They paddled around the floating wreckage for some time, but found no-one. Eventually, two other rafts were spotted, one supporting three men who appeared to be alive, the other with one man who appeared to be either badly injured or dead. They tried hard, but they were unable to get close enough to the other rafts to establish communication. Elsewhere, the sea seemed to be completely empty, and the awful truth now became clear. Of the forty-seven men on board the *Treworlas*, at least thirty-seven had gone down with her. Mercifully, their end must have been very quick, most of them probably asleep when the sea took them.

Webb conferred with Edward Beyer, who as a deck apprentice had been spending a good deal of time on the bridge, and between them they agreed that the ship had been torpedoed about 9 miles off the northern coast of Trinidad, in the region of Galera Point. Navigationally, their task was simple; merely to steer the raft in a southerly direction until they fetched up on the shore. A suitable piece of wreckage was retrieved from the sea and erected as a jury mast, and to this was lashed a square of yellow canvas found in one of the lockers. The wind was light from the north-east, and progress might be painfully slow, but at least they would be heading in the right direction.

Having set his tiny command in motion, Richard Webb turned his attention to the all-important question of sustenance. An investigation of the raft's provision tanks proved a bitter disappointment. Both tanks were leaking, and the drinking water and food they contained were all contaminated by sea water. In the absence of anything better, the water was just drinkable, but the three tins of biscuits were saturated, and were thrown overboard. Only one tin of biscuits remained edible, along with a few tins of chocolate and Horlicks malted milk tablets. Being unsure of how long it might take them to reach the land, Webb decided to ration each man to 1½ ounces of water, four pieces of chocolate, two Horlicks tablets and two biscuits per day. He issued no water on the first day.

At 0930 that morning, when a flight of three aircraft was seen approaching, it seemed that Webb's strict rationing would be unnecessary. With fingers made clumsy by their haste, the survivors struggled to open a canister of distress flares, only to find it full of water and the twelve flares it contained sodden and unusable. The raft also carried six smoke floats, but these too had been immersed in water. Five of them failed to ignite, and when the sixth, and final

139

one, flared up and orange smoke went billowing across the surface of the sea, the aircraft were already disappearing from sight.

Some three and a half hours later, the survivors were again galvanised into action by the sound of aircraft engines. A large formation of planes appeared flying at about 6,000 feet, but although they flew directly over the raft, to the pilots it must have been no more than a speck of flotsam on the face of the sea. Without any means of signalling, the survivors had no hope of being seen.

Things took a turn for the better late that afternoon. The other raft to survive the sinking, carrying three more survivors, drifted close, and while standing up to shout across Webb realised he could now see the shore. The tops of palm trees and the roofs of a few houses were clearly visible, indicating that they were no more than 4 or 5 miles off the land. They could be ashore by nightfall.

A few minutes later, it seemed to the survivors that their ordeal was almost over, when two seaplanes bearing American markings came in, flying low. The other raft set off a smoke float, and the aircraft were seen to drop lower, and began to circle the rafts. Although the planes then flew off towards the land, the survivors were convinced that they had been seen. It would be only a matter of time before rescue came.

It was then that it all started to go wrong. As the aircraft disappeared from sight, Webb's makeshift mast was carried away, and all control over his raft was lost. The wind then chose that moment to back to the west, and they began to drift back out to sea. The real test for this little band of survivors was about to begin.

For the next three days the raft drifted aimlessly, often tantalisingly within sight of the land, but unable to make progress towards it. Fortunately, the weather stayed fair, and the sea calm. Perched on their wooden platform only inches above the sea, the six men stayed dry, but all being naked with the exception of Burdett, they suffered the tortures of the damned from the hot sun during the day, and shivered miserably in the chill of the night. To add to their discomfort, the sharks found them, and began to circle the raft, at times dashing in to attempt to overturn the frail craft. The sharks were later joined by ferocious barracudas, which tried to board the raft by hurling themselves out of the water.

Using the four steel stanchions of the raft's weather screen as clubs, the men fought a running battle with shark and barracuda for hours on end. Soon, with little food to sustain them, their strength began to fail. The biscuits were almost at an end, and the remaining chocolate and Horlicks tablets were so contaminated by salt water that they were difficult for even starving men to stomach. The pemmican, which should have been the mainstay of their meagre diet, tasted so foul that no one would touch it. It can only be assumed that the early polar explorers, who are said to have thrived on the yellowish dried meat paste, had been issued with a more palatable brand than that allocated to British ships' lifeboats in the 1940s. But, in spite of all these adversities, the morale of most of the men on the raft remained high. Only the Palestinian and the Jamaican, in Webb's words, 'grumbled and complained the whole time'.

The raft must have been drifting back and forth with the tide directly under the patrol path of the American aircraft, for the planes were continually overflying them at low altitude. Apart from their now tattered strip of yellow canvas, the survivors had nothing with which to attract their attention. They were not to know that the planes – they were United States Navy aircraft – had seen them and reported their plight on the second day of their ordeal, and a rescue craft was sent out to pick them up. As luck would have it, while the raft was being blown out to sea the rescue ship was searching close inshore. After a few hours, when nothing had been found, the ship gave up the search and returned to harbour. As far as the naval authorities in Trinidad were concerned they were lost. Somewhat prematurely, all hope was abandoned for any survivors being found from the *Treworlas* by nightfall on 28 December.

Rescue, when at last it came, was largely a matter of chance. At about 10 o'clock on the morning of the 31st, two ships, one large, one small, were sighted steaming in company on a course which would bring them close to the raft. Determined that this, possibly their last chance, should not be missed, Richard Webb stood up on the raft waving Gunner Burdett's shirt, one of the few pieces of clothing they possessed. The effort all but exhausted Webb, but he was rewarded when the smaller ship, which turned out to be the US Navy escort vessel PC 609, broke away from the passenger ship she was guarding, and came racing across to the raft. Five hours later, Webb and his five companions were landed in Port of Spain. For them, the last day of 1942 had proved to be the best.

The three survivors from the other life-raft reached Port of Spain forty-eight hours later, having been picked up by an American submarine chaser on passage to Barbados.

The sands of time ran out for U-124 when, three months later, off the coast of Portugal, she attacked Convoy OS 45, and was herself sunk by the combined efforts of HMS *Stonecrop* and HMS *Swan*. Johann Mohr and his crew went down with their boat, so joining Captain Thomas Stanbury and thirty-seven men of the *Treworlas* in the realm of Poseidon.

Chapter Thirteen

The Slaughter of the Tankers

On the morning of 28 December 1942, only a few hours and some 50 miles removed from the sinking of the *Treworlas,* a convoy conference was taking place in Port of Spain, Trinidad. In a smoke-filled room at the port naval headquarters were assembled the masters of nine British and Norwegian oil tankers, together with the commanding officers of the ships of the Royal Navy's B5 Escort Group, recently arrived from New York. There was apprehension in the air as the Escort Commander spelled out the dangers and pitfalls likely to be met with on the forthcoming voyage.

Convoy TM 1, carrying in its various cargo tanks 25 million gallons of oil fuels, ranging from light crude to high-octane benzine, was shortly to set sail on a 3,500-mile voyage across the Atlantic, and into the Mediterranean. The ports of discharge for the ships had not yet been disclosed, but their masters needed no crystal ball to tell them they were bound for the coast of North Africa. Seven weeks after the brilliant success of Operation 'Torch', British and American forces now had the remains of the Axis armies bottled up on the Tunisian peninsular, but Allied supply lines were stretched perilously thin. The priority need was for fuel for the many thousands of tanks, lorries, aircraft and fleets of coastal craft involved in the massive sledgehammer operation designed to drive Rommel out of Africa once and for all. The message behind the Escort Commander's briefing was implicit. The convoy must go through.

The objective was beyond argument, but the question 'How?' was undoubtedly uppermost in the minds of the men who commanded the tankers as they made copious notes on the courses, speed and signals to be used during the voyage. It was common knowledge that the U-boats, determined to cut the Allied supply lines to North Africa, were out in the Atlantic in force. Viewed in the light of this, the convoy's escort, which consisted of the destroyer HMS *Havelock* and the Flower-class corvettes *Godetia, Pimpernel* and *Saxifrage,* looked pitifully inadequate. Air cover was to be provided by the Americans for the first twenty-four hours, but beyond that the skies would be empty for most of the crossing.

Had those assembled at the TM 1 pre-sailing conference been privy to happenings on the far side of the Atlantic, their doubts as to the success of the venture they were involved in might have been considerably raised. Under orders from Admiral Dönitz, the crack *Delphin* (Dolphin) Group of six U-boats was speeding southwards to set up a patrol line between the Azores and Madeira, directly in the proposed path of the convoy.

Captain John Andrews, master of the 9,807-ton British tanker *Empire Lytton* was among those present at the conference. His command, completed earlier in the year at the Haverton-on-Tees yard of the Furness Shipbuilding Company, was owned by the Ministry of War Transport, managed by Harris & Dixon Limited of London, and registered in Middlesbrough. Although, like most wartime-built merchantmen, she was box-like in shape, her bottom was not yet fouled, her engine not yet fatigued, and she was capable of a fair turn of speed. Her crew of forty-eight included seven DEMS gunners, who were the manning nucleus of the ship's armament of one 4-inch, one 12-pounder, four 20 mm Oerlikons, and two Marlin machine guns.

Of all the tankers in the convoy, the *Empire Lytton* could be said to be extremely well equipped to face up to the U-boats. Her only great disadvantage lay in her cargo. She carried 13,590 tons of high octane aviation spirit in her tanks, and might truthfully be described as a floating bomb, primed to explode at the slightest provocation. In times of peace, Captain Andrews and his crew would have been at considerable risk as they crossed the Atlantic. In the vicious shooting war of the time, their lives hung by a very tenuous thread.

Shortly after midday on 28 December, the escort ships having completed refuelling and restoring, preparations were made for the convoy to get under way. It was then found that the corvette *Godetia,* which had arrived from New York with two of her three boilers defective, was still not ready for sea. At the same time, the *Empire Lytton* and the Norwegian tanker *Vanja* were also experiencing problems in their engine-rooms. By 1400, the Escort Commander, having delayed the convoy's sailing as long as he reasonably could, made the decision to leave without the two temporarily immobilised tankers. The ailing *Godetia* was detailed to stay with them to act as escort when they did finally get under way.

The main body of the convoy was already out of sight when the *Empire Lytton* and *Vanja,* escorted by HMS *Godetia,* finally cleared Port of Spain. Their progress was slow, for one of the corvette's boilers was still out of action. The first indication of the enemy's presence came six hours later, when the three ships were off the island of Tobago. A Catalina patrolling overhead sighted a U-boat on the surface only 7 miles ahead of the three stragglers, and *Godetia* went in to the attack at her best speed. By the time she reached the spot, the U-boat – in all probability U-124 – had dived, and she could do no more than drop a speculative pattern of depth charges, with the inevitable negative result.

It was dawn on the 29th before the two tankers and their escort joined TM 1, which then formed up in extended order, steaming in four columns of two ships, with one ship on the starboard wing. The *Empire Lytton* took up her allotted position as rear ship of the centre column. In view of the paucity of escorts, the high octane carrier was as safe as she could ever hope to be.

The next three days passed peacefully, as the convoy, steaming on a north-easterly course, moved deeper into the Atlantic. After the oppressive heat of Trinidad, the fresh headwinds they met with were almost welcome, but combined with the prevailing adverse current, they considerably reduced the speed of the ships. Some of the older tankers, perhaps being pushed too hard, began to leave tell-tale trails of oil on the water – much to the disgust of the Escort Commander in HMS *Havelock.*

The year 1943 came in almost unnoticed, except for the good

news that *Godetia* had at last completed repairs on her second boiler. Twenty-four hours later, the seemingly fated corvette reported that the main transformer of her radar had burnt out, and she had no means of repair or replacement on board. TM 1 had lost one of its precious seeking eyes.

But the difficulties within the bounds of the convoy were insignificant compared with those building up outside. On the afternoon of 3 January U-514, returning from a successful patrol off the West Indies, quite by chance, found herself in sight of TM 1. Her commander, *Kapitänleutnant* Hans-Jurgen Auffermann, wasted no time in contacting Lorient, reporting the tankers and their puny escort to be on a course of 070° at 9 knots. Auffermann was instructed to shadow the convoy, attacking it as and when he was able. Meanwhile, the six boats of the *Delphin* Group, still meticulously combing the waters between Madeira and the Azores, were ordered south at all speed.

On the evening of the 3rd, Captain Andrews was relaxing in his day cabin below the *Empire Lytton*'s bridge, blissfully unaware of the danger threatening. The convoy was in mid-ocean, roughly halfway between Trinidad and the Azores, and was, in Andrews' opinion, barring the unlikely appearance of a German surface raider, relatively safe from attack. For the next few days, at least, he felt he would be able to relax, to shift some of the burden of his command temporarily onto the shoulders of his officers. He might even be lucky enough to enjoy several nights of uninterrupted sleep. The latter he was in need of, for when the *Empire Lytton* drew near the Canaries she would be once more entering Dönitz's lions' den.

Chief Officer Alfred Baughn, keeping watch on the bridge, was similarly contemplating a peaceful interlude. It was a fine night, and Baughn was contentedly pacing the starboard wing, occasionally lifting his binoculars to check that the *Empire Lytton* was not closing up on the ship ahead of her in the column, the 8,093-ton motor tanker *British Vigilance*. At 1845, as Baughn was seeking out her dark outline through his glasses, the *British Vigilance* erupted in a sheet of flame. Hans-Jurgen Auffermann had made his first kill.

When Andrews reached the bridge seconds later, he found that Baughn had already ordered the helm hard to starboard, and the ship was swinging clear of the funeral pyre of the *British Vigilance*. Andrews took over, bringing the *Empire Lytton* back on course when she was clear of the blazing tanker. As he completed the maneouvre, he caught sight of the low outline of a surfaced submarine close on the port bow, and etched in stark silhouette by the leaping flames.

Acting out of pure instinct, and with no thought for the highly volatile cargo below decks, Andrews hauled the ship around to port, and headed straight for the submarine with the intention of ramming. Auffermann acted with equal speed. Dark clouds of smoke spurted from U-514's exhausts, and she shot across the *Empire Lytton*'s bows from port to starboard, clearing the tanker's stem by no more than 20 yards.

But U-514 was not to escape unharmed. In the *Empire Lytton*'s starboard bridge wing, 16-year-old Apprentice Basil King, with barely six months' sea service to his name, strapped himself into the Oerlikon harness, and opened fire as the U-boat cleared the bow.

Auffermann had by now worked up his diesels to full power, and was running away from his assailant at 15 knots, but he was not fast enough. Young Basil King's aim was good, and the 20 mm cannon shells began to slam into U-514's conning tower. Simultaneously, the Panamanian-flag tanker *Norvik* opened fire with her 4-inch, bracketing the U-boat with her first two shots. Hans-Jurgen Auffermann, very wisely, decided the time had come to crash-dive and take his chances under water.

Despite the tension of the moment, Captain Andrews found it difficult to refrain from cheering as the Oerlikon shells slammed into the U-boat's superstructure. Of the 300 rounds fired by King, at least two-thirds had found their target. It was only when Andrews saw two ominous splashes under the fleeing U-boat's stern that he gave thought to the danger of torpedoes. In a last defiant gesture before he dived, Auffermann had fired his stern tubes. Andrews reacted quickly, ringing for emergency full speed and zig-zagging violently away from the scene. Another two hours were to pass before the *Empire Lytton* rejoined the convoy, taking the place of the missing *British Vigilance* in the lead of the centre column.

The remainder of the night passed without further attack, but early next morning HMS *Havelock* picked up radio signals on her

HF/DF, which indicated a U-boat nearby. *Godetia* was sent on an offensive sweep in the direction of the signals, but found no sign of the enemy. U-514 had withdrawn to a safe distance, but was still shadowing the convoy, and reporting to Lorient by W/T.

To add to his burden, the Escort Commander was now faced with another pressing problem. All the escort ships were running low on fuel, and it would be necessary for them to replenish their tanks within the next forty-eight hours. Ample fuel for this purpose was on board the *Norvik,* which carried the equipment for oiling at sea. However, the weather was steadily deteriorating, and when *Havelock* went alongside the tanker she was able to take on only six tons before the operation was abandoned in the heavy seas. The Escort Commander then decided to divert the convoy to the north in order to reach calmer weather. This enabled the refuelling to take place, but it also brought the ships closer to the U-boats of the *Delphin* Group, which were on their way south. At 1500 on the 8th, U-381, commanded by the grandiosely named *Kapitän-leutnant* Wilhelm-Heinrich Graf von Pückler und Limpurg, sighted the tankers, and alerted other U-boats in the vicinity.

When darkness descended that night, Convoy TM 1 was 550 miles to the west of the Canary Islands. The weather was fine and clear, with a light south-easterly breeze, smooth sea, and moderate swell. On the bridge of the *Empire Lytton*, Chief Officer Baughn had the watch, but Captain Andrews was hovering in the wheel-house, uncomfortably aware that conditions were ideal for a U-boat attack.

Had John Andrews been acquainted with the state of readiness of TM 1's escorts, his uneasiness would have been even greater. *Havelock*'s HF/DF was working only intermittently, *Godetia*'s radar was, of course, still out of action, and the corvette *Pimpernel*'s radar had also developed a serious fault. At that critical moment in the voyage, the long-range eyes and ears of the small escort force were partially incapacitated.

The wolves closed in at 1945, with U-436, under the command of *Kapitänleutnant* Günther Seibicke, leading the pack. Seibicke fired a spread of three torpedoes, two of which found their target in the Norwegian tanker *Albert L. Ellsworth* and the British tanker *Oltenia II.* Andrews, on the bridge of the *Empire Lytton,* was witness to their fate, watching in horror as the *Oltenia* sank like a stone, and the *Ellsworth* went up in flames.

The battle continued throughout the night, with the escorts, led by *Havelock*, fighting a magnificent defensive action. For many hours they held the U-boats at bay, but at 0315 on the 9th the wolves again broke through the thin grey cordon, and in the following fifteen minutes the Norwegian-flag *Minister Wedel* and the 10,034-ton *Norvik* were hit. Fortunately, these ships did not catch fire, and it seemed possible that, if they were not further attacked, they might be salvaged.

An hour later, it appeared that the determined depth charge attacks of the escorts had had the desired effect, for the U-boats withdrew, and all went quiet. At 0425, satisfied that the danger had passed, even if only for a while, Captain Andrews, exhausted by so many hours on the bridge, left Baughn in charge, and went below to snatch a short rest. This was not to be. While Andrews was preparing to take the weight off his tired limbs, *Korvettenkapitän* Hans-Joachim Hesse was manoeuvring U-442 into position for attack. A few minutes later, one of the two torpedoes fired by Hesse struck the *Empire Lytton* on her starboard bow.

In the master's cabin the sound of the exploding torpedo was muted, but Andrews felt the shock and heard the screech of rending metal. His tiredness forgotten, he leapt from his chair and headed for the bridge at a run, expecting that at any moment his ship and her three million gallons of high octane would turn into an ascending fireball, taking his charred ashes with her.

When he reached the bridge, Andrews found that the whole structure was covered in sticky, black fuel oil, as a result of which he was able to revise his thoughts of an early cremation. The indications were that the torpedo had hit in the *Empire Lytton*'s forward fuel tank, and its effect had been largely smothered by the thick oil. He rang the engines to stop, and sent Baughn forward to assess the damage.

As he leaned over the bridge front, peering into the darkness ahead, Andrews heard desperate cries for help coming from the main deck. He went below to investigate, and found the ship's carpenter, John Little, lying on the deck with both legs broken. Fearing that the ship might already be sinking, Andrews ordered

149

two seamen to put the injured man into one of the lifeboats and to lower the boat to the water. In the darkness, with panic never far below the surface, the boat was hurriedly lowered with the groaning carpenter lying on the thwarts. Being soaked in fuel oil, the rope falls were slippery, with the result that the forward fall ran away. The bow of the boat dropped, and John Little, unable to help himself, was catapulted into the water and disappeared before any attempt could be made to save him.

Saddened by this tragedy, for which he felt partly responsible, Andrews returned to the bridge, where he was joined by his chief engineer, Fletcher Canning, who had left the engine-room to seek information. While the two men were discussing the situation, Baughn returned with the news that the damage forward was extensive, but by no means fatal. The torpedo had struck just abaft the stem, blowing a hole roughly ten feet by four on each side of the bow. The forecastle-head was in ruins and the collision bulk-head breached. Fortunately, there was no outbreak of fire, but the ship was making water forward, although she seemed to be in no immediate danger of sinking. After some discussion with Baughn and Canning, Captain Andrews decided it would be safer to abandon ship temporarily and lie off in the boats until daylight.

The weather being fair and the sea calm, the operation of abandoning ship should have gone smoothly, but the darkness and the oil which covered everything produced a disaster. The Captain's boat was launched without incident, but Baughn's boat capsized when it hit the water, throwing its occupants into the sea. Although his own boat was already full, Andrews immediately began a search of the area for survivors. Dawn was breaking before he picked up the first man. Eleven others were eventually found, including Alfred Baughn. The chief officer was hauled on board, and for over an hour given artificial respiration, but without result. Baughn was dead.

Andrews' lifeboat now held twenty-three men, and was very much overcrowded. Although he could see at least six other men in the water, and could hear the shouts of more, he was unwilling to risk another capsize. It was now full daylight, and Andrews decided that the most sensible course of action was to return to the ship, which was still afloat, and off-load the men on board before

150

looking for other survivors. On the way back to the *Empire Lytton*, he came upon the only other lifeboat to get away, which contained just eight men, including Second Officer Ronald Moore. Andrews instructed Moore to pick up the men in the water, and carried on towards the ship with his heavily loaded boat.

The *Empire Lytton* was re-boarded shortly after 0800, and Andrews and his men were then able to clean the oil off themselves and put on dry clothes. The ship was now five feet by the head, but otherwise seemed still seaworthy. However, the corvette *Saxifrage* then appeared alongside and delivered an ultimatum. Unless Andrews was able to get his ship under way quickly and proceed at 8 knots, *Saxifrage* had orders to sink her by gunfire.

The last thing Andrews wanted was to lose his ship at this late stage, and in a desperate bid to postpone the decision, he persuaded the commander of the corvette to first search for the *Empire Lytton*'s other lifeboat and any men who might still be in the water.

When *Saxifrage* had steamed away, Chief Engineer Canning went below to examine the possibility of raising steam. On returning to the bridge, he reported that he was confident of producing up to 8 knots, but no more. By now, *Havelock* had arrived on the scene, and the Escort Commander was pressing Andrews for a decision. *Saxifrage* then returned with Second Officer Moore's boat in tow, but had found no other survivors. While Moore and his men re-boarded the *Empire Lytton*, the two warships hovered within easy gun range, their signal lamps chattering.

John Andrews appreciated that the hard-pressed escorts were anxious to dispose of the crippled *Empire Lytton* in order to concentrate their meagre resources on the tankers remaining undamaged, but he was not about to give up his ship easily. He sent Canning below to raise steam, and when that was done, to re-assess the ship's capability. Within half an hour, Canning returned to the bridge with the unwelcome news that the damage in the engine-room was worse than he had at first thought. The maximum speed he was prepared to promise was 6 knots. At 0930, for the second and last time that day, the *Empire Lytton* was abandoned by her crew, who were taken off by *Saxifrage*.

Rather than waste time on sinking her, which was liable to be a lengthy process with gunfire, the Escort Commander decided to leave the *Empire Lytton* to her fate, and *Havelock,* with *Saxifrage* in company, steamed off at full speed to rejoin the remnants of the convoy. As his late command disappeared astern, Captain John Andrews watched her sadly from the deck of the corvette, and reflected on the bravery of his men, whose valiant efforts had been in vain. Basil King, the 16-year-old apprentice, who should have been wielding nothing more lethal than a sextant, had manned his Oerlikon like a veteran gunner: the watch in the engine-room when the torpedo struck, Second Engineer John Bentley, Greaser Murray and Fireman Reid, who had remained calmly at their posts until ordered up on deck: the Estonian deckhand, whom Andrews knew only as Herman, who had supported Chief Officer Baughn in the water for two hours. Of the forty-seven men he had set sail with from Trinidad twelve days earlier, only thirty-one remained. Alfred Baughn was dead, and fifteen others, including the courageous Fireman Reid, were missing, believed drowned. As Andrews sadly turned away to go below to *Saxifrage*'s wardroom, he saw a flash and clouds of black smoke mushrooming up from the horizon astern. And now his ship had gone.

While *Saxifrage* was hurrying back to join the convoy, the U-boats were disposing of the other crippled and abandoned tankers. Herbert Schneider in U-522 sank the *Norvik* and *Minister Wedel* between 1200 and 1400, while at 1743 Günther Seibicke's U-436 came back to finish off the *Albert L. Ellsworth.*

When *Saxifrage* rejoined TM 1 after dark on the 9th, the convoy was a pathetic sight. It now consisted of just three ships, the *British Dominion*, the *Vanja* and the *Cliona.* Urged on by *Havelock*, the survivors were steaming to the north-east at their best possible speed.

And yet the massacre of TM 1 was still not complete. When darkness came on the 10th, the U-boats returned, sensing a victorious climax to their operation. Four boats penetrated the escort screen on the surface, and despite the efforts of *Havelock* and the corvettes, the *British Dominion*, fully loaded with aviation spirit, went up in a ball of fire. Torpedoes were also fired at the *Vanja* and *Cliona,* but fortunately these missed.

There is little doubt that but for the arrival on the 11th of a

Catalina flying boat and three additional escorts, Convoy TM 1 must have gone down in history as the convoy that sailed into oblivion. As it was, seven ships of 56,453 tons gross, carrying nearly 80,000 tons of precious fuel had gone to the bottom. Not one of the U-boats of the *Delphin* Group was lost.

It was later learned that the *Empire Lytton* did not succumb as easily as Captain Andrews believed. The smoke he saw on the horizon from the deck of *Saxifrage* was the result of an attempted *coup de grâce* by U-442, but the tanker was still afloat five hours later. It cost Hans-Joachim Hesse yet another expensive torpedo before, at 1838 on the 9th, the *Empire Lytton* finally sank.

U-442 outlived the *Empire Lytton* by just over a month. During that time, her only other victim was the 7,176-ton US cargo ship *Julia Ward Howe*, which she sank north of the Azores on 27 January. Two weeks later, she was surprised on the surface in the western approaches to the Mediterranean by aircraft of the US 48 Squadron, and sent to the bottom.

Chapter Fourteen

To the Bitter End

Leonardo da Vinci, the fifteenth century artist and scientist, was a man of exceptional talents, and unusually for one of his kind, also a man of great humility. His last words before he died in 1519 were said to be: 'I have offended God and Mankind because my work did not reach the quality it should have'. For a man who produced, among other things, the Mona Lisa and plans for the first helicopter, this was modesty indeed. What would Da Vinci have thought of the works his name would be associated with four centuries after his death will remain forever a matter for speculation.

Shortly before midnight on 13 March 1943, the 21,516-ton Canadian Pacific liner *Empress of Canada* was 350 miles off the coast of Liberia, sailing unescorted from the Middle East to the United Kingdom. She had on board 1,890 servicemen and crew. It was a black night, and the great ship's frothing wake cut an erratic swathe through the tranquil sea as she zig-zagged at full speed around her mean course. Her evasive action was to be of no avail, for on the stroke of midnight, as the watches were changing, a torpedo tore into her engine-room, and she came slowly to a halt. The Italian submarine *Leonardo da Vinci*, commanded by *Capitano di Corvette* Gianfranco Gazzana-Priaroggia, after a fruitless month spent patrolling these warm waters, had at last found a target for her torpedoes. Once the liner was crippled and stopped, it was easy for Priaroggia to finish her off. When she sank, she took 370 men with her. Several survivors who were in the water died of shark bites after rescue.

154

As the waves closed over the *Empress of Canada*, and she began her slow, spiralling plunge to the bottom, another British merchantman was 1,600 miles to the south-west, and following in the doomed liner's invisible wake. The 7,628-ton *Lulworth Hill*, however, was a far cry from the faded opulence of the *Empress of Canada*. Owned by the Counties Ship Management Company of London, and built in 1940 by William Hamilton at Port Glasgow, she was in outward appearance a modern tramp ship but, quite out of character, was capable of a top speed of 14 knots. She carried a crew of forty-one, supplemented by seven DEMS gunners, and was commanded by Captain William McEwan. She mounted the usual 4-inch on her poop, with four Oerlikons, two twin Marlins, two Lewis guns, and an early form of multiple rocket launcher known as a 'Pillar Box' for defence against aircraft. In addition – and this was most unusual for a merchant ship, she carried three depth charges stowed at her stern rail. How she was to use these powerful charges without doing herself serious harm was a matter for some argument.

Deep laden with 10,190 tons of raw sugar, 400 tons of rum, and 410 tons of fibre, the *Lulworth Hill* left Cape Town on the morning of 11 March, bound for Freetown, where she would join a convoy for the UK. The weather in the South Atlantic when she sailed was at its autumn best, with the South-East Trades blowing light, the skies blue, and the sun warm. There were no warnings of U-boats operating in the area, and steaming at full speed along a route recommended by the Admiralty, Captain McEwan anticipated a trouble-free passage, arriving in Freetown at some time on the 20th.

Twenty-four hours out of Cape Town, the *Lulworth Hill*'s radio officer intercepted a message from an American merchant ship reporting that she had been torpedoed not many miles ahead of the British ship's position. As a precaution, McEwan put his guns' crews and lookouts on full alert, and began zig-zagging throughout the daylight hours.

Despite the alarm, the tranquility of the South Atlantic remained undisturbed, and for the next six days the *Lulworth Hill* steamed northwards unmolested, but still maintaining her precautionary zig-zag. Then, at dusk on the 18th, when she was 500 miles north of St. Helena, a keen-eyed lookout spotted the track of a torpedo racing in on the starboard side. There was no time to take avoiding action, but fortunately the torpedo passed harmlessly astern of the ship.

Captain McEwan hit the bridge at the first shrill call of the alarm bells, and was in time to see a submarine break the surface not more than 250 yards on the starboard bow. In the lengthening shadows of the oncoming night, the long, grey shape, shedding water as it rose from the depths, had the appearance of a frightening sea-monster of the legends of old.

McEwan took the only course of action open to him, bringing his ship hard round to port to present her stern to the enemy. The *Lulworth Hill*'s gunners, already closed up on the 4-inch, acted with equal speed, opening fire on the submarine as soon as their gun came to bear. Their aim was accurate, but as the target was so close to the ship, they were unable to depress their gun sufficiently to score a hit. However, the two rounds they fired were to good effect, for the submarine immediately crash-dived. The *Lulworth Hill,* her engine making maximum revolutions, and zig-zagging with renewed purpose, made off in a south-easterly direction, seeking the cover of the night. At the same time, her radio officer was tapping out the all-too-familiar 'SSSS', informing all ships that she was under attack by a submarine.

Below the waves, *Capitano* Priaroggia checked the *Leonardo da Vinci*'s dive, and levelled off at 20 metres. The Italian commander was visibly shaken by the short shrift he had received at the hands of an apparently harmless merchantman. At his side in the control room, the *da Vinci*'s German liaison officer was furious. To him, the simple operation had been an example of Italian bungling at its worst.

The German officer had good reason to be concerned at the loss of an easy target, for at that stage of the war things were going disastrously wrong for the Axis Powers. On the Russian Front, twenty-two Wehrmacht divisions, led by Field Marshal Paulus, had only a few weeks earlier been forced to surrender at the gates of Stalingrad; in the Western Desert, Rommel's army was in full flight, while in the Pacific the Japanese had at last been prised out of Guadalcanal by General MacArthur's men. But perhaps the most bitter pill Germany had to swallow was the determined and successful assault being made on her main industrial cities by RAF Bomber Command. Up to 400 aircraft a night were laying waste to the Ruhr with thousands of tons of high explosives and incendiaries. The *Luftwaffe*, largely due to its massive commitments in Russia and the Mediterranean, no longer had the resources to mount retaliatory attacks on British cities.

The *Lulworth Hill* had been steaming at full speed for an hour before the *Leonardo da Vinci* caught up with her. By then it was fully dark, with the moon obscured by cloud, and with a fresh south-easterly blowing. Priaroggia, rather unwisely, revealed his presence to the men on the bridge of the merchantman by switching on a small searchlight. Captain McEwan passed the order to his gunners to hold their fire, and being careful to avoid stirring up a tell-tale wash, stealthily altered course until the *Lulworth Hill*'s stern was again to the enemy submarine, and she was moving rapidly away from her. A game of cat-and-mouse was on.

For another fifteen minutes Priaroggia's searchlight continued to probe the darkness searching for his prey, while the *Lulworth Hill* fled to the south-west with her boiler safety valves screwed hard down. Another hour passed, and McEwan, his eyes aching through constantly sweeping the horizon astern with binoculars, began to entertain hopes of a successful getaway. Then, at around 2300, snowflake rockets soared into the sky about 5 miles astern, and turned day into night. Priaroggia had not given up the chase. Fortunately, the *Lulworth Hill* was far enough away to be still in the shadows, and McEwan again restrained his gunners from opening fire.

Midnight came and went, with no thought of watches being changed. Every man of the ship's crew was standing to his action station – as he had been for four hours past. As the new day advanced, and the tension slowly eased, McEwan deemed it safe to send some of his men below to rest, but leaving the guns fully manned and all lookouts at their posts.

At 0345 on the 19th, in the darkest hours before the dawn when life is said to be at its lowest ebb, the silence of the night was rent by a tremendous explosion, and the *Lulworth Hill* was brought up short, listing heavily to starboard. *Capitano* Priaroggia had found his mark.

The *Lulworth Hill*'s carpenter, Kenneth Cooke, was one of those asleep in his cabin when the torpedo struck. The force of the explosion blew him out of his bunk and, dazed and shaken, he had just regained his feet when the second torpedo ripped open the ship's side. Cooke, who had taken the precaution of turning in fully clothed, stopped only to snatch up his lifejacket, before making for the deck at a run.

Both Priaroggia's torpedoes had hit forward of the bridge, breaking the *Lulworth Hill*'s back. By the time Cooke reached the boat deck, the main deck was awash, and he had only a few seconds to struggle into his lifejacket before jumping clear of the sinking ship.

In spite of the buoyancy provided by the lifejacket, Cooke found himself drawn down by the suction of the ship as she slid under bow-first. He fought his way back to the surface to find himself looking up at the stern as it lifted high in the air, the propeller still turning lazily. Then, in the grip of the increasing suction, he was dragged under again. When he broke surface for the second time, the *Lulworth Hill* had gone from sight.

It had taken less than two minutes for the ship to sink, and Cooke knew there could have been no time to launch the lifeboats. He gave thanks for the sixth sense that had made him pick up his lifejacket before leaving his cabin, but at the same time, despite the warmth of the tropical water, he felt a cold fear creeping over him as he realised that the ship had gone down over 700 miles from the nearest land. Was he alone in this great, empty ocean?

Looking around him in the inky darkness, with the waves slapping spitefully at his face, Cooke tried, unsuccessfully, to visualise in his mind's eye a distance of 700 miles. It was too vast to comprehend, and he turned his racing thoughts to how long his lifejacket would keep him afloat. Forty-eight hours, at the most. And then he remembered the sharks. There was no shortage of them in these waters. He had watched them shadowing the ship for hours – great hammerheaded brutes. He began to panic, and struck out towards the spot where the ship had gone down. There might be something of her left – a hatchboard or any piece of wreckage on which to take refuge, anything to get his legs out of the water.

A lesser man than Kenneth Cooke might have gone quietly mad

there and then, but Cooke was of that particular breed of English-
man to whom a seemingly hopeless situation presents a challenge.
He was also blessed with good luck. Within a few minutes, he had
found a cork lifebuoy, a fragile enough support, but it gave him
some security. Pushing the lifebuoy before him, he swam on, and
was overjoyed when he saw the red glow of a lifejacket light
bobbing on the waves ahead. Soon, he was drifting side by side with
another survivor, this being Able Seaman Hull, one of the *Lulworth
Hill*'s DEMS gunners.

With the sea lashing at their faces, and by its sheer persistence
threatening to drown them, the two men somehow managed to
discuss the awful predicament they were in. Hull confirmed
Cooke's assessment that there had been no time to launch boats.
Their only real hope, they decided, lay in finding one of the ship's
life-rafts, which were designed to float off if she sank. They were
about to begin their search, when they sighted a small cluster of red
lights about fifty yards off. They were not alone, after all.

They were swimming towards the lights when, with a loud
hissing of compressed air, the *Leonardo da Vinci* surfaced between
them and their goal. A searchlight was switched on, and began
slowly to sweep the sea. Accepting that life in a prisoner of war
camp was preferable to death by shark bite or drowning, Cooke
and Hull swam towards the light.

Cooke's movements were hampered by the lifebuoy, but he was
reluctant to abandon it, and consequently Hull reached the
submarine several minutes before him. Two of the crew heaved the
gunner on board, and by the time Cooke had found a handhold on
the submarine's casing, Hull had been taken below.

While Cooke was trying to recover his breath, he was suddenly
blinded by the searchlight, which was turned full on him, and he
heard a faceless voice demanding to know the name of his ship.
Buffeted against the submarine's hull by the waves and half-
drowned, he had no will to answer other than truthfully. His
questioner, whom he could now just make out, was leaning over
the edge of the conning tower, and appeared to be wearing a naval
uniform. He spoke good English, but with a strong German accent,
and Cooke naturally assumed the submarine was a German
U-boat. His questioner was, in fact, the *Leonardo da Vinci*'s SS

159

liaison officer, temporarily assigned to the submarine with the express purpose of stiffening the Italian crew's resolve, which at that stage of the war was showing signs of crumbling.

The German fired question after question at the unfortunate Cooke, who was at such a disadvantage that he could do no more than answer to the best of his ability. Then the questioning suddenly stopped, and the searchlight swung away to resume probing the darkness around them. The beam settled on what looked like a life-raft with several men clinging to it, but then suddenly the light was switched off. The submarine's diesels thundered into life, and she surged forward. Cooke, completely taken by surprise, found himself being dragged through the water. His arm, which was through a hole in the casing, felt as if it were being wrenched off at the shoulder, and his head went under water. After several agonising moments, which seemed more like an hour in purgatory, he managed to free himself. More dead than alive, he was thrown clear by the accelerating submarine's wake, and came gasping to the surface.

In a blind panic, Cooke swam after the submarine, and caught up with it when it stopped and played its searchlight on an upturned lifeboat on which six men had taken refuge. Not wishing to repeat his earlier experience, he trod water when he was within twenty-five yards of the enemy and awaited events. From his position low in the water, the submarine appeared to be huge – almost 250 feet long, he estimated. She had a very tall periscope, or mast, a large-calibre gun forward of the conning tower, and a curious square structure aft, which he took to be a seaplane hanger. Cooke had studied photographs of German submarines, and she did not match up with any he had seen. He assumed she must be Italian, although the German accent of the man he took to be her commander puzzled him.

Cautiously, Cooke moved closer, for he now heard that same guttural voice berating the men on the keel of the lifeboat. For some time the unseen man ranted against the RAF's bombing of German cities, then his voice rose to a scream with the words, 'Now you will drown!' Then, the searchlight was abruptly switched off, the submarine's diesels again rumbled into life, and she slipped away into the darkness. As the throb of her engines died away, and a

160

silence disturbed only by the slap, slap of the waves descended on the sea, the awful reality of his position came back to haunt Kenneth Cooke. He was alone in a dark, hostile world, and his chances of survival were very, very slim.

But, once again, in the face of adversity, Cooke refused to be beaten. Pushing his precious lifebuoy ahead of him, he swam in the direction of the upturned lifeboat, stopping now and again to shout, hoping to attract the attention of other survivors – if any existed. He received no answer, and soon lost his bearing in the darkness. For another half an hour he swam around in circles, still calling. He was on the point of despair, when he heard a faint answering shout. Nothing was visible, but the voice was real enough, calling out to guide him. Eventually, he found a life-raft, whose sole occupant, 21-year-old Able Seaman Colin Armitage, was only too glad to help him on board.

For what remained of the night, Cooke and Armitage paddled their raft in a systematic search of the area, stopping from time to time to listen for voices. In this way, they came upon Chief Officer Basil Scown and, with great difficulty, hauled him on board. Scown, who had been in the water for three hours, had swallowed a great deal of oily water, and was in bad shape.

The sun was well up when they sighted a second raft. It was empty, but much larger than their own, so they paddled towards it and transferred. Their new craft was of much more substantial construction, and its tanks contained eight gallons of drinking water, and a number of tins of pemmican, Horlicks tablets and chocolate. The few provisions from the smaller raft were taken on board, and the rafts were lashed together. With every hour that had passed since the sinking of the *Lulworth Hill*, Kenneth Cooke's luck had improved.

For the next few hours, the three men laboriously paddled their rafts through the wreckage-strewn area, searching for others who might have survived. Their persistence was rewarded when they at last found the upturned lifeboat Cooke had seen in the beam of the submarine's searchlight. The six men astride the keel had been joined by four others, who were floating alongside them on a damaged life-raft.

The assorted craft came together, and Chief Officer Scown,

although still very weak, took charge of the flotilla. His first action was to try to right the capsized boat, but the thirteen survivors were all so near exhaustion, that this proved impossible. Their attempts at righting the boat were not made any easier by the appearance on the scene of a number of sharks, which circled menacingly around them.

It was finally decided to abandon both the lifeboat and the damaged raft, distributing themselves on the two remaining rafts, nine men to the larger, and three to the smaller. They were cramped, but reasonably safe – for the time being. As to their future prospects, no one cared to voice an opinion, but they all had their thoughts.

A last search was made among the wreckage for more survivors and for anything that might be of use to them. The result was disappointing. They netted only a single onion, which was found floating in the oily water. By the time darkness came again, they were forced to conclude that they were all that remained of the *Lulworth Hill*'s crew of forty-six.

The thirteen survivors, six of them boys under eighteen, settled down for the night, covering themselves with the small canvas sails found in the lockers of the rafts, but sleep proved impossible. The rafts were so crowded, and the sea so rough, that it was all they could do to prevent themselves being washed overboard. Scown was in a bad way, continually retching through the effects of the oil he had swallowed, and Second Engineer Eric Ledger, who had suffered injuries to both feet, was in constant pain. All thirteen were wet, covered in oil, and thoroughly miserable.

After a couple of hours of this torture, the men gave up all thoughts of sleep, and huddled together discussing their chances of survival. Scown, the only navigator, estimated that the *Lulworth Hill* had gone down in a position roughly 700 miles east of the coast of Angola, and 900 miles south of the Gold Coast. In peacetime, the area would have been busy with ships on their way to and from the Cape of Good Hope. Now, with most ships routed well out into the Atlantic to avoid the U-boats, they were truly in the middle of nowhere, and rescue by a passing ship was unlikely. An SSSS message had been sent at the time of the first attack by the *Leonardo da Vinci* on the night of the 18th, but the ship went down so fast when she was torpedoed next morning, that no other transmission was made. It might be some days, perhaps weeks, before she was deemed overdue at Freetown, and a search was set in motion.

The only thing in the survivors' favour was that the weather in that part of the Atlantic is largely fair throughout the year, with light to moderate south-easterly winds and a total absence of gales. On the other hand, rain rarely falls, and the cloudless skies give soaring temperatures during the day, with cold nights to follow. The prevailing south-easterlies would be a help in enabling the rafts to make progress to the north, but the current would be of no help. They were under the influence of the South Equatorial Current, said to be one of the most constant currents known, in that area setting to the west at up to 20 miles a day. The rafts were in great danger of being swept out into the Atlantic.

It is probable that only Basil Scown, an experienced navigator, knew how heavily the odds were weighted against their survival. Had the others been aware, some would most certainly have given up hope there and then. As it was, when Scown put it to them, they were all prepared to make a try for the land to the north. With some difficulty due to the overcrowding, the short masts of the rafts were stepped, and the sails hoisted.

Accurate navigation of the cumbersome rafts, which had no rudders or compasses, was out of the question, and they would have to return to the ways of their early ancestors. At night, the Southern Cross would always be there, shining brilliantly against a backdrop of black velvet, and must be kept astern; during the day, with only the sun circling overhead to guide them, it would be more difficult, but they would manage. As to which way the current was carrying them, they could only guess. When dawn came next day, lookouts were posted to scan the horizon for the help they still hoped might come, and their journey began.

As day after day went by with the horizon remaining empty, morale on the rafts declined rapidly. In daylight there was no shelter from the burning sun, and at night, no matter how closely they huddled together, the cold bit cruelly into their bones. Fortunately, the rafts were well stocked with the standard lifeboat rations, pemmican, Horlicks malted milk tablets, chocolate and hard biscuits, and the water tanks contained about thirty gallons. At first reckoning, it seemed that they had ample food and water for survival. But as to how long they would be adrift was only pure guesswork. Assuming the wind continued to blow from the southeast, Scown estimated they would make progress towards the land at around 1½ knots, in which case they must be prepared for a voyage of four to five weeks at least – and that did not take into account the Doldrums, the area of calms near the Equator, which they must enter.

Chief Steward Herbert Thornton was convinced he could not survive longer than thirty days, and he made this known to the others. Basil Scown, though cheerfully shouldering his responsibilities, was seriously ill from the effects of the oil he had swallowed. The condition of Second Engineer Ledger, who was in great pain from his injured feet, was also deteriorating, as was that of one of the young boys injured in the sinking.

Ten days later, they were all still alive, but dreadfully emaciated, listless, and covered with salt water boils. Ledger and the injured boy had both developed gangrene in their wounds, and Scown was noticeably weaker. No one had the faintest idea of how far they had sailed, and the sheer hopelessness of their plight had mentally drained all of them. The only exceptions were Kenneth Cooke and Colin Armitage, who seemed to possess that extra quality that enabled them to keep a tight grip on their minds. As the Chief Officer's condition grew worse, Cooke found himself gradually taking over his role as leader of the pitiful little band.

On 6 April, when they had been eighteen days on the rafts, Basil Scown lapsed into delirium and died. There were others who outranked the carpenter, but voiced no objections when Cooke assumed command. His greatest responsibility lay in keeping a watchful eye on the food and water. Scown had set the daily ration for each man at one ounce of pemmican, one biscuit, four Horlicks tablets, three squares of chocolate, and six ounces of water. It was an insufficient, monotonous and unpalatable diet, but Cooke had little choice but to continue with it. The warm waters around them teemed with fish, but without lines and hooks the survivors had no means of catching them. Cooke fashioned a crude harpoon from a marlin spike and a length of driftwood, but while he was quite successful at spearing fish, most of them slipped off the smooth spike before they could be brought on board. He did, however, manage to land the occasional salty morsel, which was eaten raw, and with great relish.

As would be expected, the survivors' greatest enemy was thirst – and this was not helped by the salty pemmican and the sweet Horlicks tablets. Cooke caught some of the young boys sipping salt water, and took the firmest action he could to stop this dangerous practice. During the daylight hours he was able to exercise strict control, but under the cover of darkness he could do little.

Nothing could save Herbert Thornton who, as he had predicted, died on the thirtieth day. His passing signalled the beginning of the end, for thereafter death was in daily attendance on the rafts. Some died from the effects of drinking salt water, others were victims of the unrelenting torture meted out by the elements, the merciless sun by day, and the bone-chilling cold of the nights. But in many cases it was the lack of hope that killed. Physical fitness seemed to have little bearing on the sequence in which they died. Each time a man lost faith in ultimate survival, he was doomed.

By 21 April, after thirty-three days adrift, only Kenneth Cooke and Colin Armitage – ironically the original inhabitants of the rafts – remained alive. Both were strong-minded, resourceful individuals, and those characteristics undoubtedly helped them to outlive the others. Caring for the weaker men, a role they had willingly assumed, had also left them with little time to reflect on their own troubles.

When the last pathetic burial had taken place, and Cooke and Armitage found themselves alone on the raft, they resolved that having survived so far they would make every effort to live to see the land again. Their first move was to cut loose the smaller, and now superfluous, raft, which was acting as a drag on the other. Due mainly to Cooke's careful husbandry over the preceding weeks, a good supply of food and water remained – certainly enough to last the two of them for many days to come.

The harvest from the sea also increased. With practice, Cooke had become quite efficient with his makeshift harpoon, and his daily haul was rising. The near-empty raft was also proving fatally attractive to the flying fish, which flopped aboard, often three or four at a time. These were small, no bigger than sardines, but the two hungry men consumed them ravenously, leaving only the heads and wings. Their new-found freedom of movement led to the discovery of a type of mussel growing in profusion just below the waterline on the raft. These shellfish made good eating, part of the flesh containing a tiny sac of fresh water. Experimenting with a rope trailed behind the raft, they found this quickly became covered with the small molluscs. Emboldened by their good fortune, they searched the sea around them for further sources of food, and found strings of edible fish eggs. This warm-water caviar, in particular, was a very welcome addition to their monotonous diet of pemmican and malted milk tablets. As far as food and water were concerned, Cooke and Armitage were now well provided for, but their survival stilled hinged on the resilience of their minds.

As each dawn came and went, and the sea and sky remained stubbornly empty, the two men did their best not to give up hope, but their optimism eventually began to wear thin. They were now allowing themselves an increased basic diet, amounting to two ounces of pemmican, eight Horlicks tablets, five squares of chocolate, and six ounces of water. Despite this, their physical condition was deteriorating. The presence of a great number of large sharks circling the raft did nothing to ease their tortured minds. Then, on 29 April, the forty-first day of their long voyage, a flock of birds appeared overhead, and they knew they must be at last nearing land. If they could have mustered the strength to dance on their raft, Cooke and Armitage would have done so. As it was, a smile on their cracked lips was all they could muster.

At approximately 1030 next morning, the last day of April, two aircraft flew directly over the raft, but at a great height. Cooke set off two flares, which sent clouds of orange smoke billowing over the water, but the planes gave no sign of having seen them, and flew out of sight. Disappointed though they were, the men did not lose heart, for they were confident there would be other planes, perhaps ships. Their optimism was justified when, in the middle of the afternoon, two more aircraft flew over – but again without seeing their flares. They concluded that they must be within the limits of regular patrols from the Gold Coast or Sierra Leone.

The next day was one of bitter disappointment, the sky being empty, except for a few circling sea-birds. Twenty-four hours later, on Sunday 2 May, two high-flying aircraft again flew over, and Cooke set off another smoke flare, which again produced no response. A few hours later, yet another plane was sighted, only this time flying much lower. Cooke and Armitage scrambled to break out their precious supply of red distress flares, which they had been saving for such an opportunity. There was no guarantee that these flares would ignite, as they had been saturated when taken out of their so-called watertight container in the early days on the raft. Each day, the flares had been put in the sun to dry out, and stowed away again when night came. The moment of truth had arrived.

The first flare failed to ignite, but the second erupted in a brilliant red flame and clouds of red smoke which, lying low on the water, spread over an area of almost 2 square miles. The effect was immediate. The plane first flew past the raft, and then began to circle it, dropping lower with each circuit, its Morse light flashing rapidly. Cooke and Armitage were too weak to make any pretence at reading the message, but they knew that after forty-four days in which they had wandered the face of the ocean unseen, rescue was at last at hand. Tears ran down their salt-caked cheeks, and they hugged each other unashamedly.

The aircraft now swooped low over the raft, and dropped a number of packages into the sea close by. The survivors had no strength left in their arms to paddle across to the packages, but when two drifted close to the raft, they were able to reach them with Cooke's harpoon. When opened, the packages were found to contain a rubber dinghy with a full set of stores, a kite and balloons complete with gas cylinders for inflating, a portable wireless transmitter, distress rockets, and a Very pistol with cartridges. The thing they needed most, fresh water, was not there, but they were so grateful for this first contact with a world they thought they had lost that their thirst was forgotten. Night was now approaching, and anticipating that morning would bring rescue, they lay down to rest, but sleep would not come. They were too excited.

All through the following day they kept a sharp lookout for ships and aircraft, but nothing came. Exhilaration turned to disappointment, and their sleep that night was again fitful. Next day, 4 May, they decided to set up the portable transmitter. As their hands were stiff and awkward, and the instruction book had been damaged by sea water, this proved to be a long task. The balloons would not inflate, but they persevered, and were able to get the kite into the air with the aerial attached. Neither man had any experience with a transmitter, but this set was designed for such a contingency. It was sufficient for them merely to crank the generator handles and tap out a series of SOSs with the Morse key. They had no means of knowing if the radio was actually transmitting, but throughout that day, despite their weakened condition, they kept the generator going at the required speed, and sent out a steady stream of distress calls.

Next morning, their prayers were answered. A Catalina flying boat appeared, and bombarded the sea around them with dozens of packages. Paddling the heavy raft was completely beyond them, but they succeeded in inflating the rubber dinghy, and in this picked up seven packages, and brought them back to the raft. When opened, these were found to contain chocolate, barley sugar, chewing gum, tins of various foods, cigarettes, matches, distress flares, a medical kit and, most welcome of all, tins of drinking water. They also found a scribbled note from the airmen, which read:-

> *Sorry we can't get down to pick you up. Sea is too rough. Have sent signal from overhead for shore base to get a fix on you. Your signals are very clear and you have been heard in West Africa and Ascension Island. You are roughly 400 miles south of Liberia but in shipping lanes. Keep your chins up and keep smiling. Keep cracking away on transmitter, especially between hours of 11 am and 2 pm (SOS, SOS and a continuous note). You should be picked up within 36 hours. If any shipping seen on the way back to base, will direct to you.*

As they finished reading the note, the aircraft made a last run across the raft, dipped its wings, and flew off to the north.

Cooke and Armitage felt that the death sentence which had been hanging over their heads for so long had finally been lifted. Stopping only to slake their thirst with the heaven-sent water, they went back to the transmitter with renewed enthusiasm, resting only when darkness fell.

With the dawn next day they continued to transmit as they had been advised, and at 1430 a large American flying-boat came in answer to their calls for help. The sea was still too rough for the pilot to attempt a landing, but more packages were dropped. Unfortunately, they fell some miles from the raft, and were wasted. The aircraft then flew away without making any effort to communicate with the survivors.

Four days had passed since they were first sighted from the air, and the horizon still remained stubbornly empty of ships. Cooke and Armitage felt an air of hopelessness creeping over them. But throughout that day they again persevered with their distress signals, which they now knew were being listened to. The night that followed was a bad one, for the sharks came back, and spent much of the dark hours trying to overturn the raft.

It was a frightening experience, and by daybreak on the 7th the two men were completely exhausted by lack of sleep and fear. Their despair deepened into near panic when the handles of the radio's generator seized up, and they were no longer able to transmit. It was as though an invisible umbilical cord connecting them with the outside world had suddenly been cut. Then, shortly before noon, as they were debating whether to risk opening up the transmitter to free the handles, Armitage glanced seaward and, to his amazement, saw the masts and funnel of a ship on the horizon.

Not daring to speak in case the ship turned out to be a product of their tortured minds, both men reached for the hand-held distress rockets they had received from the air five days earlier. These proved to be spectacular, each rocket sending three balls of brilliant red fire skywards. The first one, fired by Armitage, resulted in a badly burned hand, and thereafter the men protected their hands with strips of wet canvas. Six rockets were launched, one after the other.

In spite of this impressive firework display, the ship did not alter course. In desperation, Cooke snatched up the Very pistol and sent up flare after flare. Coincidentally probably, this had an immediate effect. A naval ship came steaming over the horizon, and headed straight for the raft. Determined that this time they would not go unnoticed, the survivors continued to fire rockets and flares until the warship was within a hundred yards of them. Half an hour later, the emaciated Cooke and Armitage were gently lifted aboard the destroyer HMS *Rapid*.

When they were rescued, on 7 May, Cooke and Armitage had been a little short of fifty days on their raft, and had ended up 430 miles off the coast of Liberia, having covered a distance of 1,065 miles in a north-westerly direction. Much of their progress had been due to the current, but it was the effect of the south-easterly wind acting on their tiny sail that had given them sufficient northing to edge the raft in towards the land, and within range of the air patrols. Without the benefit of that scrap of canvas they would have drifted into mid-Atlantic, there to meet a lonely end somewhere between the islands of Ascension and St. Helena, where only the wheeling albatross and the patiently circling shark hold sway.

Cooke and Armitage were very near to death when they were picked up by the Royal Navy. Both men had lost almost forty pounds in weight, and their hearts were so weak that the blood had all but ceased to circulate in their veins. For three weeks they were unable to walk unaided but, under the care of *Rapid*'s doctor, and later in a Freetown hospital, they were eventually returned to full health. For their bravery and fortitude in the face of such terrible adversity, Kenneth Cooke and Colin Armitage were each awarded the George Medal. Armitage died in 1950, aged twenty-seven, a belated victim of that long voyage into the Gulf of Guinea.

As for the *Leonardo da Vinci*, she was to do little more damage to the Allied cause, sinking only one other ship, before being caught by the British destroyers *Active* and *Ness* off the Azores, and sent to the bottom on 23 May 1943. Ironically, it was on that very day that Cooke and Armitage were landed in Freetown by HMS *Rapid*.

Chapter Fifteen

Mediterranean Nightmare

The chill of the short Mediterranean winter was still in the air when, soon after dawn on 13 March 1943, the British cargo ship *Ocean Voyager* left the early bustle of Alexandria harbour astern and set course to the westward. The sky was clear, but a freshening north-westerly was busy herding the white horses across a steel-grey sea to run headlong into the bluff bows of the ship as she worked up to full speed.

After the smell and dust of Alexandria, the crisp morning air was like wine to Captain Duncan Mackellar as he studied the chart and mulled over the likely problems of the voyage ahead. Steaming at her top speed of 11 knots, it would take his ship just over three and a half days to reach her destination, the Libyan port of Tripoli, which lay 950 miles to the west. In earlier years, when peace reigned over this pleasant sea, Mackellar would have welcomed the relief afforded by the short passage through open waters. For him, it would have been a temporary escape from all the commercial and political pressures that burden a shipmaster in a foreign port – a time to step back and allow his officers to run the ship. However, in the spring of 1943, with the enemy in a spiteful mood, the Mediterranean was not a place to drop one's guard.

The German reaction to the plight of their Afrika Corps, then fleeing before the hammer blows of Montgomery's Eighth Army, had been to concentrate their ire on the thinly stretched British supply line, the merchant ships running a shuttle service with stores and ammunition from Alexandria to Benghazi and Tripoli. To that end, Admiral Dönitz had assembled in the Mediterranean twenty-three German and a dozen or so Italian U-boats. For them the *Ocean Voyager*, loaded with 2,500 tons of high explosives, 3,000 tons of aviation spirit in drums, and 1,000 tons of military stores, and sailing unescorted at the speed of a horse-drawn carriage, presented a plum target.

Built in 1942 at the Todd shipyard in California, the 7,174-ton *Ocean Voyager* was one of a breed of wartime prefabricated vessels. At a time when the U-boats were sinking Allied merchant ships faster than they could normally be built, it was fortunate that the American yards were turning out these ships at fifty-day intervals. By virtue of this mass-production, the *Ocean Voyager* was even more basic than the average tramp of the depression years, having a square-shaped hull and a triple-expansion steam engine several sizes too small for her 7,000 tons. Her crew accommodation was so utilitarian that it missed contravening the requirements of the Merchant Shipping Act of 1894 by a hair's breadth. Owned by the Ministry of War Transport, she was managed by Hogarths of Glasgow, one of the largest privately owned tramp fleets in the world, whose roots went back to 1868.

In her favour, the *Ocean Voyager* was strongly built, and her crew of forty-four, mainly Scots, were typical of the men who ran Britain's tramp ships; resourceful and tenacious. Her armament consisted of an American-made 3-inch gun mounted aft, four 20 mm Oerlikons, and six machine-guns. These were manned by nine DEMS gunners drawn from the Royal Navy and Maritime Anti-Aircraft regiment. For the passage to Tripoli she also carried two military policemen, whose role was to guard the 3,000 bags of Army mail on board.

Having successfully run the gauntlet of the U-boats, the *Ocean Voyager* arrived off Tripoli in the late afternoon of 16 March. The port, which had spent much of its time in slumber since it was founded by the Phoenicians, was humming like a disturbed beehive, with all berths occupied by a motley fleet of cargo ships discharging weapons and stores for the advancing British troops. It was at first thought that the *Ocean Voyager* would have to wait outside the port, but an anchorage was eventually found for her inside the

172

breakwaters, cheek by jowl with a throng of tankers, ammunition ships and naval vessels.

As he looked around the forest of masts and derricks around him, Captain Mackellar could not suppress a feeling of unease. His ship was hemmed in on all sides, and since being reopened to Allied ships in early February, Tripoli had been the target of frequent and determined attacks by Axis bombers. In the event of such an attack occurring within the next few days, the *Ocean Voyager*, with her lethal mixture of ammunition and high octane below decks, could be trapped like a hobbled horse in a burning stable. If that time came, he hoped that he and his men would be equal to the situation.

The first night in port passed without incident, and on the morning of the 17th barges were placed alongside the *Ocean Voyager* for the off-loading of her vital cargo. All local shore labour had long since deserted the battered port, and Mackellar had the unenviable task of ordering his crew to discharge their own cargo. As in the case of all British merchant ships, there was a clause in the Articles of Agreement, signed by both officers and ratings of the *Ocean Voyager*, which called upon them to work cargo as and when required by the Master. Under normal circumstances it is a poor shipmaster who will attempt to heap this additional burden on his crew without good cause. In this case, there was no alternative, and the *Ocean Voyager*'s officers and ratings agreed to work the ship without argument. Their philosophy was typical of the British merchant seaman of the day, preferring to get on with the job, rather than debate the merits of the case. There would be time for that later.

Under the supervision of 29-year-old Chief Officer George Stronach, derricks were rigged, winches manned, and with officers and ratings working side by side, the discharging commenced. By late afternoon on the 19th some 1,700 tons had been swung into the barges alongside, a creditable performance given that these were men unused to handling cargo. Stronach had planned to work until dark that day, but heavy rain began to fall at 1700, and he was forced to call a halt. Having worked almost non-stop since 0600 that morning, the men were tired and dirty, and there were no protests when Stronach ordered them to go below to wash and

173

rest. He considered leaving a watch on deck to look out for enemy aircraft, but decided against this, as it seemed an unfair burden for those chosen for duty. The port had been free from air attack for several days, and it seemed reasonable to take a risk – just for that night. In any case, Stronach had been advised by the authorities ashore that the air raid alarm would be sounded at least fifteen minutes before any enemy aircraft arrived over the port, giving his men ample time to get to their action stations.

At that time, George Stronach and those ashore were unaware of two crucial developments. High above the clouds, and 200 miles to the north, a force of twelve Ju-88 bombers, heavily loaded with bombs, torpedoes and parachute mines, was winging its way towards Tripoli. Meanwhile, saboteurs in the port had succeeded in cutting the wires to the air raid sirens.

Forty-five minutes later, Stronach, having bathed and eaten a good meal, was half-dozing in his cabin, when the crash of the anti-aircraft batteries ashore opening up brought him abruptly awake. He reached the lower bridge just as the bombs came raining down out of the low-hanging clouds. The *Ocean Voyager* was hit four times in as many minutes, one bomb blasting her No. 2 hatch open, while two others exploded against the bridge front. Stronach was knocked off his feet by the shock waves, and lost consciousness. As he fell to the deck, a fourth bomb exploded in No. 5 hold.

Second Engineer Hezekiah Hotham, a 58-year-old Humberside man, was on watch in the *Ocean Voyager*'s engine-room when she reeled under the blast of the bomb salvo. The lights went out, and Hotham was left deafened and fumbling for his torch. With the firemen of the watch racing up the ladders ahead of him, he reached the deck to find the ship on fire fore and aft. Moving forward to investigate, he found the bridge accommodation completely wrecked and blazing furiously. The upper part of the bridge appeared to have collapsed into No. 2 hold, and flames were leaping from the hatchway. Hotham recalled the neat rows of 250 lb bombs he had seen resting on the drums of high octane in the hold and, in spite of the heat of the fires, broke out into a cold sweat. His instinct for survival urged him to make for the ship's side rail, and throw himself into the harbour before the ship blew herself apart. But that unexplainable loyalty every seaman feels for

174

his ship asserted itself, and he looked around for help. There was a chance that the fires could be fought and extinguished before the cataclysm came.

Luckily for George Stronach, the blast from the bombs that destroyed the bridge had thrown him underneath one of the lifeboats, where he had been sheltered from falling debris. When he regained consciousness, his body ached from multiple burns and bruises, one eye was closed, and his uniform was in tatters. Otherwise, he seemed to have escaped serious injury. He got unsteadily to his feet, and set out to explore the holocaust that was once his ship.

As Hotham had already discovered, the bridge house was a blazing inferno, part of it having fallen into No. 2 hold. The cargo in the hold was on fire, with the crack of exploding small-arms ammunition adding to the roar of the flames. In the rigging abreast the hatch, the wreckage of a German bomber which had crashed into the ship was still smouldering. Further forward, Stronach could see clouds of dense white smoke pouring from No. 1 hold, while abaft the bridge No. 3 hold was also belching forth smoke and flames.

The situation was as bad as it could possibly be, but Stronach, being a Glaswegian, was not in the habit of stepping aside from trouble. Picking his way through the wreckage, he made his way down to the main deck, where he met up with Hotham. No other crew members were to be seen, and the two officers decided that the loss of life caused by the enemy bombs must have been catastrophic. However, they were of one mind as to what should be done. Hotham volunteered to return to the deserted engine-room to speed up the deck water pumps. Stronach then went forward to No. 2 hatch and coupled up a fire hose, with the intention of tackling the fire below. His efforts came to nought, for the deck service lines were fractured and only trickle of water came from the hose. The flames from the hatchway were now shooting forty feet into the air, and the *Ocean Voyager*'s predicament was too awful to contemplate. It must surely be only a matter of time – minutes, perhaps – before the bombs in No. 2 hold were set off by the heat.

At that critical point, Stronach was relieved to see his senior petty officer, Boatswain Gardiner, appear out of the smoke. Like many others, Gardiner had been resting in his cabin after the day's work when the bombs fell. Pausing only to grip the boatswain's arm in encouragement, Stronach sent him below to help Hotham. If they were to stand any chance of saving the ship, they must have more pressure on the fire hydrants.

When Gardiner had disappeared below, Stronach threw down his waterless hose, and made his way quickly aft to No. 3 hatch, where the ship's foam generating equipment was stowed. His journey was in vain, as the equipment had been smashed by the bombs. Even to the tenacious Glaswegian, the situation now looked hopeless. The aviation spirit was well alight in all holds, and the rumble of exploding drums ran the length of the ship. Flames roared and crackled, accompanied by the crash of exploding shells, grenades and bullets. It was Dante's Inferno re-enacted, and Stronach decided it was high time to evacuate any of those who might still be alive. He began a search of the ship.

Right aft, in the crew's quarters, Stronach came upon sixteen older ratings sheltering in the alleyway. Many of them were bleeding from splinter wounds, and all were very frightened. He had great difficulty in persuading them to follow him on deck, but eventually was able to bring them out to No. 4 hatch, where the motor lifeboat, which had been used for communication with the shore, was still tied up alongside. At that moment, Gardiner re-appeared from the engine-room, and Stronach put him in charge of the lifeboat, instructing him to take the injured men to the nearest naval ship for medical attention.

Having satisfied himself that the boatswain had the evacuation in hand, Stronach made his way back to the boat deck, intending to lower the port lifeboat and secure it alongside ready to take off any other survivors he might find. He realised he would need to work quickly, fearing that at any moment the burning ship would explode.

As the *Ocean Voyager*'s lifeboat davits were of the geared quadrant type, Stronach was able to swing the boat out and lower it to the water single-handed. It was only when he had the boat in the water that he realised he was not alone on the boat deck. On the raised gun platform on the port side DEMS gunner Rutherford was still at his post, manning the Oerlikon and scanning the night sky for enemy planes. Either oblivious to, or contemptuous of, the falling bombs, Rutherford had been at his gun from the start of the attack, and was probably responsible for the shooting down of the enemy plane lodged in the *Ocean Voyager*'s rigging. He had no intention of deserting his post, and waved aside the Chief Officer's invitation to take to the boat.

Stronach had no time to waste in persuading the gunner to leave the ship. He dropped down onto the main deck, and went back amidships, continuing his search for survivors. The heat from the leaping flames was searing his bare skin, and he stopped near No. 3 hatch to soak the remaining rags of his clothes with the trickle of water he was able to coax from the deck hydrant. Then he made a run for the bridge accommodation.

The devastation was even worse than Stronach had imagined, the whole of the bridge house having collapsed on itself. He hesitated, and weighed up the situation. It seemed certain that no one could still be alive in the tangled, smoking ruin that had once housed the *Ocean Voyager*'s deck officers, but he felt driven to confirm this. After several attempts, he finally forced his way into the officers' bathroom, where his persistence was rewarded when he found Second Officer Morris lying on the deck unconscious. Morris, who had obviously been taking a bath when the bombs fell, was naked, his face was covered in blood, and he had serious burns about his body. At first, Stronach feared he was dead, but he found a pulse, and then dragged the unconscious man clear of the wreckage, and out onto the deck. By that time, Morris had regained consciousness, and was able gasp out that others were still trapped in the accommodation. Stronach went back to investigate.

Flames from the inferno raging in No. 2 hold were now threatening to engulf the blackened shell of the bridge house, and Stronach, courageous though he was, realised it would serve no useful purpose to throw away his own life by entering the accommodation again. Then he heard faint groans coming from the outboard alleyway on the port side, and clawed his way through the fallen debris until he found Chief Engineer James Anderson trapped half in and half out of a cabin porthole. Anderson, who was clearly in terrible pain, explained that the bulkheads of the cabin had fallen in, trapping both his legs, and while attempting to escape through the porthole, the heavy steel deadlight had fallen on his back, and he was unable to move.

The Chief was a big man, and Stronach, choking on the black smoke, and seared by the flames leaping around him, had great difficulty in extricating him. Somehow – he never did quite understand how he succeeded – he levered up the heavy deadlight, prised the groaning Anderson out of the porthole, and lowered him, none too gently, to the deck. He then dragged him aft to No. 3 hatch, where he had left the semi-conscious Morris. He then tied a rope around Anderson's waist, and prepared to lower him over the side into the boat. But Stronach's own strength was now failing, and he was unable to lift the engineer over the rail. Rutherford, who was still manning his Oerlikon, and firing whenever an enemy plane came into his sights, saw the Chief Officer's difficulty, and left his post to lend a hand. Hotham appeared on deck at the same time, and between them the three men lowered the two injured men into the waiting boat. Stronach then instructed Rutherford to take the boat to safety.

By now, the situation in the harbour was becoming almost as bad as it was on board the burning *Ocean Voyager*. The bombs were still falling, and a small Greek tanker anchored nearby had been sunk, and was spewing blazing petrol onto the water. Into this roaring furnace three German bombers then crashed, adding to the horror of the night. Much of the surface of the water in the harbour was ablaze, and the flames were drifting purposefully towards the *Ocean Voyager*.

While George Stronach had been engaged in his gallant rescue attempts on board, Boatswain Gardiner was faced with the unenviable task of taking his lifeboat and its sixteen injured and frightened passengers away from the ship. He was unable to find the key to start the boat's engine, and he was forced to calm the men, and persuade them to ship the oars. This he eventually did – assisted, no doubt, by the fire raging on three sides of the boat. The men wanted to row to a nearby American ship, which had so far escaped the bombs, but Gardiner knew this ship was also loaded with ammunition, and had no intention of boarding her. After some argument, Gardiner's wisdom prevailed, and the men rowed in some semblance of unison towards a British destroyer, which took them on board. The wounded were given medical attention, and hot drinks and dry clothing appeared as if by magic.

But the night of agony was not yet over for these survivors. Half an hour after their rescue, the destroyer was hit by an aerial torpedo, and began to sink. Fortunately, there were now plenty of small craft at hand, and the *Ocean Voyager*'s men were taken off and landed ashore.

Back aboard the blazing ship, Stronach and Hotham continued their search for survivors. They were particularly concerned for Captain Mackellar, who had not been seen since the first bombs fell. Returning amidships, they made determined efforts to penetrate the bridge accommodation, but were forced back by debris, flames and smoke. They were finally forced to agree that if Mackellar was lying somewhere under the wreckage he was either dead, or would die soon, for there was no way they could reach him.

There was no good reason why Stronach and Hotham should not take steps to safeguard their own lives, but they were both stubborn men, and had their minds set on making one last effort to save the ship. Hotham volunteered to return to the engine-room in the hope that he would be able to increase the pressure on the deck service water, and while he awaited developments, Stronach carried on looking for survivors. It was then that, in the orange light of the dancing flames, he came across the body of Captain Duncan Mackellar lying on the port side of the deck. Mackellar's injuries were extensive, and he had most probably been killed outright by the exploding bombs. There was nothing more Stronach could do for him, other than say a silent goodbye.

Crossing to the starboard side of the deck, Stronach continued his search, and found Third Radio Officer Frankland lying in the scuppers. A quick examination showed Frankland to have severe head injuries and a broken leg, but he was still alive. Slipping his arms under the wounded man's shoulders, Stronach dragged him towards the ship's side. It was then that he saw a life-raft, paddled by two more survivors, just pulling away. He persuaded the men to come back alongside, and Frankland was put aboard.

At Stronach's back, the fire in No. 3 hold had reached a spectacular peak, with smoke and flames billowing from the hatchway accompanied by the crack of exploding ammunition. The bulkheads of the hold were glowing white-hot, and as that hold contained a quantity of 1,000 lb bombs, Stronach reluctantly concluded that it was time to go. He went to the top of the engine-room, and called to Hotham to come up on deck.

Before abandoning the ship Stronach made one last round of the decks. His persistence was rewarded when he stumbled over Greaser O'Shay, who was lying unconscious on the starboard side of the after deck. O'Shay was badly burned, but still alive. When Hotham arrived on deck, the two men carried the greaser to the ship's side, only to find that the last life-raft had drifted away. The *Ocean Voyager* was now blazing furiously from stem to stern, and time was running out for the three men left alive on board. Stronach and Hotham hurriedly tied a lifejacket on O'Shay, and un-ceremoniously threw him over the side. It was the only way to give the unconscious man a chance to live.

Stronach then dived into the sea, and swam after the dis-appearing raft. When he clambered aboard, he found that the two very demoralised occupants had lost their paddles. He wasted no time in commiserating, and bullied the men into paddling with their hands towards a burning lighter. Stronach was aware that the lighter had on board ammunition discharged from the *Ocean Voyager* earlier in the day, but he desperately needed some means of propelling the raft, and planks of dunnage wood on the deck of the lighter were all there was within reach. He finally put the raft alongside, boarded the lighter, and despite the heat and flames, rummaged around until he found pieces of wood suitable for use as paddles. He then took the raft back to the ship, where Hezekiah Hotham was taken off, and O'Shay pulled out of the water.

The burning oil on the water of the harbour was now closing in around them, while smoking debris rained down on their heads from the erupting holds of their ship. Fear lent strength to their arms, and they paddled clear of the oncoming flames, and out into the darkness of the smokescreen which had been laid across the harbour to confuse the enemy bombers. For the next half hour they wandered aimlessly through the thick, black fog looking for safety. The indomitable Stronach used his whistle to signal for help, and at last a naval launch, which had been patrolling the perimeter of the burning oil, came to their rescue. The six men were put ashore at 2030, the injured rushed to hospital, and the others accommodated at the Merchant Navy Club about a mile from the harbour.

It would seem that, for George Stronach and Hezekiah Hotham the long Mediterranean nightmare had come to an end, and that they would now be able to enjoy the sleep of the just. But the *Ocean Voyager* had not finished with those who had tried so hard to save her. A little before midnight, she blew herself apart with an explosion so great that the blast wave partly demolished the Merchant Navy Club a mile inland. Stronach and Hotham were rudely jerked out of their exhausted sleep, and spent the next few hours digging out one of the *Ocean Voyager*'s firemen, who had been trapped by a falling wall.

When daylight came, there was little to be seen of the *Ocean Voyager*. Parts of her bow and stern lay half-submerged off the quay, but most of her remains were scattered all over the harbour and town. One of her boilers, crushed like a huge tin can, was found more than two miles from the wreck. A number of ships in the harbour had suffered damage from her flying debris.

The reckoning in human terms of the bombing of the *Ocean Voyager* made grim reading. Captain Duncan Mackellar had been killed outright, and Greaser O'Shay later died of his burns. Four men, Third Officer Norman Wright, First Radio Officer Samuel Smyth, Chief Steward Percy Appleton and one of the military policemen were missing, and twelve others were injured. Undoubtedly, had it not been for the efforts of Chief Officer George Stronach, Second Engineer Hezekiah Hotham, Boatswain Gardiner and Gunner Rutherford, many more would have lost their lives. Stronach, badly burned and bruised, with splinters in one eye which rendered him partially blind, had throughout shown magnificent leadership and stubborn courage in the finest Nelsonian tradition. Hotham was to say of him: 'I would like to place on record a tribute to Chief Officer G.P. Stronach, who displayed exceptional courage in remaining on board to rescue so many survivors, who would otherwise have lost their lives. His cool bravery in the face of overwhelming odds was outstanding, and throughout he was under the impression that he was doing nothing more than his duty. Despite the almost incredible feats which he performed, his only fear was that he had perhaps not done enough.' Boatswain Gardiner had this to say: 'There is no doubt at all that Chief Officer Stronach displayed incredible heroism in remaining on this blazing inferno for such a long time, fully knowing that the ship was likely to blow up at any minute. Many of the ship's personnel owe their lives to his cool courage, fortitude and complete disregard for his own personal safety.'

Hezekiah Hotham, although he was nearing his sixtieth year, on that awful night had showed the bulldog-like determination and casual bravery that have been characteristic of British Merchant Navy engineer officers for generations. Chief Officer Stronach put on record: 'Although aged fifty-eight, this officer displayed magnificent courage and initiative such as is not generally found, even in younger men. Without his untiring help, it would have been physically impossible to have rescued any survivors. I consider his gallant action in going into the engine-room and staying there to attend to the pumps was truly magnificent, as he was fully aware of the many and extreme dangers, including that of a major explosion, which might have occurred at any moment.' Stronach's praise of Gunner Rutherford was no less generous: 'The gallantry and cool bearing of DEMS Gunner R. Rutherford were also magnificent and inspiring. After all the younger members of the crew had jumped overboard, he went to his gun and continued to repel the attack completely unaided. His unselfish action and complete disregard for his own personal safety were a wonderful example to all and were in accordance with the highest traditions of the Service to which he belongs.'

The *Ocean Voyager* was barely a year off the slipway when the catastrophic explosion ripped her apart in Tripoli harbour on the night of 19 March 1943, but she and her men did not die in vain. Other ships followed close in her wake, loaded to their marks with sufficient ammunition and supplies for Montgomery's army to keep up the momentum of its advance.

On 12 May, having been driven onto the Cape Bon peninsula with their backs to the sea, 240,415 German and Italian troops laid down their arms. The final battle of the Western Desert had been won.

Chapter Sixteen

Appointment off Minicoy

In early September 1943, the Indian Ocean, sometime haunt of Henry Every, William Kidd, and a host of their piratical contemporaries, was once more a place full of dangers for the lone merchantman. Throughout the preceding months of the year, a wide-ranging force of enemy submarines, estimated to be seven German and eight Japanese, had reaped a rich harvest amongst those whose paths crossed this lonely sea. Of the increased number of Allied ships bringing supplies to India for the planned re-entry into Burma by Lord Louis Mountbatten's forces, at least fifty-seven, totalling 337,169 tons gross, had been sent to the bottom. The Royal Navy, which had kept the peace in the area for centuries past, was strenuously engaged elsewhere, and could spare only a handful of old cruisers and armed merchantmen for convoy escort duty. It was inevitable, therefore, that many merchant ships were left to fend for themselves. One such unfortunate was the 5,150-ton *Larchbank*.

Owned by Andrew Weir & Company of London, and built on the Clyde in 1925 by Harland & Wolf, the *Larchbank* was a solidly-built, twin-screw motorship designed for extended voyages, and therefore geared to self-sufficiency. In her younger days, she had managed a steady 12 knots, but age and the rigours of the trade had long reduced her to a laborious plod that rarely exceeded 10 knots. Under the command of Captain William McCracken, she was crewed by nineteen British officers and forty Lascar ratings. Added to her normal complement for the duration were ten DEMS gunners, and on her current voyage, two Royal Navy petty officers 'on special assignment', and five Lascar seamen taking passage back to India following the loss of their own ship. This gave her a total complement of seventy-six.

The *Larchbank* had loaded in the American east coast port of .Baltimore for Calcutta, and carried several thousand tons of railway iron, four tanks, two amphibian trucks, various military stores and, on deck, two motor torpedo boats, the latter in the care of the RN petty officers.

Thirty days out of Baltimore, the *Larchbank* left Aden on 1 September, bound for Colombo, where she would bunker before continuing her voyage to Calcutta. Her route lay through the Gulf of Aden to a position close northward of the forbidding island of Socotra, thence through the seventy-mile-wide channel between the Laccadive and Maldive Islands, and so south-east to Colombo. With the South-West Monsoon still blowing, the weather for much of the 2,000-mile passage was likely to be anything but favourable. As soon as she drew clear of the Horn of Africa, the *Larchbank* could expect to be beam-on to the strong south-westerly winds and rough seas generated by the deep summer depression lying over northern India. A predominantly overcast sky, with frequent heavy rain squalls would give little opportunity for sun or star sights, reducing navigation to the realms of educated guesswork. In the season, even in times of peace, the passage was rarely an enjoyable one; with German and Japanese submarines known to be active, it appeared less attractive still. Making, at best, 10 knots, the *Larchbank* would be extremely vulnerable throughout. Granted, she was well armed, mounting a 4-inch, a 12-pounder and five Oerlikons, and her ten DEMS gunners were highly trained, but as Captain McCracken was aware, all this considerable firepower would be useless against a submerged U-boat.

One thousand miles to the east, deep in the Arabian Sea, the Japanese submarine I-27 cruised hopefully under a grey, rain-laden sky. In the conning tower, her commander, Toshiaki Fukumura, braced himself as the trimmed-down boat buried her bows in yet another huge comber, and rose again, streaming water like a half-tide rock. The strain of the long patrol was beginning to show on Fukumura's normally impassive face. I-27 was running short of

184

fuel and provisions, and ominous cracks were appearing in the morale of his well-disciplined crew. Since the sinking of the 6,797-ton American freighter *Alcoa Prospector* in the Gulf of Oman two months back, the horizon had remained empty of suitable targets. Fukumura was reaching the point where he would gladly have wasted one of his precious torpedoes on any down-at-heel Arab dhow in the interest of breaking the awful monotony of the patrol. Yet, such was his luck, he had failed to flush out as much as a fishing canoe.

On the evening of Thursday 9 September, the *Larchbank* was in the vicinity of Minicoy Island, a low, sandy atoll which marks the northern end of the Eight Degree Channel, one of the deep-water routes through the Maldive chain. She was just over 400 miles from Colombo, having crossed the Arabian Sea without molestation.

Soon after 2000, Second Engineer Pain and Junior Fourth Engineer Goodall emerged from the engine-room with their white boilersuits grimy and soaked in sweat. The four-hour watch they had just completed below in temperatures in excess of 100° F had been the equivalent of a sustained Turkish bath. Stopping only to pick up two cups of tea and a plate of sandwiches at the pantry, the two men moved out onto the after deck, grateful for the touch of the cool evening air on their clammy bodies. It was a fine, clear night, with – for the first time since leaving Aden – the heavy clouds having cleared away to reveal the tropical night sky studded with a million twinkling stars.

Pain and Goodall settled themselves side by side on the tarpaulin-covered hatch-top to watch the new moon rise, sipping at the hot, strong tea, and biting with relish into the cold beef sandwiches. No words passed between them, but their thoughts were in tune. It was at a time like this that all the hardship and discomfort involved in life at sea seemed suddenly worthwhile. No man safe on shore could ever experience such blessed peace and contentment at the end of a day's work.

The silver crescent moon was only a hand's breadth above the horizon, when the two watchkeepers were joined by Captain McCracken and Chief Engineer James Ford, who were also sampling the pleasant night air. For ten minutes or so the four men chatted amiably, the main topic of their conversation being the shore-going attractions offered by the port of Colombo, where McCracken estimated they would arrive at noon on Saturday. On this occasion, the engineers would be fully occupied taking bunkers during the short stay in port, but they had memories enough of Mount Lavinia, the Galle Face Hotel, and other less salubrious haunts. Colombo was a good place for a run ashore.

At about 2030, the little group split up, McCracken and Ford to continue their walk, Pain and Goodall going to their respective cabins. After a quick shower in tepid water, 34-year-old Douglas Goodall turned in on top of his bunk wearing only a pair of shorts. The temperature in the tiny cabin was only marginally less than in the engine-room, over which it was situated. Before dropping off into an uneasy sleep, Goodall's thoughts turned to his wife Elizabeth and their small house overlooking the Firth of Forth. Drowsily, he wondered if the soft rain was falling there now as it had been on the day he left. Or was the sun shining down out of a clear autumn sky, turning the normally steel-grey waters of the forth to an inviting blue? It had been that way when they first met. How many more months would it be before he saw Elizabeth and Scotland again?

Out in the darkness of the night on the *Larchbank*'s port side, the ghostly shape of I-27 glided through the water unseen, as Toshiaki Fukumura continued his patient search for another victim. Fukumura's long-standing frustration had not been eased by a disastrous encounter with an American merchantman, the 7,176-ton *Lyman Stewart*, forty-eight hours earlier. Of the five torpedoes fired at the freighter, only one had hit – and that proved to be a dud. Fukumura had then surfaced, and opened fire with his deck gun, but could inflict only minor damage on the ship before she escaped. He had caught up with the elusive American again in the early hours of that morning, but once more his attack failed miserably. The *Lyman Stewart* had gone on her way virtually unharmed, leaving Fukumura and his crew suffering from severe loss of face.

On the *Larchbank*'s bridge, Third Officer Bockam, officer of the watch, haunted the port wing, his eyes straining to pierce the darkness ahead. The night was quiet, disturbed only by the muted thump of the ship's two 6-cylinder diesels and the creaking of her derricks in their crutches as she rolled in a heavy swell. The stand-by quartermaster moved into the shadows of the wheelhouse to strike four bells. Ten o'clock, halfway through the watch. Having listened to the bells repeated by the lookout man on the forecastle head, indicating he was still awake, Bockam decided it was time to break the monotony of the watch with a cup of tea. He took a last look around the horizon before retiring to the chartroom – and suddenly froze. Crossing the ship's bow close ahead, moving swiftly from port to starboard, was a long, phosphorescent trail. It might be only be a cruising porpoise, but Bockam was not prepared to speculate. He lunged for the alarm button – and as he did so, a second line of bubbles came racing in towards the *Larchbank*'s port side. This time, Fukumura's torpedo did not fail to explode.

Douglas Goodall awoke from his fitful sleep with the crash of the exploding torpedo ringing in his ears. He shot bolt upright in his bunk, dazed and wondering if it was another of those horrendous nightmares that so often haunt those who lived and slept cheek by jowl with violent death in that awful war. Then, the ship shuddered violently, and the air was filled with the stench of burning oil. Goodall realised that this was no bad dream, but stark reality.

He rolled clear of his bunk, and with an instinctive reaction romantics might make much of, reached for the framed photograph of his wife that lived on the chest of drawers alongside the bunk. As he did so, the ship lurched heavily to starboard, and the photograph slid off the polished top of the chest, to fall with a splintering of glass on the deck. Aware that, if he were to save his life, he had no time to waste, Goodall struggled into his lifejacket, falling against the bulkhead, and then out into the alleyway as the *Larchbank* gave another lurch.

The alleyway was awash, but the lights were still on, and Goodall was relieved to find himself in the company of Chief Engineer Ford and two engineers of the 8 to 12 watch, who had just evacuated the engine-room. Having ascertained from the watchkeepers that the ship had been torpedoed on the port side, in way of No. 4 and No. 5 holds, Ford led the way on deck. As they passed the engine-room door, he paused to pull the emergency stops of the main engine fuel valves. Following the Chief and the others, Goodall

187

tripped over the bodies of two officers lying in the alleyway, but dared not stop to identify them.

The after deck of the *Larchbank* resembled a battlefield; derricks were broken and bent, and hatchways stripped of their boards and tarpaulins. The motor torpedo boat stowed on top of No. 4 hatch was hanging drunkenly over the side, secured only by a few frayed lashings. A red glow emanated from the open holds, and the ominous crackling of flames could be heard from below. The plates of the main deck were awash with cascading, foaming water.

The four engineers scrambled up the ladder to the boat deck, where they separated, the watchkeepers going to their station on the starboard side, Goodall and Ford to the port, forward lifeboat. There they found the Deck Serang and one of the Lascar seamen in the act of lowering the boat, which was fully manned. Ford ordered the two Indians into the boat, and he and Goodall took over the falls.

The boat was safely lowered to the water, but owing to the heavy swell running its occupants were unable to release the after fall block. As they struggled, the boat lifted on the swell until it was level with the boat deck. When the swell subsided again, the boat was left hanging bow-down, suspended by the after fall. Ford and Goodall watched helpless as the Lascars fought in vain to clear the jammed block. The next swell smashed the hanging boat against the ship's side, breaking it in two, and spilling the screaming men into the dark, angry water below.

Horror-stricken, the two engineers raced to the after end of the deck with the intention of jumping over the side, for it was clear that the *Larchbank* would not stay afloat for many more minutes. They stood at the rail, hesitating, for neither man could swim. Then the decision was made for them, when a wall of green water slammed against the ship's side, surged upwards, and swept them off their feet.

Goodall ended up in the starboard scuppers, and before he could regain his feet, the *Larchbank* gave a slow roll, and slid beneath the waves, taking him with her.

Fortunately, Goodall did not panic, but held his breath as he went down and down into the gloomy depths, drawn by the powerful suction of the sinking ship. He had always scoffed at tales of dying men seeing the events of their lives flashing before their eyes, but that was exactly what he experienced now. At last, when his lungs were on the point of bursting, the *Larchbank* released her hold on him, and he shot to the surface. Luckily, he came up close to a packing case, which supported him while he regained his breath. The sea around him was covered in floating wreckage, and where the *Larchbank* had been, there remained above water only her fore-topmast, on which a red light still shone eerily. Then, that too was gone, as the broken ship began her last journey into the depths.

The new moon was now high in the sky, and casting sufficient light for Goodall to see a small life-raft bobbing on the waves twenty yards away. Being unable to swim, the engineer was reluctant to relinquish his hold on the packing case, but the raft beckoned temptingly. After hesitating for a moment or two, he kicked clear of the case, and paddled furiously across the intervening stretch of water. When he reached the raft and dragged himself aboard, he was completely exhausted. But he had little time to dwell on his physical state, for he heard shouts close by. He was soon helping aboard the raft the *Larchbank*'s engine-room serang and one of her sailors.

For the next hour, the three men lay side by side on the heaving raft, miserable, but glad to be alive. Then the sound of paddles was heard, and a larger life-raft came into sight. On board were Third Radio Officer Glendenning, Chief Motor Mechanic John Ives, one of the petty officers in charge of the MTBs the *Larchbank* had carried, a deck apprentice, and two more Lascar seamen. It was decided to lash the two rafts together, and they lay drifting side by side to await the coming of daylight.

With dawn on the 10th came a strong south-westerly wind, which quickly whipped up an angry sea. By 0800, it had become so rough that the rope joining the two rafts snapped, and they drifted apart. Douglas Goodall and his two companions were alone again.

Noon brought fresh hope. One of the *Larchbank*'s lifeboats, containing Chief Engineer James Ford and twenty-three other men, drifted into view. Ford, who had spent two hours into the water after the ship sank, brought the boat alongside Goodall's raft, and they were later joined by the other raft. Assembled, it would seem, were the only survivors of the sinking of the *Larchbank,* seven officers, one RN petty officer, three DEMS ratings, and twenty-two Indian seamen. Forty-three men, including Captain McCracken and all his deck officers, were missing.

The lifeboat was overcrowded, it had lost its rudder, and its engine was out of action due to being under water. It was, in fact, no more seaworthy than the two rafts. James Ford, being the senior surviving officer, decided that as the three craft were unable to help each other, it would be best to split up, each then making the best possible progress to the east, where the land lay. It was agreed that whoever was picked up or reached the land first would send help for the others. Within minutes of parting, they had lost sight of each other in the troughs of the swell.

Junior Fourth Engineer Douglas Goodall, unexpectedly finding himself elevated to command, albeit of a tiny wooden life-raft, resolved to do his utmost to bring his craft and her crew of two to safety. He was realist enough to accept that the *Larchbank* had gone down so quickly that there could have been no time to send an SOS, and that no rescue ship or aircraft was likely to be searching for them. The only route to safety lay due east, over 200 miles of rough seas to the coast of India. As the raft's only means of propulsion was by paddle, this would be no mean feat. They would, however, be aided by the South-West Monsoon drift current, which at that time of the year, although weak, flowed eastwards. Goodall, being an engineer, was not aware of the current's existence, but what he lacked in knowledge he made up for in determination.

When he came to examine the meagre resources at his disposal, Goodall's confidence received a severe shock. The underside of the raft had been damaged when it floated clear of the ship, resulting in the puncturing of one of its two fresh water tanks, the contents of which were polluted by sea water. The other tank had lost water through evaporation, or some other means, and contained no more than four pints. In the food tank, Goodall found one pound of biscuits, one tin of chocolate, two six-ounce tins of pemmican, and one tin of malted milk tablets. With careful rationing, the food should last the three of them for many days, but the lack of drinking

190

water would be a critical factor in their fight for survival. There was some comfort to be found in the raft's gear locker, which yielded a canvas weather screen and stanchions, three sleeping bags, a torch, a tin of red distress flares, two measuring spoons, and four graduated drinking cups. After some deliberation, Goodall set the daily ration for each man at one ounce of water, three malted milk tablets, two biscuits, and one spoonful of pemmican. He hoped that this would ensure their survival for at least twenty days. If they had not been picked up or reached the land by then, they would escape through death.

It was not physically possible for three men to paddle the raft continuously, so Goodall allocated specific hours during daylight for this. He had no means of measuring what progress they were making, but, using the sun as a guide, he endeavoured to keep the raft on an easterly course. The days passed slowly and monotonously, with the small raft rising and falling uncomfortably on the interminable swell. Goodall kept an account of the passing of the days by scratching a mark for each sunrise on one of the boards of the raft. On the fourth day it rained, and using the canvas screen, they collected half a gallon of water, thus doubling their chance of survival.

By 19 September, when they had been ten days adrift, it became apparent to Goodall that his rationing of the provisions had not been strict enough. There remained only three pieces of chocolate, the pemmican, biscuits and malted milk tablets having all been consumed. Goodall then suggested to his fellow survivors that they attempt to catch some of the small fish that swam around the raft. The Indians were not enthusiastic, grumbling that they had neither fishing tackle nor bait. Goodall was not deterred. In his youth, he had spent many a happy hour 'tickling' trout in the Scottish burns, patiently coaxing the speckled fish against the bank, and into his hand. Lying face down on the raft – just as he had done on the banks of a stream in his schooldays – he succeeded in trapping one of the small tropical fish against the side of the raft, and with a dexterity born of desperation, scooped it on board. He quickly followed this with another, then using a scrap of empty biscuit tin, he skinned the fish and cut them into small pieces. The Indians at first refused to eat, fearing that they might be poisoned. When

Goodall demonstrated that the raw fish was harmless, even palatable, they joined the feast with the enthusiasm of starving men at a laden table.

On the following day, Goodall caught six more fish, and found they were less salty if boned and dried in the sun. From then on, he provided daily meals from the sea for all, but the water was running short. To add to their troubles, a number of large sharks had begun to follow the raft, perhaps sensing that the three men were growing weaker. As the days passed, the ugly predators – Goodall counted nine of the brutes – grew bolder, and attacked the raft, seeking to overturn it. As their craft had only a few inches of freeboard, this was a frightening experience for the survivors. At night, the sharks changed their tactics, swimming close to the raft and slamming the water with their tails, so that the occupants were constantly lashed by spray. The obvious intent was to wear the survivors down by keeping them wet, miserable and sleepless. It was a ploy that might have worked, had it not been for the defiant Douglas Goodall, who fought the sharks off with a weather screen stanchion, and persuaded the others to join him. But their evil tormentors never gave up.

It rained again on the night of the 22nd, enabling the men to quench their raging thirst, and to collect sufficient water to last a few more days. Throughout, Goodall had kept the fresh water ration at one ounce per man per day, which was barely enough to wet their parched throats, but just sufficient to sustain life. It was fortunate that the weather was humid, for they perspired little, and so preserved their bodily fluids.

A moment of ecstatic hope came on the morning of the 23rd, when a ship was sighted. But although Goodall burned red distress flares, she sheered off, and steamed away. The men on the heaving raft were near to tears with disappointment and frustration, but Goodall did not allow them to give up hope. This first sighting of a ship must mean that, at long last, they were in the shipping lane, and others might follow in its wake.

Goodall's hopes were not realised. For three long days and nights no ship came in sight. Only the persistent sharks kept company with the three emaciated men who sprawled listlessly on their tiny floating prison. Then, at sunset on the 26th, the roar of aircraft engines was heard, and a Sunderland flying boat was seen skimming low over the water. The survivors were roused from their stupor and galvanised into frantic action. They burned flares, waved and shouted until they were hoarse, but the giant aircraft flew past without deviating. As the raft must have been directly in the rays of the setting sun, Goodall concluded it was unlikely they had been spotted.

The night that followed was one of sheer misery, for although the weather had improved considerably, the number of sharks cruising around the raft had increased to more than a dozen, nine of which were very large and menacing. During the dark hours, the assaults on the raft grew more frequent and frenzied. It was as though the predators sensed that they were about to be cheated of their prey. Next morning, it seemed that the sharks' fears might be realised, for a ship appeared over the horizon to the north. With his heart thumping, Goodall fumbled one of the last remaining flares out of the tin, ignited it, and held it high above his head, while the others waved and shouted like madmen. They all cheered when the ship altered course towards them, and Goodall set off more flares, but their hopes were crushed when she veered away, ignoring their signals. The ship was soon hull-down on the southern horizon, zig-zagging blissfully towards her destination.

Douglas Goodall, by now hardened to disappointment, was determined not to let despair get the better of him. For as long as he was able to catch fish – now the survivors' only source of food – and for as long as the water held out, there was still hope. The water posed the greater problem, for it had not rained for five days, and they were down to less than one pint between the three of them. As it turned out, five more days were to pass without rain or any further sign that help was at hand. When, on the afternoon of 2 October, another ship was sighted to the north, and heading towards them, Goodall was certain they must now be directly in the path of ships using the Indian coastal shipping lanes. There were no more distress flares left, and he made a crude signal flag from a paddle and a scrap of canvas. When the ship came near, he waved his flag vigorously, and continued to do so

193

for the next hour. It was to no avail. The ship again sailed past, completely ignoring them.

The two Indians had now reached the point where, through physical weakness, thirst, and sheer disappointment, they had lost all will to continue the struggle. But Douglas Goodall refused to admit defeat. When the ship was out of sight, he balanced himself erect on the raft, and searched all round the horizon. To his great relief, he saw another vessel coming in from the west, coming their way. He goaded the others into taking up the paddles to keep the raft in the path of the approaching ship, and took up his improvised flag again. After what seemed like an age, the ship, a large four-masted cargo vessel, was seen to alter towards them. She was soon abreast the raft, with her crew lining the rails and cheering. A voice boomed out from her bridge, 'All right, lads! We will stop and pick you up.' These were the sweetest words Goodall had ever heard. With a triumphant cry, he hurled his flag at the still circling sharks, and sat down on the raft, his mind at ease for the first time in twenty-three days.

The Danish motor vessel *Panama* launched a lifeboat, and half an hour later Goodall and the two Indian seamen were on board the ship being welcomed by her master, Captain Frederiksen. Their raging thirst was first slaked, then they were provided with hot baths, clothing, and food in plenty. That night, they slept the sleep of the exhausted between clean, cool sheets. Characteristically, Douglas Goodall's last thought before dropping off was that he would soon be able to return to sea in a ship of his own. The sudden loss of the *Larchbank* and the twenty-three days of hell he had endured had not broken his spirit.

As to the rest of the *Larchbank* survivors, the six men on the larger raft had already been picked up by the Norwegian ship *Tahsinia* off Colombo on the morning of 27 September. Chief Engineer James Ford and the twenty-three men in the disabled lifeboat had landed on the Indian coast on the night of the 28th. In all, thirty-three men survived the sinking of the *Larchbank*, but one of them, a Lascar seaman, died after arrival in Colombo.

Toshiaki Fukumura shifted his hunting ground to the Gulf of Aden for a while after torpedoing the *Larchbank*, and there he sank four more ships. Six months later, on the afternoon of 12 February

1944, I-27 was patrolling to the west of the Maldive Islands, when she sighted a small convoy.

Convoy KR 8, nearing the end of its 2,500-mile passage from Mombasa to Colombo, was steaming in three columns of two ships. In the van, ziz-zagging wide on each bow, were the British destroyers *Petard* and *Paladin,* who had joined that morning, while the ocean escort, the ageing cruiser HMS *Hawkins,* had dropped back to a less demanding role as lead ship of the port column. The Indian Ocean was on its best behaviour, with a light north-easterly breeze, blue sky and unlimited visibility; ideal for the sunbather, but dangerously benign for a convoy of KR 8's calibre. The five merchant ships, under the direction of the Convoy Commodore in the 7,513-ton *Khedive Ismail*, were all packed with troops. They were fat, sitting ducks, wandering across the oily swells at a very vulnerable 13 knots.

Unaware of the importance of his targets, Fukumura began painstakingly to manoeouvre I-27 into position for an attack.

From the open bridge of HMS *Petard,* out on the starboard bow of the convoy, the Officer of the Watch searched ahead with his binoculars, the hot sun beating down on his back. Thoughts of tall, ice-frosted glasses on the terrace of Colombo's Galle Face Hotel were high in his mind when he turned aft to cast an eye over the convoy. His idle thoughts vanished when he caught sight of the periscope breaking the surface astern and to starboard of the serenely sailing merchant ships.

Petard's alarm gongs were already shattering the peace of the afternoon when two torpedoes slammed into the side of the *Khedive Ismail*, sending twin columns of dirty water and debris soaring skywards. The trooper, which had a total complement of 1,590, including sixty-one Army Nurses and twenty-six WRNS on board, heeled drunkenly over to starboard, and within two minutes had sunk stern-first.

With *Hawkins* giving cover, the remainder of the convoy scattered to the east, while *Petard* and *Paladin* raced in to attack with depth charges. They were too late, for without waiting to observe the result of his torpedoes, Fukumura had immediately dived deep. There followed a long cat-and-mouse game, with the two destroyers patiently stalking the enemy submarine, from time to time dashing in to drop patterns of depth charges, and churning the once-placid ocean into an angry battlefield. But Fukumura was a wily foe, and after an hour the escorts lost all contact.

The Senior Officer Escort, in HMS *Hawkins*, was by now becoming concerned for the safety of the other troopships, and signalled *Paladin* to rejoin him, leaving *Petard* to continue the search for the enemy. On her way back to the convoy, *Paladin* lowered her boats near the wreckage-strewn area marking the end of the *Khedive Ismail*, and proceeded to pick up survivors. Of the 1,590 on board, only 201 men and 6 women were rescued from the water alive.

After carrying out a wide sweep to the westwards that yielded no trace of the enemy, *Petard* returned to assist *Paladin* in the rescue work. While both ships were thus engaged, a large bubble of air welled to the surface close north-westwards of the wreckage. This might merely have been air escaping from the sunken ship; on the other hand, a submarine blowing her tanks would produce a similar effect.

Petard immediately broke away from the rescue operation, and began sweeping with her Asdic in the vicinity of the bubble. No contact was made, but the destroyer persisted, searching in ever-widening circles. *Petard*'s commander was on the point of taking her back to the convoy when, with a great gush of compressed air, I-27 suddenly surfaced 1½ miles off the destroyer's starboard quarter.

By this time, *Paladin* had recovered all survivors of the *Khedive Ismail*, and was already steaming to assist *Petard* in the search. With the Japanese submarine on the surface, and apparently stopped, both destroyers raced in to attack with all guns blazing. *Petard*, being closest to the enemy, made a run across her stern, hurling depth charges set to explode at 50 feet from her port thrower. These seemed to have no noticeable effect on the submarine.

I-27 was now under way, and some of her crew could be seen scrambling from her conning tower, obviously intending to man the 5-inch deck gun. Fukumura did not intend to give up without a fight. But the heavy machine-guns of the attacking destroyers cut his gunners down before they reached their gun.

It was then that the attack went seriously wrong for the British ships. While *Petard* moved away from the surfaced submarine in order to bring her guns to bear, an over-enthusiastic *Paladin* closed in on the enemy at high speed, signalling that she intended to ram. *Petard*'s commander, the senior officer on the spot, considered ramming too drastic and potentially dangerous an action to take at this point, and signalled *Paladin* to hold back. His signal was received too late, and in attempting to abort the attack at the last minute, *Paladin* sheered away, put herself across I-27's bow, and was herself rammed by the submarine. She retired from the fray with her engine-room, steering gear flat, and after magazine flooded.

The fight now became a battle of wits between I-27 and *Petard*. Although the submarine was plainly in serious trouble, down by the stern and unable to man her 5-inch deck gun, she still had her bow and stern tubes. These worried *Petard*'s commander. For the next hour the two adversaries stalked each other, with I-27 running in wide circles, striving to bring her tubes to bear on the destroyer. *Petard*, twisting and turning at high speed, fired some 300 rounds of 4-inch, smashing the submarine's deck gun and riddling her conning tower, but being short of armour-piercing shells, she was unable to hole I-27's pressure hull. The British commander considered closing the range to lob depth charges, but the threat of the enemy's torpedo tubes and the danger of repeating *Paladin*'s disastrous collision made him keep his distance.

Darkness was now coming on, and fearful that her quarry might escape with the setting sun, *Petard* herself was forced to resort to using torpedoes. Even then the Japanese submarine proved difficult to sink. In the mad ring-a-ring-of-roses she was caught up in, six of the destroyer's torpedoes missed their target, but the seventh found its mark, and I-27 blew up. When the tall column of water thrown up by the explosion subsided, the submarine had gone, leaving only a patch on the water to mark her going. A few minutes later, there was a violent underwater explosion, and more oil and scraps of wreckage came to the surface.

Toshiaki Fukumura and his men had lost the three-hour-long battle, but they had taken the honours. As they spiralled down to their last resting place they left behind them a scene of devastation and confusion. The *Khedive Ismail* had gone, taking almost 1,500 souls with her, the destroyer *Paladin* was crippled and in danger of sinking, and the convoy had scattered. I-27 would be remembered for a long time to come.

Chapter Seventeen

When Will We Learn?

We had experienced a full gale, and run the gauntlet of an attack by U-boats. And now we were homeward bound. It may have been a lack of visibility in the increasing darkness; it may have been merely foolish imagination. But as I walked along the deck towards the door of the engine-room I could have sworn I saw the shape of a ship. A British tramp she was, and her torn hull lay very low in the cross-seas. Her broken masts, her emptied lifeboat davits were ghostly mockeries of what they had been. And then a group of misted figures gathered from nowhere about her mainmast and hauled aloft a shadowy rag. I fancied I could hear that infinitely brave little group shout: 'The enemy had none of that colour!' And the tattered remnants of a Red Ensign fluttered in the night wind . . .

As quick as it had come, the vision was gone. I had a feeling, out there in mid-ocean, that it was tragic the British Houses of Parliament could not send all those politicians, and the British industry all its experts and planners concerned with post-war policies, on one voyage in a salt-water tramp. Just one voyage, preferably between Britain and America, where they would see the real effects of an enemy torpedo on a ship carrying food and supplies; where they would see the shattered seamen and shattered ships. Some of those ships should never have been afloat. But they were. And they went bravely on, voyage after eight-knot voyage, showing the Flag to an ever-decreasing number of astonished and awe-stricken crews of Hitler's U-boats.

These poignant words were written over sixty years ago by journalist and ship's engineer Warren Armstrong. World War II was then drawing to a close, a war which Great Britain had embarked on with a fleet of over 4,000 merchant ships. When that bitter conflict ended and the final reckoning was made, 2,246 of those ships and 28,180 men had fallen to the enemy – twenty ships a week going down at the height of the Battle of the Atlantic. Britain had survived, but only through the supreme efforts of her merchant seamen, who had kept the sea lanes open at such great cost. Yet no one heeded the advice given by Warren Armstrong and so many others who had been in the thick of it. As the first peal of the Victory bells rang out, politicians, planners and industrialists – not one having tasted life in a salt-water tramp – smartly turned their backs on Britain's Merchant Navy. All the sacrifices of those six punishing years, when Britain had been kept fed and armed for war, had been in vain. Those gallant, unsophisticated men, one in every three who had set sail from these shores, had died for nothing.

The danger was not immediately apparent, for with a broken world to mend, the post-war years brought about a boom in shipping. Britain's merchant fleet prospered and grew fat again. By 1950, the Red Ensign flew over a quarter of the world's ships, and looked set to regain its former eminence. The lot of the merchant seaman improved dramatically. Most of the old ships had gone, sent to the bottom by the enemy's torpedoes. Their replacements would win no awards for excellence of build, but there was a new mood of generosity abroad. This change of attitude came not through any sudden surge of gratitude on the part of the nation or her shipowners, but as a direct result of the grievous losses suffered by the Merchant Navy during the war. The industry had lost a third of its trained workforce in the space of six years, and was, in 1945, scraping the bottom of its manpower barrel. Accommodation, for officers and men, became more spacious, and amenities were improved; many of the new-age ships boasted the hitherto unheard-of luxury of fresh water piped to all cabins. Food, always an important part of a seaman's life, took a turn for the better.

Curry and rice for breakfast and scouse for tea were out. Refrigeration had arrived, and with it bacon and eggs, green salads, and meat that needed no strong spices to disguise its rottenness. For the first time in history, British merchant seamen were guaranteed pay between voyages, and awarded two days' leave for every month on articles. After a brief tussle between unions and owners, the £10 a month extra the men had been paid in recognition of their willingness to run the gauntlet of the U-boats was added to their basic wage. From then on, wages and conditions of service went into an upward spiral in line with those ashore.

British merchant shipping peaked in 1975 at 50 million tons, and then, faced by competition from ships sailing under flags of convenience and manned by cheap crews, it went into terminal decline. Today, in 2006, a mere 282 ships totalling less than five million tons, remain British owned and sailing under the Red Ensign. More than two-thirds of Britain's exports and imports, and almost all her coastal trade, including the oil from the North Sea, is now carried in foreign-flag ships. One major consequence of this decline is that in the many overseas conflicts Britain has been involved in over the past twenty-five years, her merchant fleet, for the first time in its long history, has been found wanting, with no ships available to fetch and carry for the Armed Forces. This has resulted in the nation suffering the gross humiliation of having to go cap in hand to America for ships, or landing the taxpayer with huge bills for foreign tonnage chartered in as war transports. At long last, apathy has achieved what six years of world war and the might of Hitler's U-boat Arm failed to accomplish. How Warren Armstrong's ghosts of yesteryear must now weep in their cold graves.

In those few ships left sailing under the Red Ensign another revolution is taking place. Modern technology enables the shipowner to safely man a 50,000-tonner with a crew of twelve, but while this may cut costs dramatically, it has inevitably led to the basic seafaring and engineering skills being abandoned. A rudimentary knowledge of computers now counts for more than the ability to handle a sextant or change a blown exhaust valve. This, in the eyes of the faceless bureaucrats of Brussels, was excuse enough, to deliver the *coup de grâce* to British shipping as it had been known for many hundreds of years. On their dictat, and with the eager connivance of the British Government, it is now legal for a ship sailing under the Red Ensign to be owned in another country, and manned by foreign seamen, something unprecedented in the long history of shipping. To quote a typical example, a large container vessel recently involved in a serious collision was found to be British registered, but foreign owned, and with a mixed crew of South Koreans, Turks, Ukranians, Bulgarians, Yugoslavs and Romanians. A Marine Accident Investigation Branch report on the incident revealed that the Yugoslav chief officer on watch on the bridge and the Turkish lookout man had no common language, and could not communicate, other than by signs, while none of the watchkeeping officers understood the operation of the engine controls on the bridge – and these officers held certificates of 'equivalent competency' issued by the UK Government. Nearly 500 such ships, totalling 11 million tons gross, already exist, proudly circling the world under the Red Ensign, and their number grows day by day. This means that, in effect, the Red Ensign has now become a flag of convenience to be ranked alongside the prostituted flags of Liberia, Panama, and half a dozen others of similar repute.

As I write, Britain's last recognisable major shipping company, P & O, whose ships followed in the wake of the great East Indiamen, dominating the world's trade routes for more than 150 years, is up for grabs – for sale to the highest bidder with no strings attached. And so another jewel in Britain's maritime heritage is tossed into the dustbin of history. Ironically, the only shipping that now seems to arouse public interest in this island kingdom of Britain is that of a byegone age. No expense is spared when it comes to prising the rotting hulks of sailing ships out of the mud for preservation, but the plight of the disappearing merchant fleet, once the driving force of Britain's economy, is ignored. This is the ultimate betrayal of the men of Sam Plimsoll's Navy, who fought and died on every ocean to ensure the survival of their nation and their fleet all those years ago.

Bibliography

Admiralty, British, *British Vessels Lost at Sea* 1939–45, Patrick Stephens 1984

Armstrong, Warren, *Salt Water Tramps*, Jarrolds 1945

Bates, Lt. Cmdr. L.M., *The Merchant Service*, Frederick Muller 1945

Beaver, Paul, *U-boats in the Atlantic*, Patrick Stephens 1979

Bryant, Arthur, *The Turn of the Tide*, Collins 1957

Churchill, W.S., *The Second World War Vols 1–6*, Cassell 1948–52

Costello and Hughes, *The Battle of the Atlantic*, Collins 1977

Course, Captain A.G., *The Deep Sea Tramps*, Hollis & Carter 1960

Cresswell, Captain John, *Sea Warfare 1939–45*, University of California Press

Hocking, Charles, *Dictionary of Disasters at Sea During the Age of Steam*, Lloyd's Register of Shipping 1969

Hope, Stanton, *Ocean Odyssey*, Eyre & Spottiswoode 1944

Hurd, Sir Archibald, *Britain's Merchant Navy*, Odhams Press 1943

Jones, Geoffrey, *Defeat of the Wolf Packs*, William Kimber 1986

Lund, Paul and Ludlam, Harry, *PQ 17 Convoy to Hell*, W. Foulsham 1968

Mason, David, *U-boat, The Secret Menace*, Macdonald 1968

Middlemiss, Norman L., *The British Tankers*, Shield Publications 1995

Ministry of Information, *Merchantmen at War*, HMSO 1944

Montgomery, Michael, *Who Sank the Sydney?* Leo Cooper 1989

Muggenthaler, Karl-August, *German Raiders of World War II*, Robert Hale 1978

Poolman, Kenneth, *Periscope Depth*, Sphere Books 1984

Robertson, Terence, *The Golden Horseshoe*, Evans Bros. 1953

Rohwer, Jürgen, *Axis Submarine Successes* 1939–1945, Patrick Stephens 1983
Roskill, Captain S.W., *The War at Sea*, HMSO 1947
Showell, J.P. Mallmann, *U-boats Under the Swastika*, Ian Allan 1973
Slader, John, *The Fourth Service*, Robert Hale 1994
Terraine, John, *Business in Great Waters*, Leo Cooper 1989
Thomas, David, *The Atlantic Star 1939–45*, W.H. Allan 1990
Woon, Basil, *Atlantic Front*, Peter Davies 1941

Index